D1487983

SHORTLIST

Prague
2008

WHAT'S NEW | WHAT'S ON | WHAT'S BEST

www.timeout.com/prague

Contents

Prague by Area

Essentials

Published by Time Out Guides Ltd
Universal House
251 Tottenham Court Road
London W1T 7AB
Tel: + 44 (0)20 7813 3000
Fax: + 44 (0)20 7813 6001
Email: guides@timeout.com
www.timeout.com

Managing Director Peter Fiennes
Editorial Director Ruth Jarvis
Deputy Series Editor Dominic Earle
Financial Director Gareth Garner
Editorial Manager Holly Pick
Accountant Ija Krasnikova

Time Out Guides is a wholly owned subsidiary of Time Out Group Ltd.

© **Time Out Group Ltd**
Chairman Tony Elliott
Financial Director Richard Waterlow
Time Out Magazine Ltd MD David Pepper
Group General Manager/Director Nichola Coulthard
Managing Director, Time Out International Cathy Runciman
Time Out Communications Ltd MD David Pepper
Production Director Mark Lamond
Group Marketing Director John Luck
Group Art Director John Oakey
Group IT Director Simon Chappell

Time Out and the Time Out logo are trademarks of Time Out Group Ltd.

This edition first published in Great Britain in 2007 by Ebury Publishing
A Random House Group Company
Company information can be found on www.randomhouse.co.uk
10 9 8 7 6 5 4 3 2 1

For further distribution details, see www.timeout.com

ISBN 13: 978184670 0231
ISBN 10: 1-84670-023-X

A CIP catalogue record for this book is available from the British Library

Printed and bound by Firmengruppe APPL, aprinta druck, Wemding, Germany

The Random House Group Limited makes every effort to ensure that the papers used in our books are made from trees that have been legally sourced from well-managed and credibly certified forests. Our paper procurement policy can be found on www.randomhouse.co.uk

Prague Shortlist

The **Time Out Prague Shortlist 2008** is one of a new series of guides that draws on Time Out's background as a magazine publisher to keep you current with what's going on in town. As well as Prague's key sights and the best of its eating, drinking and leisure options, it picks out the most exciting venues to have opened in the last year and gives a full calendar of events from September 2007 to December 2008. It also includes features on the important news, trends and openings, all compiled by locally based editors and writers. Whether you're visiting for the first time in your life or just the first time since 2007, you'll find the *Time Out Prague Shortlist 2008* contains all you need to know, in a portable and easy-to-use format.

The guide divides central Prague into six areas, each containing listings for Sights & Museums, Eating & Drinking, Shopping, Nightlife and Arts & Leisure, and maps pinpointing all their locations. At the front of the book are chapters rounding up these scenes city-wide, and giving a shortlist of our overall picks in a variety of categories. We include itineraries for days out, plus essentials such as transport information and hotels.

Our listings give phone numbers as dialled from within the Czech Republic. To call from abroad, preface them with your exit code and the country code, 420.

We have noted price categories by using one to four dollar signs ($-$$$$),

representing budget, moderate, expensive and luxury. Major credit cards are accepted unless otherwise stated. We also indicate when a venue is NEW, and give Event highlights.

All our listings are double-checked, but places do sometimes close or change their hours or prices, so it's a good idea to call a venue before visiting. While every effort has been made to ensure accuracy, the publishers cannot accept responsibility for any errors that this guide may contain.

Venues are marked on the maps using symbols numbered according to their order within the chapter and colour-coded according to the type of venue they represent:

❶ Sights & Museums
❶ Eating & Drinking
❶ Shopping
❶ Nightlife
❶ Arts & Leisure

Map key

Major sight or landmark	
Railway stations	
Metro stations	Ⓜ
Parks	
Pedestrian zones	
Churches	✚
Steps	
Area name	JOSEFOV
Tram routes	

Time Out Prague Shortlist 2008

EDITORIAL
Editor Will Tizard
Copy Editor Anna Norman
Researcher Hela Balínová
Proofreader Marion Moisy

DESIGN
Art Director Scott Moore
Art Editor Pinelope Kourmouzoglou
Senior Designer Henry Elphick
Graphic Designer Gemma Doyle
Junior Graphic Designer Kei Ishimaru
Digital Imaging Simon Foster
Ad Make-up Jodi Sher
Picture Editor Jael Marschner
Deputy Picture Editor Tracey Kerrigan
Picture Researcher Helen McFarland

ADVERTISING
Sales Director/Sponsorship Mark Phillips
International Sales Manager Fred Durman
International Sales Consultant
  Ross Canadé
Advertising Sales Time Out (Prague):
  ARBOmedia.net Praha
Advertising Assistant Kate Staddon

MARKETING
Marketing Manager Yvonne Poon
**Sales & Marketing Director, North
America** Lisa Levinson
Marketing Designer Anthony Huggins

PRODUCTION
Production Manager Brendan McKeown
Production Co-ordinator Caroline Bradford
Production Controller Susan Whittaker

CONTRIBUTORS
This guide was researched and written by Hela Balínová, Jen Harris, Frank Kuznik, Mimi Rogers, Radka Slába, Will Tizard, Jacy Ynsua and the writers of *Time Out Prague*.

PHOTOGRAPHY
All photography by Elan Fleisher, except: pages 11, 21, 39, 44, 46, 47, 54, 80, 114, 131, 136, 150, 157, 166 Helena Smith; pages 13, 34, 49, 50, 56, 59, 60, 62, 65, 69, 70, 79 (bottom), 84, 95, 96, 100, 102, 116, 122, 146 (left), 152 CzechTourism; pages 18, 26, 43, 79 (top), 111, 113, 129, 142, 143, 147, 148, 158, 159, 161 Will Tizard; page 41 Gallery of the City of Prague; pages 63, 66, 74, 76, 98, 99, 127 Rene Jakl; page 73 William Ferris; page 149 Adrian Stout; page 160 Sex Appeal Party Agency.

The following images were provided by the featured establishments/artists: pages 2 (top left), 28, 31, 32, 33, 36, 38, 103, 134, 169.

Cover photograph: Charles Bridge. Credit: Clay McLachlan/Getty Images.

MAPS
JS Graphics (john@jsgraphics.co.uk)

Thanks to Chris Davies, Nick Draper and Taryn Walker.

About Time Out

Founded in 1968, Time Out has expanded from humble London beginnings into the leading resource for those wanting to know what's happening in the world's greatest cities. As well as our influential what's-on weeklies in London, New York and Chicago, we publish more than a dozen other listings magazines in cities as varied as Beijing and Mumbai. The magazines established Time Out's trademark style: sharp writing, informed reviewing and bang up-to-date inside knowledge of every scene.

Time Out made the natural leap into travel guides in the 1980s with the City Guide series, which now extends to over 50 destinations around the world. Written and researched by expert local writers and generously illustrated with original photography, the full-size guides cover a larger area than our Shortlist guides and include many more venue reviews, along with additional background features and a full set of maps.

Throughout this rapid growth, the company has remained proudly independent, still owned by Tony Elliott nearly four decades after he started Time Out London as a single fold-out sheet of A5 paper. This independence extends to the editorial content of all our publications, this Shortlist included. No establishment has been featured because it has advertised, and no payment has influenced any of our reviews. And, for our critics, there's definitely no such thing as a free lunch: all restaurants and bars are visited and reviewed anonymously, and Time Out always picks up the bill.
For more about the company, see www.timeout.com.

Don't Miss
2008

Sights & Museums

Prague tourist authorities, confronted for the first time in 2007 with visitor numbers that weren't growing, have done much soul searching. In fact, they've been working on marketing and spin control for quite some time, with results that have sometimes been curious, from expensive TV commercials playing up the lax Bohemian lifestyle to logo contests. Not surprisingly, these haven't connected to visitors nearly as effectively as the message of cheap flights, cheap alcohol and cheap sex.

But the Czech Tourism agency is not out to draw more stag parties from Birmingham. They want quality visitors. The kind of folks who are into culture, designer hotels and big restaurant tabs.

Yes, having studied up on how other capital cities keep their attractions fresh, Prague's civic leaders have decided that the way forward is 'experience tourism,' defined as the kind of thing that involves visitors in a unique process that's wholly apart from gazing at castles (or strip club windows). Slated to open to the public in autumn 2007 (check out the website of the Prague Information Service for details, www.pis.cz), the impressive network of subterranean conduits beneath Old Town was being frantically renovated as this guide went to press and multilingual guides were

St Vitus's Cathedral p11

SHORTLIST

Best progressive
- Futura (p87)
- Jewish Museum (p98)

Best views
- Astronomical Clock (p94)
- Old Town Bridge Tower (p101)
- Petřín hill (p53)

Best castling
- St Vitus's Cathedral, Prague Castle (p63)
- Vyšehrad (p138)

Best outdoor
- Letenský zámeček (p156)
- Rowing on the Vltava
- Vojanovy sady (p78)

Best architecture
- House of the Black Madonna (p98)
- Municipal House (p117)
- Old-New Synagogue, Jewish Musuem (p98)

Best secret
- Museum of Decorative Arts (p101)
- Museum of the City of Prague (p101)
- Wallenstein Gardens (p78)

Most Kafkaesque
- Golden Lane (p58)
- Spanish Synagogue (p100)
- Church of Our Lady before Týn (p94)

Best curated
- House at the Golden Ring (p97)
- Municipal Library (p101)
- Rudolfinum (p117)

Best historic
- National Museum (p124)
- New Town Hall(p124)
- Old Town Hall (p102)
- Schwartzenberg Palace (p65)

being trained in every aspect of fluid dynamics, international architecture and tunnelling terminology.

City officials hold out equal hope for Prague's municipal water station (well, it is in a lovely big pre-war building by the river south of the Nové Můsto district) and the mechanisms that drive the Petrin Hill funicular in Malá Strana. As may be apparent, Czechs are master engineers and apparently assume most visitors will be as fascinated as they are by the gears and shafts that move large quantities of people, water or waste around.

Meanwhile, most of Prague Castle's (p56) displays still consist of dusty mimeographed illustrations with Russian in prominent use, and many of the labels in the city's incredible number of museums are still Czech-only. True, some areas of the castle have been fully redone with exhibitions geared towards international audiences, such as the

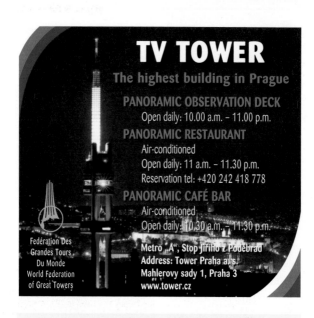

kid-friendly Story of Prague Castle, which occupies the cellars of the Old Royal Palace (p59). The displays, which mirror the sprawling nature of the palaces themselves, stretch out over a dozen rooms and feature exciting insights into the lives that have occupied this special space since 3200 BC. Though the roots of the castle itself extend back to a mere 900 AD, the hill now known as Hradčany was clearly of sacred significance to pagan peoples, as shown by the funerary rituals that still have scientists puzzled.

The country's greatest icon, meanwhile, is currently caught in the middle of an ancient struggle between church and state. The communist regime under Klement Gottwald, the first Soviet-backed hardliner who seized power in 1948, seized all property belonging to the Church and made priests state employees in order to keep them under close watch. Now, over 17 years after the Velvet Revolution, the courts are still deciding who should run and own St Vitus's Cathedral (p63), along with hundreds of other chapels and churches throughout the country.

Many are in states of severe disrepair because local authorities, although technically still the owners (the Church has been in line for having its property restored since 1989), are hesitant to invest in buildings they know they won't be able to hang on to for much longer. At St Vitus, this has meant that the greatest share of renovations have been taken on by international foundations rather than local bodies. For a while, when the Church had won the latest ruling, they were charging a special entrance fee to St Vitus of 100 Kč in the hopes of

Astronomical Clock p94

earning some maintenance dosh but the state has since won control again and done away with this extra levy.

Meanwhile, even the tombs under the cathedral, containing the greatest Bohemian leaders in history, the Přemyslid clan, including Charles IV, St Ludmila and St Wenceslas I, still remain in what amounts to a concrete bunker.

In all fairness, everyone from the late Renaissance Swedes to the Nazis and Soviets have been carting off Prague's most valuable treasures for centuries, so if the Castle cupboards seem bare these days, it's shouldn't be surprising. Still, it seems a bit sad that the most exciting developments tend to come from abroad, such as the return of four priceless artefacts from the court of Rudolph II, which will take pride of place in the Prague Castle Picture Gallery in April 2008. A myth allegory by Hans von Aachen, two pictures by Bartholomeus Spranger and a work by Dutch sculptor Adrian de Vries, on loan from a British collector, made headlines in Prague this year.

The city's other key sites, at least, have been working to stay fresh, such as the Museum of the City of Prague (p101), which has finally restored its incredibly elaborate paper model of the city.

If that sounds a bit dry, you might put the new Museum of Music (p77) on Karmelitská street in the Malá Strana district higher on your list. Its shows, with colourful, noisy interactive displays, have been a hit with local and visiting crowds since it opened its doors.

Others, like the Jewish Museum (p98), the city's second most visited attraction, have been running city-wide multi-venue shows in concert with other museums and galleries, such as the museum's centennial in 2005, which carried on into 2006. And Prague's National Museum (p124), centered at the top of Wenceslas Square, has gone as far as incorporating smells into its exhibits, such as the recent olfactory sensation on mammoth hunters, complete with primordial scents.

Unfortunately, the other Prague museum that's always been a hit with younger visitors, the Technical Museum in the Holesovice district, closed for extensive reconstruction in spring 2007 and will be shuttered for at least a year. The kid-friendly Zoo Praha (p153), however, is looking better than ever – in fact Czech Television recently based a reality show on the activities of its gorillas, which has been a success with audiences.

Most people experience Prague mainly by walking its streets, which are conveniently compact (Old Town, with its Astronomical Clock, is just two kilometres across) and, despite record commercial growth, remain little changed from their appearance centuries ago. Luckily or not, the city was taken by the Germans in 1938-39 without a fight, and survived World War II with barely a scratch.

Tickets and information

The latest state of the city's main attractions, together with new exhibitions, is reliably posted on the Prague Information Service website (www.pis.cz), while the Prague Tourist Card is a worthwhile investment if you're planning to see much more than Prague Castle (note, though, that it does not cover entry to the Jewish Museum, the National Gallery or all the sites of the National Museum). It does cover four days of visits to dozens of other venues plus public transport for the price of 750 Kč, or 490 Kč for students. Pick it up at the Prague Information Service on Old Town Square or at the main railway station, Hlavní Andreaží.

U Zlatého tygra p16

Eating & Drinking

It's been a year of hallmarks for Prague foodies and bar patrons. The latter group, which has always been well-catered for in the capital of Bohemia, was presented with a host of new venues that expanded the range and quality of pours available to them – something worthy of toasting.

Among the highlights was the opening of Bukowski's (p151), a British-style pub, complete with carpets and impressive woodwork, but known to cognoscenti as a good deal more. Already full of Prague's most notorious characters before it legally opened, this Žižkov district bar represents not just a promising grill bar in a non-touristy locale but a return to the fold of Glen Emery, founder of the legendary Jo's Bar.

Anyone who visited the city in the early 1990s and thirsted for something beyond the ubiquitous smokey, not-so-friendly local probably ended up here at some point, or at one of Emery's other ventures that followed, such as the long-since closed Repre – where people like Joe Strummer would turn up for gigs despite wiring so bad the power went out during his first set. It's been years since Emery, a former miner and lumberjack from British Columbia, tended bar and the scene has been sorely missing colour and a reliable magnet for Prague's craziest barflies as a result.

And that, after all, is the essential distinction of going out in the Czech capital; perhaps because of its concentrated centre, or

because it's got some kind of cosmic vortex, half the fun is about who you run into in this city. And in that respect, this year's bar and restaurant additions promise much – nearly all feature colourful crowds of regulars and great rapport between staff and clientele.

Pubs and bars

Other drinking-related developments have accompanied the favourable omen of Bukowski's: Černá Kočka, Bílý Kocour (p147) is another great addition to Žižkov, this one Czech-owned and operated, with a well-stocked cocktail bar and satisfying grill-bar food – a new development in Prague, to be sure. Until recently, bars assumed you were there just to drink, and pubs that do feature food generally have very similar menus of pork, goulash and schnitzel and kitchens that close at 10pm – many a night owl has found himself tipsy without intending to be for sheer lack of food.

Another classic Žižkov living room bar is Hapu (p148) – also Czech-owned and, while not much to look at, serving the district's best cocktails to an interesting crowd of international regulars. It's no coincidence that its management has been involved in the opening of Bukowski's (whose name, by the way, was chosen wisely – it seems that every kid in the region knows and holds dear the alcoholic poetry of Charles Bukowski, so this bar has instant name recognition).

In Old Town, meanwhile, a quiet street just two blocks from Old Town Square holds another great hole-in-the-wall bar where cocktails are also the speciality: Čili (p105). Though it doesn't reach the heights of the more visible mixed drink bars like Tretter's and Ocean Drive (p110), this dark little place serves sincerity with its generous pours and has a strong local following.

DON'T MISS: 2008

SHORTLIST

Best new
- La Casa Argentina (p107)
- Le Degustation (p107)
- Oliva (p130)

Best views
- Kampa Park (p83)
- Palffy Palác (p83)
- Rio's (p138)

Best museum cafés
- House of the Black Madonna (p98)
- Kampa Museum (p77)

Best hotel dining
- Alcron (p126)
- Allegro (p102)
- Hotel Mandarin Oriental (p169)

Best beer gardens
- Letenský zámeček (p156)
- Park café (p140)
- Žofin (p126)

Best wine bars
- Le Terroir (p108)
- Monarch (p108)

Best pubbing
- U medvídků (p110)
- U Vejvodů (p110)

Best coffeehouse
- Franz Kafka Café (p106)
- Kavárna Obecní dům (p106)

Most Czech
- Kolkovna (p106)
- U Maltézských rytířů (p85)
- U modré kachničky (p110)

Best scene
- Bukowski's (p151)
- Fraktal (p153)
- U Malého Glena (p86)

The same is true of the Tato Kojkej art bar (257 323 102), in an old mill in Malá Strana's Kampa Park – just without the cocktail expertise (but with a lot more sofas). This district is clearly studying up on the lush life, with another little bar and club – Popocafepetl (p86) – that's packed nightly and features live music acts (of varying pedigree). (Popocafepetl has a sister in Žižkov of the same name, that's better on atmosphere and pub grub – the two should not be confused).

But have no fear that timeless bohemian pubs of old are dying out. With 500 years' experience as brewmasters and beer guzzlers, Czechs are not about to give up their old-style beerhalls. The traditional working-class district of Žižkov remains pub heaven, famed for having more pubs per capita than any other place on earth, with many concentrated on Bořivojova street. They remain firmly in place, even in Old Town, as U Zlatého tygra (p110), the pub that functioned as the late novelist Bohumil Hrabal's receiving room, can attest. What's more, this venerated place, where foreigners may have to endure the stares of the ageing local regulars, features an underground tank, making for some of the finest Pilsner tapping around. And, even up by Prague Castle, the Czech President knows his office is just a five-minute walk from the ageless U Černého vola pub (p67).

And the city still offers the finest pub crawling – in terms of both affordability and quality – in the world. You can savour the workhorses of *pivo* – Pilsner Urquell, Radegast, Staropramen, Budvar and Gambrinus – just about anywhere. Then head for the speciality bars for less well-known Czech beer delights: Letenský zámeček for Bernard, U Černého vola for Kozel, and so

on. And those without much on their menus will usually offer some trad beer grub like smoked meat platters and/or the magnificently smelly pivní sýr (beer cheese).

Cafés

Café culture in Prague offers everything from old-style dark, elegant coffeehouses of the Vienna school to American innovations and shrines to mocha frappuccino. The kavárna in Prague has long been at the centre of intellectual life and, with secret police now gone, some new places have slipped right into this role, such as the delightfully Mitteleuropa-feeling Café Dinitz (p105), while some classics have rebounded. The cosy Café Montmartre (p104) has bounced back from the bon vivant days when it hosted black masses during the 1930s. The Slavia (p109), meanwhile, where dissidents like Václav Havel and Jiří Kolář once planned and plotted, has been slightly too cleaned up, alas. Meanwhile, expat caffeine addicts often get their fix at Fuzion, Ebel Coffee House, Kava Kava Kava and the Globe Bookstore & Coffeehouse.

Places such as the ethereal Dahab (p105), which looks to all the world like a movie set harem, signify the highest form of a different Prague phenomenon – the *čajovna* or tearoom. This quintessential example comes fully equipped with Persian pillow seating, jangly belly dancing, steamed couscous, mint tea and houkahs. A more recent addition is the spacey vegetarian tearoom (with houkahs, of course) known at Lehká hlava, or light head, which features such add-ons as ginger carrot soup and couscous.

Dining

The culinary world, being a bit more complicated to perfect, evolves more slowly, of course, but Prague has also seen positive precedents here: Le Degustation (p107) has presented Old Town with its first three-plus-hour experience of truly refined dining, while Café Savoy (Vítězná 5, 257 311 562, www.ambi.cz) offers elegant, creative flourishes, and good neighbourhood ethnic offerings are quietly attracting diners to Himilaya (p106) and Kabul (p106).

Of course, going out to eat anywhere in the former Eastern Bloc can still often be described as an adventure. It can still be a challenge, incredibly enough, to get yourself noticed, seated, given a menu and get your order in.

But the city's veteran venues are still going strong and stand out from the old-school ones as much as they do from the host of new ones that seem to equate sharp Mylar furniture with quality. Evocative neglected mansions like Palffy Palác (p83) still top many visitors' lists of memories to savour, while the microbrew restaurant Pivovarský dům still merits *New York Times* mentions with its friendly update of the classic gruff Czech pub, complete with delicacies like smoked meat-filled dumplings. Two more central such places with far more seating space have also proven their staying power, the Budvar microbrewery U Medvídků and the antique-style brewery restaurants U Vejvodů, both steeped in bohemian atmosphere.

These places feature the best elements of the still (mercifully) unchanged neighbourhood pub, invariably serving pork knuckle, schnitzel (known here as *řízek*), beef in cream sauce (*svíčkova*), and endless cheap half-liters of lager (the sour and beloved Pilsner Urquell when you're in luck). They remain a working-class treat to be savoured, where you sit at communal tables, you can cut the air with a knife, and your

waiter, after working a traditional 12-hour shift, looks about to pass out.

A few genuine gems at the high end have also proven their merits with imaginative gusto, such as Aromi, Opera Garden, the Four Season's Allegro, the beloved French Le Bistrot de Marlène, and the wine bar Le Terroir. Prague's venturesome expat community has further enriched the mix with satisfying brunches, bagel shops, and Sonoran Mexican food, at places like Radost FX, the ever-popular Bohemia Bagel and Picante, a cheap, all-night fast food joint that serves the best Mexican in town. And vegetarians in this meat-loving town have reasonable options at Country Life and Radost FX. Otherwise it may come down to *smažený sýr*, the fried cheese served at most pubs, but mind they don't slip ham (*šunka*) in.

Tipping and etiquette

At pubs and beerhalls, tables are often shared with other patrons who, like you, should ask '*Je tu volno?*' ('Is it free?') and may also wish each other '*dobrou chut*' before tucking in. Prague dines with a relaxed dress code and reservations are necessary at only the new generation of upscale spots in town. Many waiters still record your tab on a slip of paper, which translates at leaving time into a bill. Pay the staff member with the folding wallet in their waistband, not your waiter (the phrase '*Zaplatím, prosím*' means 'May I pay, please?'). A small cover charge and extra for milk, bread and the ubiquitous accordion music are still in practice at many pubs, as is tipping by rounding the bill up to the nearest 10 Kč. At nicer places, 10-15 per cent tips have become the rule. While you should have little trouble making a phone reservation in English at modern establishments, at other places it might be easier to book in person.

La Casa del Habano p21

Shopping

If there's one thing Czechs are living for these days, it's shopping. Shopping for new careers, new mates, new lifestyles – and more than a little real estate. They may, in fact, prove to be the EU's best new consumers and certainly one of its most promising markets, considering the size of this country of 10.2 million.

The only possible problem with this is that, by and large, everyone wants to be on the customer side of the counter rather than the service one. And the country's reputation for hanging on to communist-era attitudes, in which the customer was always wrong, is one the authorities are still trying to shake off. Thankfully, this is proving easier than ever before.

There's also no denying that Prague is a treasure trove of the past. Head down any narrow side street, even in the old centre of town, and you'll find amazing knick-knacks, antiques and artefacts, from gorgeous books with engraved illustrations to art deco jewellery and vinyl recordings of forgotten Czech pop.

If you're under strict orders to bring home Bohemian crystal or a puppet – and there are good reasons the country is famous for both – then just about any of the dozens of highly visible shops selling these will do. There's very little difference in quality or price, at least in central Prague, and goods can generally be shipped home safely and reliably.

English is spoken widely, if sometimes begrudgingly, at just about all shops in the centre of Prague, and credit cards are in widespread use these days, though you'll probably find welcoming smiles and offers of 'How may I help you?' fairly rare. Shops also have longer opening hours now than those you'll find outside the touristy areas. Note that straying even a little outside the city centre may mean shops that close at noon on Saturdays, and don't open at all on Sundays.

The majority of the big stores are multinationals come to spruce up the shopping scene. They've found a welcoming public, especially for the clothing shops that sell inexpensive but fashionable gear. The average Czech salary is still low compared to those of other European countries, and retailers are mindful of their market. The shopping mall concept has been extremely well-received, with mammoth ones spread around the outskirts of town. Smaller ones can be found at Palác Flora and Nový Smíchov, where half the fun is watching newly flush Czech consumers looking as content as you'll ever see them.

Aside from the chance to witness the massive consumer boom, you can also pick up some excellent bargains, especially leather goods and high-quality sports clothing and equipment (Czechs and Slovaks being both born entrepreneurs and wilderness freaks). Also excellent value is local music, particularly classical recordings on the respected Supraphon label. These sell for about half the price they do in Western Europe and are available at most music shops. (Bontonland on Wenceslas Square has the most comprehensive collection, with listening stations.)

SHORTLIST

Best new
- Antique v Douhé (p112)
- Monarch (p108)
- Toalette (p113)

Best design
- Modes Robes (p112)
- Pavla & Olga (p112)
- Tatiana (p113)
- Fashion Galerie No.14 (p133)

Best souvenir
- Antikvariát Kant (p132)
- Dr Stuart's Botanicus (p112)
- Le Patio (p135)

Best retro
- Antique Ahasver (p86)
- Art Deco (p112)
- Bazar Antik Zajímavosti (p132)
- Bric a Brac (p112)
- Kubista (p112)

Best music
- Pohodli (p113)

Best food/wine
- Cellarius (p134)
- Havelský Market (p94)

Best read
- Antikvariát Kant (p132)
- Antikvariát Galerie Můstek (p132)
- Big Ben Bookshop (p112)
- Globe Bookstore and Coffeehouse (p133)

Best specialist
- Beruška (p133)
- Foto Škoda (p133)
- Květinařství U Červeného Lva p86
- La Casa del Habano (p112)
- Svara's Hexenladen (p135)

Best museum gift shops
- Prague Castle (p56)
- National Gallery (p153)
- Museum of Decorative Arts (p101)
- House of the Black Madonna (p98)

Meanwhile high-end retailers like Cartier, Hermès, Louis Vuitton, Christian Dior and Versace, plus shops such as luxe cigar emporium La Casa del Habano, have all picked up on the high demand for status items in the Czech Republic and opened branches in Prague. Of course there's no strategic reason to hit these stores here, where goods are no cheaper and the catalogue's quite a bit thinner. Knock-offs have followed right behind; many filling street markets with shoes, purses and the like, sporting the look and the 'label'. Often enough, Czech celebs can be spotted picking up the copycat goods, which can still usually pass muster at social gatherings at this stage of the game.

When entering a shop, the salesperson will ask '*Máte přání?*' ('Do you have a wish?'). While ringing up your purchases, they may ask '*Ještě něco?*' ('Anything else?') or '*Všechno?*' ('Is that all?'). Say '*Kolik to stojí?*' to find out what something costs.

Garnets and amber

Every jeweller worth his weight in carats offers these in Prague, but those with distinctive settings are the ones worth noting. Garnets and amber are impossible to miss, featured prominently among the crystal and nesting dolls that line the tourist shops. The city of Turnov, in North Bohemia, is garnet central, where the original and true Bohemian garnets hail from. This stone is celebrated for its fiery red colour and its light-reflecting qualities. Its supposed curative effects include the ability to overcome sorrow, bring vitality

Palác Knih Luxor p22

and instil feelings of joy in the wearer. The fashion dates back at least to the Renaissance days of Emperor Rudolf II, who counted many garnet-encrusted pieces in his collection, as did Russian tsarinas in the 1800s, who used them to decorate their dresses.

Art Cooperative Granát, a production facility in Turnov, produces 3,500 different designs, and employs master craftspeople to create new ones every year. They come set in gold-plated silver, sterling silver, 14- or 18-carat gold. The Granát facility is the only legal mining operator in the country so always ask for a manufacturer's certificate. True Bohemian garnets will be marked with G, G1 or G2.

As for the Baltic's signature stone – amber – it's not a mineral at all but prehistoric tree resin. It also has healing properties: it is believed to fight depression, attract joy and promote wellbeing. Again, fakes abound in the many shops scattered around town so remember: real amber floats, like a bar of soap, in salt water. Glass and plastic are the most common fakes, but amber is warmer to the touch.

For book lovers, the city abounds with *antikvariáts*, fusty places full of old Czech tomes, ornate Bibles, photos, maps, magazines and postcards. Palác Knih Luxor on Wenceslas Square (www.neoluxor. cz) has a great selection of English books and Czech art titles. The bazars (second-hand shops) are also fun for a browse. For native crafts with local colour, try Manufaktura (p112) – at first sight, it looks touristy, and is found in prime tourist locations (including the airport), but it's worth a second look for natural soaps, herbal essences and old-fashioned homewares. Dr Stuart's Botanicus (p112) is another specialist in Czech-made organic

products, from soaps and shampoos to cooking oils and candles. Art is another excellent buy, and it needn't be from a vendor on Charles Bridge. Many galleries scattered around the city offer serious bargains on one-of-a-kind items, as do museum gift shops like Prague Castle (p56) or the National Gallery (p153). And, of course, never underestimate the power of Czech alcohol. A liqueur like Becherovka, bitters like Fernet, plum brandy like Slivovice or a beer like the beloved Pilsner Urquell will keep the Prague memories flowing.

Shopping areas

As is typical in most cities, avoid the central shopping areas unless you are rushed or need classic souvenirs. This especially applies to Hradčany and the area around Prague Castle. Staré Město is a little better, especially as you drift towards Nové Město, and many backstreets contain rewarding second-hand junk and book shops. High fashion and high prices can be found on Pařížská, which you should hit on a sunny day for its tree-lined pavements and inviting outdoor cafés. Mall central, as well as many other chain stores, can be found along Na příkope. Wenceslas Square can pretty much be skipped for shopping – nothing too unique, but some old standbys if you're looking for crystal. The streets on either side of Wenceslas Square are great for a wander, especially the further out you go. Beware of some shady characters, however, especially at night. Souvenir seekers should stroll any of the streets leading out from Old Town Square, as well as the Malá Strana area near Charles Bridge. Moving further out to Karlín and Holešovice will reward antique junkies, but every neighbourhood boasts a hidden surprise or two.

Roxy p26

WHAT'S BEST
Nightlife

Prague's clubbing scene is heating up, to be sure, though the city is far from one of Europe's great nightlife capitals. The preferred way to spend a night out, sitting in a pub or wine bar while conversing and regaling, is still something the hottest DJ in town can't compete with. And, though scholarly research confirming this has not turned up as yet, many theorise that the deeply entrenched beer culture somewhat precludes the rise of clubbing as a major pursuit; after all, alcohol is a powerful sedative.

Still, those up for carousing and shaking it about will find more than enough options around, and their variety and the physical space they inhabit make for satisfying tales the morning after.

And, often enough, someone to wake up next to. It is a thriving society of flexible mores after all, where little stigma is attached to intoxication and which hosts the largest number of atheists per capita in the world. Seize the moment, then, and do as the Czechs do: live as if there's no tomorrow.

Clubbing

Prague features some impressive summer raves and one-off parties in vast old tram factories, but is otherwise not really on the circuit of Europe's great clubbing cities. That said, there are always new ventures popping up and there's usually something wild going on that you'll have to catch on your mobile phone camera to believe.

Within a block of Wenceslas Square there are three new venues that represent the spectrum well enough. The slickest of these, the KU Bar Café (p107), is an unabashed magnet for the new generation of tanned, fit Czuppies in designer gear from head-to-toe, but it's still an amusing place to visit for all that – and the right place to meet Italian tourists wearing their sunglasses all night.

Petrovič (p115), a cellar bar and live music venue, represents the latest wave of the westward Russian invasion. Prague is now a hugely popular destination for Muscovites in search of a lower cost of living and a safer environment, and many of them can be seen, along with a healthy Ukrainian contingent, at venues like this. Ever fans of fashionable clubbing garb, the colourful crowd sets the new standard for putting on a show while taking one in.

And on Wenceslas Square itself, in the basement of the building that is topped by Duplex (the main drag's biggest disco), is Hot Pepper's (p135). This one's on the itinerary of every stag party in Prague in the last year (which is an awful lot of itineraries) because of its Vegas-style striptease acts and lap-dance artists. The place is strangely innocent compared to the many brothels that operate openly in the vicinity of – and sometimes on – the square, offering no sex for sale, though there are levels of intimacy to the table dances that have a sliding price scale. Between that, the wacky theme acts and the light and smoke machines, this place is entertaining enough to almost justify the entrance scam (free with a free first beer – but the small one you pay for costs 200 Kc: about ten times the usual rate).

Otherwise, most Prague clubs fall into one of three categories:

SHORTLIST

Best for preening
- Celnice (p105)
- Duplex (p135)
- KU Bar Café (p107)

Best dance mixes
- Mecca (p156)
- Roxy (p115)

Best late bars
- Blue Light (p81)
- N11 (p115)
- Vertigo (p116)

Best local scene
- Akropolis (p156)
- Cross Club (p156)
- DJ night, Lucerna Music Bar (p135)

Best cruising
- Chateau (p105)
- Marquis de Sade (p108)
- Radost FX Café (p130)

Best pop discos
- Duplex (p135)
- Face to Face (p156)
- Misch Masch (p156)

Best anarchy
- Klub 007 (p68)
- Újezd (p86)

Best for students
- Nebe (p135)
- Tulip Café (p132)

Best for discretion
- Darling Club Cabaret (p135)
- Hot Pepper's (p135)

Best gay bars
- Friends (p115)
- Saints (p142)
- Valentino (p143)

Best for live music
- Malostranská beseda (p86)
- Metamorphis (p108)
- Petrovič (p115)
- Popocafepetl (p86)
- U staré paní (p116)

DON'T MISS: 2008

trendy brushed steel and recessed lighting, with a crowd out of a toothpaste commercial (Vertigo, Celnice, Solidní nejstota, Radost FX) ; smoke-filled, glorified pubs with neo-hippies in dreadlocks (Meloun, Ujezd, Guru); and full-on pop disco infernos (Duplex, La Fabrique, Lucerna Music Bar on Fridays and Saturdays).

A sub-category of this last group is made up of places that American students doing a year abroad have adopted as their own, such as Cross Club, Nebe, Double Trouble and the bars Tulip and Marquis de Sade. This last well-worn stalwart has changed hands recently but reports of its death were exaggerated.

Of course, all but the mega pop discos (which Prague also has in the teen-filled Face to Face) are subject to fickle fashions, noise ordinances and avaricious landlords. All these factors may explain why the city still has, much to the frustration of its growing ranks of club cognoscenti, only a handful of truly respected survivors of any

size: the Roxy, Mecca, Radost FX and Akropolis, which is really a series of bars and a live stage. It's probably also telling that none of these has really changed much in years, but that's also because they've all had high standards from the start and have managed to keep up with trends, sound systems, atmosphere and ideas.

Just try to keep an open mind and embrace the fact that Czech crowds still go mad for ABBA, loads of hair gel and silly dance caverns, where someone might at any time hop up on the bar and start stripping off. But then, these are what form those only-in-Prague moments.

And, of course, there are those incredible venues – if the tram factory's occupied, you may end up in the Parukarka bunker (yes, it's really a Cold War bomb shelter) or the National Memorial, a hilltop Soviet-era mausoleum. Now that's something nobody in London or New York is going to experience this weekend.

Parukarka bunker

Gay

Many of the best-run clubs – and certainly those with the best soundtracks – are, not surprisingly, the gay clubs. These too are fairly few in number but the trade-off is that they're concentrated around the old centre and most are quite welcoming to anyone. Valentino (p143) in Vinohrady is a new state of the art venue, with three floors of mad clubbing, including darkrooms, while the American-style Friends (p115) on a quiet street in Staré Město is as amiable as its name, with a grown-up, cosy quality and 200 square metres of up-all-night dancefloor with great sound, providing a break from the city's many gritty grope clubs frequented by German businessmen.

Managing it all

A time-honoured strategy for Prague clubbing is to start pretty much anywhere in the old centre and move on to other venues to check whether you've missed anything, stopping off at any number of dodgy late-night bars and pubs along the way to refuel. U Medvidků has a bar on one side that's open till 3am, N11's (p115) open all night and a vast number (too many to mention here) of holes-in-the-wall will present themselves as you migrate. Thus, unless a supreme party or DJ is rolling in to town, there's no real need to make a detailed plan in advance. If you did, you'd probably discover that the event's been moved or the club's dark for some reason anyway – that's just how Prague works.

What hot tips and info there are tend to be in the free pocket-sized 'zines you'll find lying all over town. Try venues like U Malého Glena, Tulip or the Globe Bookstore and Coffeehouse (p133).

The names – and only the names – of these change like the rate of your socks, but at press time *Think Again* was as good as any and *Prague in your Pocket*, a 150 Kč investment available at the Globe, is usually plugged in and quite comprehensive. Otherwise, the Czech-language www.techno.cz has comprehensible DJ names, styles, dates and addresses – hundreds of them, in fact, including every major clubbing event for the next month. Other useful sources – in English – are the expat websites that you may have already turned to for amusing forums on dating, laundry or all the other sundry concerns of life in Prague, namely www.expats.cz and prague.tv. *The Prague Post*'s site, www.prague post.com, has comprehensive food and drink listings and its Night & Day section has all the best in music, film and festivals, but there's no systematic clubbing coverage there at present.

As with clubbing anywhere, the good stuff only just starts to get rolling around midnight, which happens to be when the Prague metro shuts down. Don't fret: the city centre is small and by-and-large safe and you may just be able to walk back to your room if it's anywhere near the centre. Otherwise, taxis – at least the reputable ones like AAA (14014) are still cheap and night trams run till 5am on all the main routes from the centre to outlying areas. Hopping aboard one of these in booze-loving Prague is another experience you're not likely to forget in a hurry, though a clothes peg for your nose or a high state of intoxication yourself might be the best preparation for a night-tram ride.

Less exhausting might just be ordering a Red Bull and holding out till the regular trams and metro start up again at 5am.

I served the King of England

Arts & Leisure

The arts are all too often neglected in countries focusing on catching their economies up to their neighbours', and if you speak to any Czech filmmaker, painter, scribe or musician, they're likely to tell you that's just what's happened in Prague. Some go so far as to get nostalgic about the days when, yes, all plays, movies and books had to be approved by fusty bureaucrats who had bizarre lists of requirements – but an artist could actually make a living and have a decent flat.

Czechs are fast learners, however, and have learned all about corporate sponsors, as the logos festooning film festivals, major exhibitions and concert programmes all attest. In fact, some, like the Czech National Symphony Orchestra, are thriving in the brave new world, recording in studios the orchestra installed in an old community hall (and leasing it out for decent fees), then going on world tours. Film festivals like One World and Febio Fest grow every year, attracting thousands (while banks, drug companies and car-makers get high-profile appearances on opening night). Filmmaking is bouncing back too, with heavy product placement – Jiří Menzel missed his chance for this with his period adaptation *I Served the King of England*. Gallery Art Factory (p123), meanwhile, has expanded its marketing onto Wenceslas Square, hosting outdoor shows from international creatives.

Literary festivals, such as the Prague Writers' Festival in June, have always been a strong tradition in the city, and most still draw star authors, willing to be talked into giving lectures.

Some older cultural institutions, meanwhile, are still going strong (if others have fallen by the wayside), such as the top-rated Prague Spring (www.festival.cz), the best of the local music festivals. At 62 years old in 2007, this month-long festival consists of concerts around town, and still draws the likes of Murray Parahia and Jordi Savall. And the National Theatre (p137) recently pulled off one of its biggest coups, with Milos Forman directing *A Walk Worthwhile* in the same venue in which his sons, Petr and Matěj, have had recent hits of their own.

The State Opera (p138), which has been less successful in attracting sponsors, managed a novel conception of *La Traviata* this season, with 1920s-style sets and standout performances, even as it struggled to get energetic performances out of its musicians. This last example shows where new and old overlap: most orchestra members are still state employees who earn so little they must hold second jobs, making discipline and performance-quality an issue. The flipside is culture that's still sheltered from the free market and that is remarkably affordable. Yes, the National Theatre and State Opera may close for long summer breaks just when demand is high, but when they're open, you can get a prime seat for as little as 200 Kč.

The city's newest classical gala, the Prague Music Festival, mixes popular faves with serious Czech composers, while the Prague Proms has also proven a hit, adding touches like late-night jazz sessions with local stars. Meanwhile another respected edition, Prague Autumn, www.prazskypodzim.cz, remains a strong presence on the scene.

SHORTLIST

Best repertory cinema
- Evald (p137)
- MAT Studio (p137)
- Světozor (p138)

Best on stage
- National Theatre (p137)
- State Opera (p138)
- Švandovo divadlo (p88)

Best classical music
- Chapel of Mirrors (p117)
- Prague Symphony Orchestra, at Municipal House (p117)

Best rock
- Archa Theatre (p117)
- Lucerna Music Bar (p135)
- Vagon (p116)

Best jazz
- AghARTA (p137)
- U Malého Glena (p86)
- U staré paní (p116)

Best modern art
- House at the Golden Ring (p97)
- Hunt Kastner artworks (p160)
- Kampa Museum (p77)
- National Gallery Collection of 19th-, 20th- and 21st-Century Art (p153)

Best spectator sport
- Football at AC Sparta Praha (p158)
- Hockey at T-Mobile arena (p160)

Best active sport
- Shooting pool at Café Louvre (p45)
- Skating at Letná (p152)
- Tennis at Tenisový klub Slavia Praha (p160)

Grandest venues
- Municipal House (p117)
- National Theatre (p137)
- Rudolfinum (p117)

DON'T MISS: 2008

Visual arts

On the art scene, two competing megashows were going head to head in summer 2007. The Prague Biennale, organised by the editors of Italian magazine *Flash Art International* (www.praguebiennale.org) and held in the factory hall known as Karlin Studios, won out for edginess over the National Gallery's International Biennale of Contemporary Art, held at Veletržní palác. Meanwhile, an 'anti-biennale' sprung up in 2006, an off-year for the other biennales, called Tina B – an acronym for This Is Not Another Biennale (www.tina-b.com), which is slated to return with force in 2008.

A flurry of artist-run spaces like Futura (p87) are also claiming their glory with fascinating, fresh shows.

Staging a coup

Early summer now sees exciting shows of contemporary dance, when twin festivals showcase home-grown talent. Czech Dance Platform (www.divadloponec.cz) reprises the best of the previous year every April. In June, Tanec Praha (www.tanecpha.cz) juxtaposes new Czech works with headliner performances by visiting dance troupes.

Autumn brings more great festival events: Four Days in Motion (www.ctyridny.cz) selects a new and unorthodox site every year – for instance, an abandoned factory – to stage avant-garde dance and physical theatre pieces. But contemporary dance is on the programme year-round at experimental venues like Roxy's (p115) Galerie NoD and Alfred v Dvoře and Divadlo Ponec (www.divadloponec.cz). And keep an eye out for the local companies for the excellent cutting-edge theatre-dance like Déja Donné (www.dejadonne.com). And if an established foreign contemporary dance troupe is touring Europe, a stop at the Archa Theatre (p117) will be on its itinerary. For classical dance fans, the National Theatre ballet company (performing at both the National and Estates theatres) and the State Opera's resident company offer a steady diet, from standards like *Swan Lake* to occasionally inspired originals.

DON'T MISS: 2008

National Theatre p29

National Theatre pieces tend to be more polished and sophisticated, the State Opera more bold and colourful.

As for theatre, most plays are in Czech, but English-language performances grow in number every year. The Prague Fringe Festival (www.praguefringe.com) in early June is a circus worthy of its namesake in Edinburgh, with dozens of visiting performers filling multiple venues around town.

Performers occasionally visit Prague for 'off-Fringe' nights other times of the year, usually held at Palác Akropolis. The star of the English-language scene is Švandovo Divaldo (p88), a refurbished theatre in the city's Smíchov district that's managed to retain its friendly, funky atmosphere in smart new surroundings. Eight to ten plays are on at any time, about half of which have English subtitles. The theatre also stages progressive concerts and conversation nights with visiting celebrities like Michael Nyman.

During the summer, consider a visit to one of the 'Shakespeare at the Castle' performances (old.hrad.cz). These are in Czech but most audiences should be able to follow a staple like *Romeo and Juliet* in any tongue. And there's nothing like experiencing *Hamlet* staged in a castle as twilight turns to darkness and church bells toll. Or, for family fun, don't forget the mainstays of Czech theatre for export: black light and puppetry, available in many venues throughout the city. You won't be able to miss the signs for these in Old Town in tourist season.

Tickets and information

Many box office clerks have a rudimentary command of English, but you're better off buying tickets through one of the central agencies. These accept credit cards (unlike many venues), you can book via their websites or by telephone in English and there are numerous outlets throughout the city. Bohemia Ticket International (Malé náměstí 13, Staré Město, 224 227 832/www.ticketsbti.cz) is the best agency for advance bookings from abroad for the National Theatre, Estates Theatre and State Opera. Ticketpro at Old Town Hall (p102) also sells tickets for some events. Ticket touts cluster at many events so you can often get into sold-out (vyprodáno) performances, although for a price. Wait until the last bell for the best deal. For the latest art, film, theatre and dance listings, pick up a copy of *The Prague Post* (www.praguepost.com) or drop into your nearest branch of the Prague Information Service or check out its website www.pis.cz.

Archa Theatre p31

Calendar

Collegium Marianum, Summer Old Music Festival p37

There are 12 public holidays in the Czech Republic. Except for Easter Monday, the dates are fixed, with the sliding holiday concept not employed – that is, when they fall on a weekend, the following Monday is a normal business day.

Public holidays are highlighted here in **bold**.

September 2007

8 **Mattoni Grand Prix**
Staré Město
www.pim.cz
An offshoot of the Prague Marathon (p36), despite the confusing name, with a 5km women's run and a 10km men's race.

12 Sept-1 Oct **Prague Autumn**
Various venues across Prague
www.prazskypodzim.cz
Festival of world-renowned classical talents, based around the Rudolfinum.

12 Sept-20 Oct **Tina B**
Various venues across Prague
www.tina-b.com
An acronym of This Is Not Another Biennale. This 'anti-biennale' showcases contemporary art in surprising locations around Prague.

Mid Sept **International Aviation Film Festival**
Various venues across Prague
www.leteckefilmy.cz
Festival of war and action films with famous pilots and war heroes present.

Late Sept **Burčák arrives**
Various pubs across Prague
Cloudy, half-fermented, early-season wine from Moravia is served from jugs during this month-long festival.

28 **Czech Statehood Day**

October 2007

Ongoing Prague Autumn (see Sept); Tina B (see Sept)

Easter

Mid Oct **Festival of Best Amateur & Professional Puppet Theatre Plays**
Various venues across Prague
www.pis.cz
Innovative puppetry festival.

28 Anniversary of the birth of Czechoslovakia
Various venues across Prague
www.ifp.cz
Fireworks and a public holiday mark independence from the Habsburgs.

November 2007

2 **All Souls' Day**
Olšany Cemetery, p146
Czech families say prayers for the dead.

Mid Nov **French Film Festival**
French Institute
www.ifp.cz
Indie and pop French movie overload, some with English subtitles.

17 Anniversary of the Velvet Revolution
Wenceslas Square p126, and also on Národní třída, Nové Město.
Flowers are laid near the equine statue, with a memorial to student protesters.

December 2007

5 **St Nicholas's Eve**
Staré Město
www.pis.cz
Trios dressed as St Nicholas, an angel and a devil grill children about who's been naughty and who's been nice.

Mid Dec **Christmas Markets**
Wenceslas Square, p126, and Old Town Square
www.pis.cz
Stalls with crafts and Czech Christmas food and drink spread the cheer.

24 Christmas Eve/Midnight mass
St Vitus's Cathedral, p63
old.hrad.cz
The finest Christmas observance in Bohemia fills the (cold) Gothic church; bring your thermal underwear.

25 Christmas Day

26 St Stephen's Day

31 **New Year's Eve**
Wenceslas Square, p126
'Silvestr' sparks off a plethora of fireworks and flying bottles. Bring your helmet.

January 2008

1 New Year's Day/Prague New Year's Concert
Rudolfinum, p117
www.czechphilmarmonic.cz
Czech Philharmonic's annual concert.

February 2008

Early Feb **Days of European Film**
Various venues across Prague
www.eurofilmfest.cz
Ten days of flicks from across Europe, many with English subtitles.

Mid Feb (7th Sun before Easter) **Masopust**
Various venues in Žižkov
www.palacakropolis.cz
A weekend of street parties, concerts and feasts.

Feb **One World Human Rights**
Various venues across Prague
www.oneworld.cz
Festival of documentaries and features on human rights, some in English.

Feb-Mar **Matějská pouť**
Výstaviště, p153
www.pis.cz
St Matthew's Fair marks the arrival of
warm weather with cheesy rides for the
kids at a run-down funfair.

March 2008

Ongoing Matějská pouť (see Feb)

20-24 **Easter**

24 **Easter Monday**
Staré Město
www.pis.cz
Men whack women on the backside
with sticks; women douse men with
water and give them painted eggs.

Mar **Febiofest**
Palace Cinemas, Anděl
www.fest.cz
The city's biggest film fest offers a
huge scope of world cinema.

Mar-Apr **Prague Jazz Festival**
Various venues
www.agharta.cz
Prague's hottest jazz fest brings in the
likes of John Scofield. Mainly at
Lucerna Music Bar (p135).

April 2008

Ongoing Prague Jazz Festival
(see Mar)

30 **Witches' Night**
Petřín Hill, p78
Halloween and Bonfire Night in one.

May 2008

Ongoing Prague Jazz Festival
(see Mar)

1 **Labour Day**
Letná, p152

1 **May Day**
Petřín hill, p78
Czech lovers of all ages kiss in front
of the statue of Karel Hynek Mácha.

8 **VE Day**
Letná, p152
Czechs now celebrate the Allied victory
more openly, with American Jeeps join-
ing the memorials to the Red Army.

May Day

What does a fervently no-longer-
communist country do about a
holiday like 1 May? It's easy to
cancel the tank parades and
allow the children to stay home
instead of making them march
behind Socialist Youth banners.
But what of the old folks who
just won't let this celebration
go? Even America celebrates
Labour Day! – they just do it on
the first Monday of September.

More worrying still, what of the
new generation of Communists
who add to the numbers of
pensioners who go to Letná
park to moan about the cost of
groceries each May Day? In fact,
the party still polls high-enough
numbers to get into Parliament
and was cautiously considered
during the months it took for
the four-party coalition of Prime
Minister Mirek Topolánek to
form in 2007 (they didn't make
it in, and remain in opposition).

Well, as one group discovered,
the Communists don't own May
Day. Hence, the Confederation
of Political Prisoners, an anti-
communist group dedicated to
chronicling the crimes of the pre-
1989 regime, has lately been
outflanking the red retirees.
Recently they applied for the
Letná park demonstration permit
before the Communist Party did,
and managed to get use of their
favourite gathering spot for 1
May. The poor Communists had
to move to a nearby park and
hold an indignant rally there.

The conservatives even turn
out for the new 'First of May
Without Communist' rallies.
So how are they supposed
to be any fun *now*?

Fringe benefits

Random Accomplice

The first time you encounter outsize, demented-looking walking puppets on the Charles Bridge in the dead of night, it's bound to cause a slight pause. But a quick check of your calendar may be all you need to reassure yourself that you haven't lost your mind or slipped into another dimension.

If it's May, it's probably just the Prague Fringe Festival, spilling its delightful madness onto the streets again. This event, inspired by the Edinburgh original, fills a lot more than theatres, obviously, and incorporates performers for whom anything can be a stage. Nor are they all even doing what's normally considered theatre: bands, comics, children's events and even film make up many of the 180 or so performances that this hit festival brings each spring.

Performers pour in from the United States, Canada, Australia, Ireland, the UK, France and Denmark and, with good

performance spaces at a premium, some take over coffeehouses, some jazz clubs, some castle catacombs. And all offer audiences in this theatre-crazed city a chance to see more spontaneity and interaction than you normally get in a year.

From smouldering lounge-singing by Maria Tecce to street-poetry by guitarist Stephen Brandon or traditional hyperkinetic Mediterranean folk by Tarantella, Taranula, the music acts offer a rich complement to the thespian action. Theatre troupes range from Venezuela's Passport, performing gripping political polemics, to experimental stuff from folk like the critically acclaimed Americans Quick Silver Productions, complemented by local dance and movement companies. Comedy, meanwhile, ranges from standup talents good enough to have spawned a new comedy nights section of the festival, to the in-your-face cabaret antics of the UK's Topping & Butch.

Former English teacher and longtime Prague resident Steven Gove, a Scottish expat, set the wheels turning for Prague Fringe in 2001, and the fest has steadily picked up steam to the point where it's now one of the most anticipated events on the cultural calendar.

What's more, the fest has become a sort of family reunion for fans and artists from around the world, as reflected by the launch in 2007 of the Fringe Club, a space to gather for after-show frolics and to catch up with performers. Cue the lights!

May **Prague International Marathon**
Various venues across Prague
www.pim.cz
Those not up to the full 42km (26-mile) race can try the 10km race.

May **Four Days in Motion**
Various venues across Prague
www.ctyridny.cz
Excellent fest of international dance and visual theatre, in unusual venues.

May **Khamoro**
Various venues across Prague
www.khamoro.cz
Concerts, seminars and workshops on traditional Roma culture.

Last weekend May **Mezi ploty**
Around the Psychiatric Hospital, Bohnice
www.meziploty.cz
Events by professional, amateur and mentally or physically disadvantaged artists over two days.

May **Prague Fringe Festival**
Various venues across Prague
www.praguefringe.com
The newest theatre fest fills venues like Vyšehrad with cabaret to multimedia.

Mid May-early June **Prague Spring**
Various venues across Prague
www.festival.cz
The biggest and best Prague music festival draws international talent.

June 2008

Ongoing Prague Jazz Festival (see Mar); Prague Spring (see May)

1-4 **Prague Writers' Festival**
Various venues across Prague
www.pwf.cz
Czech and international literati gather to read and hobnob.

June **Respect**
Various venues across Prague
www.respectmusic.cz
Celebration of world and ethnic music.

June **Tanec Praha**
Various venues across Prague
www.tanecpha.cz
A top-flight international gala of modern dance with recitals in Prague's major theatres.

June **United Islands of Prague**
Střelecký ostrov, Žofín (p126)
www.unitedislands.cz
Popular weekend of rock, jazz and folk music on the city's river banks.

July 2008

Ongoing Prague Jazz Festival (see Mar)

5 **Cyril and Methodius Day**

6 **Jan Hus Day**

July **Prague Proms**
Various venues in Staré Město
www.pragueproms.cz
A new series of classical concerts, opera and jazz.

July **Summer Old Music Festival**
Various venues in Staré Město
www.tynska.cuni.cz
Renaissance and baroque music on period instruments, in historic settings.

August 2008

Ongoing Prague Jazz Festival (see Mar)

Mid Aug **Letní Letná**
Letná park, p152
www.letniletna.cz
Theatre, music and circus fest attracting Czech and European talents.

September 2008

Ongoing Prague Jazz Festival (see Mar)

Mid Sept **Prague Autumn**
Various venues across Prague
www.prazskypodzim.cz
See Sept 2007.

Sept **St Wenceslas Sacred Music Festival**
Various venues across Prague
www.sdh.cz
Sacred music festival held at half a dozen chapels, churches and cathedrals across Prague.

Late Sept **Burčák arrives**
Various pubs across Prague
See Sept 2007.

28 **Czech Statehood Day**

Prague Spring p37

October 2008

Ongoing **Prague Jazz Festival**
(see Mar)

Mid Oct **Prague International
Jazz Festival**
Various venues across Prague
www.pragokoncert.cz
Mix of local and international jazz masters at some of the city's top clubs.

**28 Anniversary of the birth
of Czechoslovakia**
Various venues across Prague
See Oct 2007.

November 2008

Nov **FAMU Festival**
Academy of Performing Arts
www.famufest.cz
FAMU students' best work is screened.

**17 Anniversary of the
Velvet Revolution**
Wenceslas Square, p126, and on
Národní třída near No.20
See above Nov 2007.

Mid Nov **Alternativa**
Archa Theatre, p117
www.alternativa-festival.cz

Underground film, music and stage
performances.

Mid Nov **French Film Festival**
French Institute
www.ifp.cz
See Nov 2007.

December 2008

5 St Nicholas's Eve
Staré Město
www.pis.cz
See Dec 2007.

Early Dec **International Festival
of Advent & Christmas Music**
Various venues across Prague
www.orfea.cz
Choirs and choruses ring in the season.

24 Christmas Eve/Midnight Mass
St Vitus's Cathedral, p63
old.hrad.cz
See Dec 2007.

25 Christmas Day

26 St Stephen's Day

31 New Year's Eve
Wenceslas Square, p126
See Dec 2007.

Itineraries

Laterna Magika
Národní třída 4
Praha 1
www.laterna.cz
info@laterna.cz

box office:
224 931 482
group orders:
222 222 041
fax: 222 222 039

LATERNA MAGIKA´s

secret is in its mixture of film and live performance. The continuous search for novelty and originality stemming from the combination of these elements lies at the heart of the ensembles creative work.

House of the Stone Bell p42

Green Line Art & Architecture

Prague gets swoons for its architecture from many who wouldn't know a cubist building from a petrol station; and rightly so. It doesn't take a scholar to appreciate both the overall sense of wondrous ornament to the city, and the fact that it's not particularly concerned with orderly commerce, particularly on Old Town's knotted lanes. Better yet, many of the most stunning structures are homes to even more breathtaking art within.

This art and architecture itinerary will take a full day if you hit all the buildings and galleries listed here – quite a marathon, which could easily lead to sensory overload, so feel no compunction to do them all and by all means

stop off for a pint at any of the iconic beerhalls along the way. Some Prague galleries still lack English-language signage or helpful guides, but the following are quite progressive. Just don't go on a Monday, when museums and galleries are closed.

Start at the Jiřího z Poděbrad metro on the green line, which shares the same square with the **Church of the Sacred Heart** (p143), an overlooked modernist wonder. Built by the Slovene iconoclast Josip Plečnik, the man who made over Prague Castle for the first independent Czechoslovak state following World War I, the brick church features twin obelisks, an ancient icon much-loved by

Plečnik and installed in Hradčany too, and the black and white brick patterns that are meant to suggest a king's mantle. Don't miss the immense rose window, which features a single ramp within; you could ride a bicycle to the top if you felt inclined to.

Now hop on the metro towards the centre, being sure you buy your 20 Kč ticket if you'll be riding for an hour or less (a safer bet for this tour is the 80 Kč 24-hour pass; both are available from the overcomplicated ticket machine inside the metro station). Ride two stops to the Muzeum station and exit on **Wenceslas Square** (p126). Towering above you is the **National Museum** (p123), but that's not where you're headed. Quirkier rewards await two thirds of the way down the square on the right-hand side (as you face away from the museum), at No. 15: **Gallery Art Factory** (p123). One of the most engaging galleries in town, this space invariably hosts low-budget (that is, fresh and provocative) international modern art, Slovak artists and the annual Sculpture Grande show, which covers the street in big, bizarre offerings like Superman crashing into the pavement.

At the bottom of Wenceslas Square, turn right down shopping heaven Na Příkopě, and walk four blocks to the enormous **Municipal House** (p100). This gorgeous art nouveau masterpiece has a small gallery on the top floor that consistently features compelling modern work, from photo shows to the commercial art of Karel Čapek's brother, Josef. Getting to it is half the fun, causing you to glide through the fabulously ornate bronze-and-oak entryway under an impressive Atlas hoisting a massive crystal globe. There's also a classic Vienna-style

coffeehouse on the ground floor, complete with tinkling grand piano and precious little cakes on trolleys. More substantial white-linen fare can be had at the oppulent French Restaurant, also on the ground floor.

From here, turn west down Celetná. At the corner of Ovocný trh, a former fruit market, stands something unique in the world: Prague's most definitive example of cubist architecture, the **House of the Black Madonna** (p98), a fine, bevelled Josef Gočár creation that was first opened in 1912 as a department store. It's now a cubism museum, café, shop and bookstore (the cubist porcelain ashtrays can't be beat).

Continue down Celetná to **Old Town Square**. Unless it's winter, early morning or late at night, it probably doesn't pay to tarry long here, thanks to the roving packs of tourists who gather to watch the **Astronomical Clock** (p94) put on its hourly show. The pickpockets they attract are another disincentive (but you won't be bothered as long as you don't have camcorders hanging off you). At the east end of the square next to the Týn Church you'll spot a tall, battered sandstone building, the only one on Staroměstské náměstí with its original Gothic façade visible; all the others were prettied up with baroque makeovers by Habsburg burghers during the Counter-Reformation. Head for the one that wasn't: the **House of the Stone Bell** (p98). This lovely old gallery, arranged around an ancient courtyard, also goes in for inspired contrast, hosting shows like the Zvon Biennale of Young Artists or showcasing digital installations exploring perception and subjectivity.

If that doesn't make your head spin, it's definitely time for lunch. Try the handy **Café Ebel** down the unnamed passage between the Stone Bell and the Týn Church for a little light quiche and powerhouse coffee. More serious noshing probably doesn't go well with gallery walking marathons (don't worry, though – all of Old Town is only a square kilometre and, though the streets are all winding, it's flat).

Thus restored, head north on Týnská to one of the most easily overlooked and interesting of the city's small, basement galleries, the **House of the Golden Ring** (p97). Find the entrance on the right-hand side midway up the street next to the café. Art from various media and periods is thoughtfully organised here by theme, rather than by artist or country, making for fresh work to mull as you digest.

Continue up Týnská and go left down Masná, passing (if you can resist entering), the delectable expat institution **Bakeshop Praha** (p103), until you hit Vězeňská. Have a look to your right and acquaint yourself with Jaroslav Rona's surrealist sculpture that is Prague's first real tribute to Franz Kafka (that is, one not printed on a T-shirt or postcard – Czechs have issues with Kafka), a hulking, dark bronze figure erected in 2002.

Now continue west down Široká street to your last stop, the magnificent (but still manageable) **Rudolfinum** (p117). Prague's greatest kunsthalle, and the only major exhibition space dedicated to this genre of changing major shows, the former parliament building may be housing a Chinese art show or a Cindy Sherman photo collection, but whatever's on is sure to surprise and reward.

If Pilsner's needed at this point, you won't have to go far. There's the classically unreformed pub **U Rudolfinum** across Křižovnická, catty-corner from the gallery. On

Rudolfinum

the corner of Kaprová you're back at Staroměstská metro, where you can now ride one more stop to the west on the green line to Malostranská. Here, just outside the metro exit, is the **Wallenstein Riding School** (p81) situated at Valdštejnská 3. Part of the **Wallenstein Palace** complex, this National Gallery space holds some of Prague's most popular and well-attended exhibitions, often highlighting Czech artists you won't see anywhere else, like National Revival-era patriot František Ženíšek, modernist Václav Špála and symbolist Max Švabinský. And if you've made it this far, you certainly have earned a fine riverside meal at **Palffy Palác** (p83), 100 metres south down Valdštejnská, where even the cuisine is museum-worthy.

To art in all things!

Jan Žižka equestrian statue p46

Soviet Souvenirs

The signs are still all around, if you know where to look: still looming over Wenceslas Square like ghosts are the names of communist state companies with their utilitarian ring still good for a frisson. Orwell himself could hardly do better than a name like Strojimport or Dům mody, meaning, simply, House of Fashion. The latter, long since turned into offices and modern retail spaces that line the south side of the top of this bustling boulevard, still features a frieze of proletarian labourers hoisting bolts of fabric and running sewing machines.

This tour of the surviving icons of the bad old days will take a half day, relying on a mix of walking, trams and the metro – probably the single best surviving Soviet contribution to Czech society in itself.

It's appropriate, then, to start at the **Anděl metro stop**, which was once named Moskva, or Moscow. At the top of the escalator leading out to Nadrážní street, you can still see the murals of heroic workers marching towards their bright destiny. Filmmaker Jan Svěrák was so transfixed by this image that he used this backdrop in his Oscar-winning *Kolja*, about an ageing Czech Romeo who finds himself suddenly saddled with a Russian boy. The Soviets, as part of their post 1968 'Normalization' programme, began work on the Prague's metro in a kind of sister city exchange with the Russian capital, with metro stops in Moscow named after Prague and vice versa. It must be said that the system is still clean, fast, efficient and cheap after all these years, even if the high-speed Russian escalators are almost all gone, replaced with (presumably safer, if slower) modern ones.

Like the metro in Russia, Prague's was designed to double as a civil defence facility, which could be sealed in case of nuclear attack. Rumours, later proven false, circulated widely during the floods of 2002 that the water that took out downtown metro stations got in because someone forgot to close the nuclear doors. One truth, however, was that dozens of cheap coffins, which had been kept in metro station storage rooms with nuclear war in mind, were discovered bobbing inside by clean-up workers.

From the Anděl metro station, hop on a 20 tram north four stops to **Hellichová**. From here, walk east two blocks to Nosticova and turn left. After two blocks, the street ends at a garden wall on the south end of **Maltežské náměstí**. Follow it east a few metres to where it's covered in graffiti and pick out the benificently smiling John Lennon image. The original Beatle has long since faded away, but new ones are always emerging on the **Lennon Wall** (p77), where students first painted him, lit candles and sang protest songs after his assassination in New York in 1980. The communist authorities, troubled by this, kept cleaning the wall, but up would pop John anew every time, until the wall became a locus for dissidents who later grew in strength, becoming a force that helped to bring down the regime in 1989.

Head back to the tram stop and hop on the 22 or 23 in the opposite direction to cross the Vltava river, getting off at **Národní divadlo**. Continue east for one block, keeping to the right side of **Národní** street, where you'll find a short colonnade. Under the columns lies a plaque honouring the students who faced down the riot police on 17 November 1989; people still place flowers and

candles here on the anniversary of the Velvet Revolution.

At this point, consider lunch or a refresher at the **Café Louvre** (Národní 22, 224 930 949), a grand old Bohemian eatery where the city's literati once hung out (and a favourite of dissidents, of course, back in the day). Then continue east up Národní three blocks to **Můstek**, the square at the bottom of Wenceslas Square. As you pass by the giant Tesco supermarket, try to picture it as it once was, as the communist regime's biggest department store, then known as Maj, or May (as in 1 May, international day of the worker). Before 1989, little was sold from this space that anyone wanted – but tyres, pipes and tiles were in abundance.

At **Wenceslas Square** (p126) have a gander up the great boulevard and try to imagine Soviet tanks firing into the **National Museum** (p123), which sits so majestically at the top. They mistook the building for the Czech Parliament when they rolled into town in 1968, putting a brutal end to the reforms Alexander Dubček had allowed during the Prague Spring. They wouldn't leave for 21 years. Communist central planners also came up with, aside from Strojimport and Dům Mody, the noisiest, most polluted thoroughfare in the city, which cuts the top off Wenceslas Square running between the top of the boulevard and the National Museum. Plans for a ring road have been discussed for years, but Prague seems no closer to having one than when the monster freeway was built through the town centre.

Walk halfway up Wenceslas Square, taking note of the smoked meat (*maso uzeniny*) shops that still satisfy old party members (and hordes of other Czechs), and hop on the metro's green line in the Můstek

One of Staré Město's many *maso uzeniny* shops p45

station. Ride three stops in the direction of Depot Hostivár and get out at **Jiřího z Poděbrad**. From here, pass the Church of the Sacred Heart and head up Milešovská two blocks north towards the bizarre radio tower you see looming over the Zizkov district.

The **Zizkov Tower** (p147), which artist David Černý has covered with crawling black babies, was the pride of Soviet engineering in the 1980s, and used to jam western radio signals. Sensitively constructed on top of a former Jewish cemetery, part of which still survives, the tower now sports a bar and observation tower that must be experienced to be believed. From inside, you get a commanding view not only of the city, but of the **National Memorial** (p146), also known as Vitkov, fronted by the massive **Jan Žižka equestrian statue**. This building once served as resting place for first working-class president, Klement Gottwald, and a host of other high party officials. These days it's rented out

for parties by the Czech Technical University, which owns the lease.

Now settle into the sci-fi surrounds of the tower restaurant and have yourself a meal of schnitzel and beer, just as any good working-class party member would, and see if you can feel the winds of change.

If, afterwards, you'd like a close-up look at the National Memorial, which is covered in Soviet-era bronze bas-reliefs of brave Russian soldiers being greeted by grateful Czech peasants, be advised that it's a further 20-minute hike to the north through potholed streets, then a steep walk up the hill. If you're up for it, however, walk two blocks north on Čajkovského, cross Seifertova and continue north on Miličova two blocks, turning left on Prokopova. Go two blocks north to cross Husitská and you're on the narrow lane Pod Vítkovem.

From here, summon a proud worker's energy and haul yourself up the hill towards the glorious future of the proletariat!

Toalette p48

Old Town Charmer

The Staré Město district, long devoid of young Czechs – with the exception of punters visiting the few well-hidden pubs and clubs – is now being reclaimed by locals. And meandering **Karolíny Světlé** street, just north of the high street of Národní, is one of the first significant patches to be won back.

This walk could be done in 20 minutes with only window shopping, but that would deprive you of the chance to check out, handle and barter over unique goods that are a world away from the tourist tat. It would also deny you the opportunity to shoot the breeze with relaxed local shop owners – by and large colourful Bohemians who have an interesting collection of tales about their origins and experiences in the Czech Republic's rapidly evolving world of capitalism.

Little, winding Karolíny Světlé is studded with designer boutiques,

galleries, an antique shop or two and characterful food and drink spots. The enchanting lane is the place to source original gifts, while gauging the state of the artisan community and its efforts to balance commercial success with keeping the faith.

That trade-off is at an intriguing stage these days with much promise for the future, as Czechs wean themselves off big-box stores and off-the-shelf lifestyles imported from the West. Nowadays, a growing number are willing to pay a few crowns more for an old desk-lamp, an asymmetric handmade dress or an exotic meal of Afghan food.

Note that some shops mentioned here are only open on weekdays, so plan this itinerary accordingly.

Starting at the corner of Národní and Karolíny Světlé, head north one block into Old Town (Národní street forms the southern border of the district) and follow the cobblestone street directly to **Nábytek ProByt**, which stands at a Y in the road (Krocinova 5). Vladimír Chilko, the impresario of this unique furniture and housewares shop, clearly believes in practical uses for gorgeous pieces. He's filled his capacious shop, which he opened three years ago, after returning to his native Czech Republic from Germany, with handmade glass, ceramics, iron, woodwork and furnishings. Many items are antiques but more are 'antiqued': furniture newly created by local craftsfolk is aged convincingly and stained or painted in faded, homely tones. The work is a hit with many touring celebrities who perform at the nearby National Theatre.

Take the left fork now to continue down Karoliny Světlé, noting on your left the art space **Galerie Kai de Kai** (Karoliny Světlé 9, no phone), open just weekdays, as is still typical of many small Czech shops. It's worth getting your timing right to catch a glimpse of the work of **František Skála**, one of the most outlandish and intriguing artists on the local scene today, who employs found material, such as broken car mirrors and industrial machine parts, to ironic effect. His surreal interiors fill art rock haven the Akropolis club (p146), and his bizarre trailer opened every film at the Karlovy Vary International Film Festival in 2006, causing a stir with audiences.

Next on the left, Monika Burdová's cosy clothes boutique **Toalette** (p115) mixes whimsical local designs, including her own, with select second-hand finds. Colourful creations by apparel artists encourage a lingering visit. Burdová, who established the shop five years ago, believes cool togs should also be functional and adaptable. 'It depends on the girl,'

she says, holding up a glistening green sweater. 'She can put it on over jeans or wear it to the theatre. I think that fashion is play.' Across the street from Toalette, at No.12, stands the source of many of these design inspirations, the **MarLen fabric store**, with bolts of an impressive range and texture and some unexpected ready-to-wear stuff.

If refuelling is rising to the top of the agenda, **Kabul** (p106) can fulfil that need with its affordable Afghan dishes. Book ahead if you're planning to visit this one-room eatery during the midday rush.

Once recharged, manoeuvre yourself a few doors to the south. At No.5, on the west side, is a spot that will ensure your kids are as hip as their parents – **Bim Bam Bum**. Only open on weekdays, from 2pm to 5pm, the shop features a range of appealing togs for tots.

Back on the east side are two upscale fashion boutiques favoured by Czech celebs: **Alice Abraham**, at No.18, and **Pavla & Olga** (p113), at No.30. The posh and spatially challenged Abraham shop (www. aliceabraham.com) doesn't fuss too much about practicality but offers gloriously cool haute couture pieces for women (evening gowns, skirts, tops, jackets) made from quality materials (brocade, suede and silk feature heavily). Prices reflect the swank clientele but are no more outrageous than, say, Lyon or Munich rates, and still well below Paris- and Rome-style extravagance. Pavla & Olga, one of two Prague boutiques owned by the Machálková sisters, is great for accessories, and features more affordable creations that appeal to young and old alike.

As you wrap up the tour, toast your achievement at **Duende** (p106), a local café-bar that's always abuzz with creative, world-hopping types. Sip a grappa and contemplate what shopping tells us of a place's culture.

Prague by Area

St Vitus's Cathedral p63

Hradčany & western Malá Strana

From any open space or high ground in Prague, the Castle complex looms over the city, centred on the spire of St Vitus's Cathedral. As the president's office and the seat of the archbishopric, it remains the political, spiritual and national heart of the Czech Republic. It's also the top tourist attraction in town, even if church-state struggles have resulted in neglect over the years.

The Přemyslid dynasty founded **Prague Castle** in the ninth century, choosing the strategic hilltop as a suitable site for a fortification. Continuously occupied since then, it's changed shape and form a dozen times, following the fortunes and successors of this family, which also ruled parts of Poland but died out in 1306. Like many royal lines of the time, their claim to the throne

rested on a myth, this one holding that Libuše foretold the founding of a great city where Prague now stands, and sent her horse forth to find a ploughman to be her mate in populating its leading class. Few historical details have survived about the reality of the family, its power base or decrees, but it's hoped that excavations going on around the castle grounds will fill missing gaps with the aid of DNA analysis of bones found in royal graves.

Breathtaking city views can only really be had from the gardens and courtyards around the castle, but a trip up the Gothic St Vitus tower solves that – and even from the ground, its flying buttresses and portals never cease to inspire.

The coronation of Charles IV and the Nazis' march through the gates are just two moments in

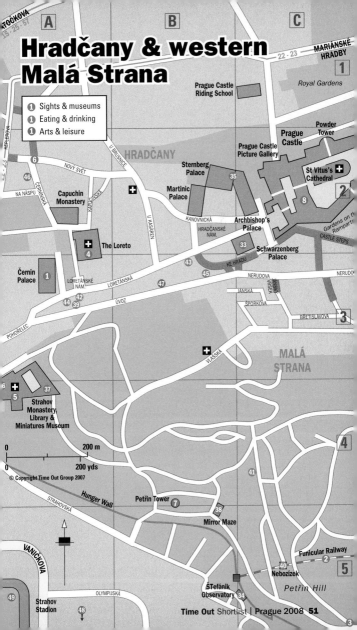

Hradčany & western Malá Strana

STOCKOVA 15 · 25 · 57

A · **B** · **C**

MARIÁNSKÉ HRADBY 22 · 23

1

Royal Gardens

1 Sights & museums
1 Eating & drinking
1 Arts & leisure

Prague Castle Riding School

HEFENICKA

HRADČANY

Powder Tower

Prague Castle

Prague Castle Picture Gallery

Sternberg Palace 35

Martinic Palace

St Vitus's Cathedral

8

2

46

NOVÝ SVĚT

ČERNÍNSKA

KAPUCÍNSKA

U BRUSNICE

U KASAREN

NA NÁSPU

Capuchin Monastery

KANOVNICKÁ

HRADČANSKÉ NÁM.

Archbishop's Palace

Gardens on the Ramparts

CASTLE STEPS

4 The Loreto

33

Schwarzenberg Palace

KE HRADU

43

Černín Palace 1

LORETÁNSKÉ NÁM.

LORETÁNSKÁ

47

45

NERUDOVA

NERUDO

JANSKÁ

ŠPORKOVA

JANSKÝ VRŠEK

44 42
39

ÚVOZ

3

BŘETISLAVOVA

POHOŘELEC

VLAŠSKÁ

MALÁ STRANA

6 5 37

Strahov Monastery, Library & Miniatures Museum

4

0 · · · 200 m
0 · · · 200 yds
© Copyright Time Out Group 2007

41

STRAHOVSKÁ

Hunger Wall

Petřin Tower 7

38

Mirror Maze

Funicular Railway 2

40

Nebozízek

5

VANIČKOVA

49

OLYMPIJSKÁ

Strahov Stadion

48

ŠTefánik Observatory 34

Petřin Hill

Hradčany's 1,000-year history that are likely to give you goose bumps. Czechs take great pride in having had the castle finally returned to public use after the Velvet Revolution. The complex continues to undergo major makeovers and renovations, with a dozen rooms now open to the public beneath the **Old Royal Palace**, the first modern development worthy of such a national treasure.

The rest of the district comprises the surrounding streets, which stretch north and west from the castle across the hilltop. It's quiet and less touristy than the castle itself, and the Nový Svět, or New World, pocket of streets is particularly enchanting.

The castle complex is open to the public until midnight and the best chance of avoiding throngs of tourists is to visit during the evening, when the place is at its most romantic. It's dark, but quite safe. The castle grounds do warrant lengthy (daylight) strolling, however; you'll find a fair number of options for refuelling in the near vicinity and a handful of terrace restaurants visible below. Otherwise, there are richer pickings down the hill in Malá Strana.

Hradčany owes its grand scale and pristine condition to a devastating fire in 1541, which destroyed the medieval district, and to the frenzied period of Counter-Reformation building that followed the Protestant defeat at the Battle of White Mountain in 1620. Little has changed here in the last two centuries.

The area's focal point is **Hradčanské náměstí**, one of the grandest squares in the city, lined with imposing palaces built by the Catholic aristocracy, anxious to be close to the Habsburg court. Empress Maria Theresa had a grand spring clean in the mid 18th

Loreto p55

century, consolidating the castle grounds and opening up the square to a view of Malá Strana, the Strahov Gardens and Petřín hill.

Sights & museums

Černín Palace

Černínský palác
Černínská 5 (no phone). Metro Malostranská, then tram 22, 23.
Map p51 A3 ①
This enormous, unprepossessing structure, with its imposing grey façade, articulated by a line of 30 pillars, was commissioned in 1669 by Humprecht Johann Černin, imperial ambassador to Venice; its construction expenses ruined the family. Gestapo interrogations were later conducted here during the Nazi occupation. Its curse surfaced again in 1948, when Foreign Minister Jan Masaryk, the last major political obstacle to Klement Gottwald's communist coup, had a fatal fall from an upstairs window a few days after the takeover.

What lies beneath

There's more to Prague Castle than meets the eye. Below the complex lies a vast underground network of tunnels, built by the communists during the Cold War, which is sealed to all but Castle engineers. Sadly, there are no plans to allow public access. However, there is hope for the royal tomb that sits below St Vitus's Cathedral (pictured). The space is also currently off limits, but with word awaiting from the courts on whether the situation will change. Access rests on official resolution of the tug-of-war between the Catholic Church and the Czech state. It seems these two battling titans are still sorting out the legacy of President Klement Gottwald, who seized all Church property after making himself Soviet-backed top dog in 1948.

But the most likely area of Prague's underground to first be made accessible to the public is the space that was the source of St Vitus's Cathedral's stones (and those of the surrounding Castle). The Prague 9 district City Council is at work on a tourist-orientated plan to open up 400 metres (1,312 feet) of sandstone caves, formed from the mining of the stone.

Aside from providing building blocks for palaces and cathedrals, ancient miners used to break off chunks of the soft white mineral to sell as a cleaning agent for floors and dishes, a brisk trade that explains why the caves go so far underground. This stopped only a century ago as resources ran out and (illegal) Prague residents moved in. No one is really sure how extensive the underground network is because of the many cave-ins that occur due to the softness of the sandstone.

The plans might, however, deprive the district's growing homeless population of a place to sleep at night, but that's not troubling Prague 9 officials, who say the current illicit use of the caves (said to be extensive) raises both safety and hygiene issues.

For now, like many other Prague districts, the honeycombed secrets are there to be discovered any time someone cares to get to work with a pick and shovel.

Funicular

Petřín hill, Karmelitská 1. Metro Malostranská. **Map** p51 C5 ❷
Newly restored and gliding again, this feat of engineering is 118 years old in 2008 and still offers a lazy (and fun) way up to the top of the hill from Újezd, running roughly every ten minutes March-Oct from 9am until 11.20pm and every 15 minutes in winter season, stopping halfway up the hill before continuing to the top. Your tram and metro tickets are all you need.

Karel Hynek Mácha

Petřín hill (257 315 212). Tram 12, 22, then funicular railway. **Map** p51 C5 ❸
This tragic romantic poet – the unofficial patron saint of lovers – has a statue in the park where every young couple in Prague (or so it seems) turns out on 1 May to smooch. Any lad who hesitates when his girl suggests this is not long for this world – or certainly not long for the relationship.

Loreto

Loretánské náměstí 7 (220 516 740/ www.loreta.cz). Metro Malostranská, then tram 22, 23. **Open** 9am-12.15pm, 1-4.30pm Tue-Sun. **Admission** 110 Kč; 90 Kč reductions. No credit cards. **Map** p51 A2/A3 ❹
Probably the most outlandish baroque fantasy in Prague, the Loreto contains the bearded St Wilgefortis, the skeletons of another two female saints and the highest concentration of cherubs to be found anywhere in the city. The heart is a small chapel, the Santa Casa, supposedly the home of Mary in Nazareth until it was miraculously flown over to Loreto in Italy by angels, spawning a copycat cult all over Europe. This one, dating from 1626-31, boasts two beams and a brick from the 'original', as well as a crevice left on the wall by a divine thunderbolt that struck an unfortunate blasphemer. The famous diamond monstrance, designed in 1699 by Fischer von Erlach and sporting 6,222 stones, is in the treasury.

Miniatures Museum

Muzeum miniatur
Strahovské nádvoří 11 (233 352 371). Metro Malostranská, then tram 22, 23. **Open** 9am-5pm daily. **Admission** 50 Kč; 20 Kč children. **Map** p51 A4 ❺
This obsessive collection on the grounds of Strahov Monastery lets you in on monkish work with the aid of magnifying glasses and microscopes. Portraiture on a poppy seed, a caravan of camels painted on a grain of millet, a prayer written out on a human hair, and minuscule copies of masterpieces by the likes of Rembrandt and Botticelli.

Nový Svět

New World
Černínská. Metro Malostranská, then tram 22, 23. **Map** p51 A2 ❻
From Černínská to the streets north of it, behind the Loreto, some of the prettiest and quietest lanes in Hradčany are known as the New World. The quarter was built in the 16th century for Prague Castle staff; its tiny cottages are now the most prized real estate in the city. Going down Kapucínská, you pass the Domeček, or Little House, at No.10, once home to the notorious Fifth Department – the counterintelligence unit of the Defence Ministry. Tycho Brahe, the Danish alchemist known for his missing nose and breakthroughs in accurate observations of orbits, lived at No.1, the Golden Griffin.

Petřín Tower

Rozhledna
Petřín hill (257 320 112). Tram 12, 22, then funicular railway. **Open** *Jan-Mar, Nov-Dec* 10am-5pm Sat, Sun. *Apr, Sept* 10am-7pm daily. *May-Aug* 10am-10pm daily. *Oct* 10am-6pm daily. Closed in poor weather. **Admission** 50 Kč; 40 Kč children. **Map** p51 B4 ❼
This copy of the Eiffel Tower offers spectacular views over the city. The tower was erected in 1891 for the Jubilee Exhibition, as was the neighbouring mock-Gothic castle that houses the amusements below. Its fiercest opponent was Adolf Hitler. The view of St Vitus's Cathedral includes the complete

Petřín Tower p55

building, not just the usual vista of a set of spires poking over the top of the rest of the castle. Just try not to think about the way the tower sways in the wind.

Prague Castle
Hradčanské náměstí (224 371 111/ old.hrad.cz). Metro Malostranská, then tram 22, 23. **Open** *Apr-Oct* 9am-5pm. *Nov-Mar* 9am-4pm daily. **Admission** 50-350 Kč; 30-175 Kč reductions; 520 Kč family, for two days. **Map** p51 C2 ❽
Founded around AD 870 by Přemysl princes, this impressive if sombre collection of buildings has been extended, torn down and rebuilt over the centuries. The final touches, including the present shape of St Vitus's Cathedral, were not added until the early 1900s, thus the complex feels like an enormous festival of architectural styles, stretching all the way back to the Romanesque era. The grandiose façade enclosing the castle is down to Empress Maria Theresa's desire for coherence but the outcome of Nicolo Pacassi's monotonous concept is uninspiring. Václav Havel did his best to enliven the palace, opening it to the public and hiring the costume

designer from the film *Amadeus* to remodel the castle guards' uniforms.

There's no charge to enter the grounds, but you will need a ticket to enter the Old Royal Palace (which now features the excellent Life at Prague Castle exhibit), the Basilica of St George, the Golden Lane, the Powder Tower and the choir, crypt and tower of St Vitus's Cathedral (except Jan-Apr & Oct-Dec, when the tower is closed and the Golden Lane is free of charge). Entrance to the art collection of St George's Convent and the Toy Museum is extra. It's a stiff walk up to the castle from Malá Strana's Malostranská metro station. The least strenuous approach is to take the No.22 tram up the hill and get off at the Pražský hrad stop. There are a handful of adequate cafés within the castle complex, if you don't mind paying double the usual prices.

Ball Game Court
Míčovna
U Prašného mostu (224 373 579/ old.hrad.cz). Metro Malostranská, then tram 22, 23. **Open** Events only. **Admission** Varies. **Map** p57 C1/C2 ❾

Prague Castle

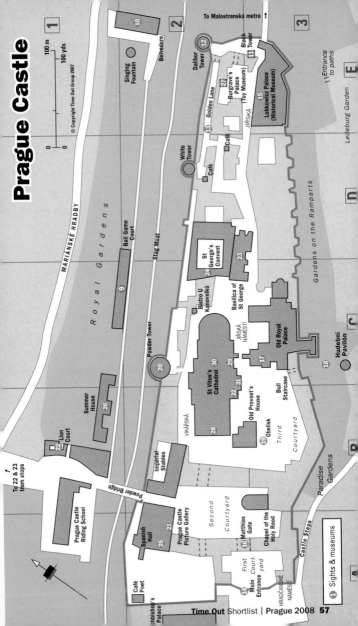

1 | 100 m
100 yds

© Copyright Time Out Group 2007

To Malostranská metro ↑

MARIÁNSKÉ HRADBY

Royal Gardens

Stag Moat

Singing Fountain

10

Belvedere

Ball Game Court

9

Dalibor Tower 12

Golden Lane 13

Burgrave's Palace (Toy Museum) 27

Black Tower 11

JIŘSKÁ

Lobkowicz Palace (Historical Museum) 15

Entrance to paths

Ledeburg Garden

White Tower

Café

Café

St George's Convent 24

Basilica of St George 23

Gardens on the Ramparts

Powder Tower 20

Summer House 26

Bistro U Kanovníků

JIŘSKÁ NÁMĚSTÍ

Old Royal Palace 17

Hudební Pavilón 18

St Vitus's Cathedral 30

32 31

Old Provost's House 29

Obelisk 19

Bull Staircase

VIKÁŘSKÁ

28

Third Courtyard

Lion Court 22

Imperial Stables

To 22 & 23 tram stops

Powder Bridge

Prague Castle Riding School

Second Courtyard

Spanish Hall 25

Prague Castle Picture Gallery 21

Matthias Gate 16

Chapel of the Holy Rood

Paradise Gardens

Castle Steps

First Courtyard

Café Poet

Main Entrance

HRADČANSKÉ NÁMĚSTÍ

Archbishop's Palace

1 Sights & museums

On the southern side of the Royal Gardens, overlooking the Stag Moat, lies this Renaissance former hall. Built in 1563-69 by Bonifác Wohlmut, it was originally conceived for Habsburg tennis matches, but hasn't seen sport for centuries. It's now periodically open for exhibitions and, despite awful acoustics, concerts. Look carefully at the elaborate black-and-white sgraffito above the figure of Justice (tenth from the right) and you'll spot some façade work modified under the old regime, which now contains a hammer and sickle.

Belvedere
U Prašného mostu (224 371 111/ old.hrad.cz). Metro Malostranská, then tram 22, 23. **Open** Events only. **Admission** Varies. **Map** p57 E2 ⑩
At the eastern end of the Royal Gardens, this stunning Renaissance structure was built by Paola della Stella between 1538 and 1564. It was commissioned by Ferdinand I as a gift for his wife, Anne – a loveshack away from the skullduggery of life in Prague Castle. But the long-suffering Anne never got to see 'the most beautiful piece of Renaissance architecture north of the Alps' – as the city's gushing tourist brochures invariably call it. She drew her last breath after producing the 15th heir to the throne. Occasional art shows are held.

Black Tower
Černá věž
Na Opyši (no phone). Metro Malostranská, then tram 22, 23. **Map** p57 E3 ⑪
The first reward for reaching the top of the Old Castle Steps (Staré zámecké schody), which lead up from the park just east of the Malostranská metro station, is this blocky tower above the east entrance to Prague Castle. To the left of the entrance gate, where decorated palace guards stand all year, is a prime viewing spot over the red tiled roofs, spires and domes of the Lesser Quarter.

Dalibor Tower
Daliborka
Zlatá ulička (224 371 111/old.hrad.cz). Metro Malostranská, then tram 22, 23. **Map** p57 E2 ⑫

The former prison rooms, which housed an inmate who lent his name to the tower, can't be entered but standing beneath it you can just imagine Dalibor, later portrayed in Smetana's opera, amusing himself by playing the violin while awaiting execution. Crowds of onlookers turned up at his execution to weep en masse.

Golden Lane
Prague Castle, Zlatá ulička (224 371 111/old.hrad.cz). Metro Malostranská, then tram 22, 23. **Open** Apr-Oct 9am-5pm. Nov-Mar 9am-4pm daily. **Admission** 50 Kč. **Map** p57 E2 ⑬
The tiny multicoloured cottages that cling to Prague Castle's northern walls were thrown up by the poor in the 16th century out of whatever waste materials they could find. Some contend that its name alludes to a time when soldiers billeted in a nearby tower used the lane as a public urinal but a more likely source is the 17th century goldsmiths who worked here. The house at No. 22 was owned by Kafka's sister Ottla, and he stayed here for a while in 1917, reputedly drawing the inspiration from the streets for his novel *The Castle*. If he rewrote it today, he'd call it *The Souvenir Shop*.

Hradčanské náměstí gates
First courtyard. Metro Malostranská, then tram 22, 23. **Map** p57 A2 ⑭
Linking the Castle's first courtyard with the outside world is this gateway that has been dominated since 1768 by Ignatz Platzer's monumental sculptures of battling Titans. They create an impressive, if not exactly welcoming, entrance. The changing of the guard takes place in this courtyard, a Havel-inspired attempt to add some ceremonial pzazz to the castle. The change is carried out on the hour every day from 5am to 10pm, but the big crowd-pulling ceremony, complete with band, takes place at noon.

Lobkowicz Palace
Lobkovický palác
Jiřská 3 (224 371 111/old.hrad.cz). Metro Malostranská, then tram 22, 23. **Open** Apr-Oct 9am-5pm daily.

Nov-Mar 9am-4pm daily. **Admission** 100 Kč. **Map** p57 E3 ⓯

One of several palaces in town owned by the influential Lobkowicz family, who did not fare well under the communists. This one, which was finished in 1658, now houses the Historical Museum, for which a separate ticket is required – the Prague Castle two-day pass doesn't cover this collection of displays on the roots of the Czech lands' power players.

Matthias Gate

Matyášova brána

First courtyard (224 371 111/old.hrad. cz). Metro Malostranská, then tram 22, 23. **Open** *Apr-Oct* 9am-5pm daily. *Nov-Mar* 9am-4pm daily. **Admission** free. **Map** p57 A2 ⓰

To reach Prague Castle's second courtyard, stoll through this impressively over-the-top 1614 portal, topped by a double-headed German Imperial Eagle, a symbol of the old Habsburgs that has remained despite the family's changing fortunes. The eagle, of course, pleased Hitler when he came to stay in 1939.

Old Royal Palace

Starý královský palác

Third Courtyard (224 371 111/old. hrad.cz). Metro Malostranská, then tram 22, 23. **Open** *Apr-Oct* 9am-5pm daily. *Nov-Mar* 9am-4pm daily. **Admission** 50-350 Kč; 30-175 Kč reductions; 520 Kč family, for two days. **Map** p57 C3 ⓱

Part of the ticketed Castle tour, the palace offers three areas of royal chambers above ground level, all with badly photocopied engravings for displays, most with more Russian text than English, and, in the cellar, an exquisite, gorgeously presented new permanent exhibition focusing on palace life. The new displays inhabit the 12th-century Romanesque remains of Prince Soběslav's residence. A worthwhile highlight at ground level is the Vladislav Hall, which was designed by Benedict Ried at the turn of the 16th century, and which was where Václav Havel was sworn in in 1990. Its exquisitely vaulted ceiling represents the last flowering of Gothic art in Bohemia.

Prague Castle p56

Belvedere p58

Paradise Gardens
Rajská zahrada
Below third courtyard (224 371 111/ old.hrad.cz). Metro Malostranská, then tram 22, 23. **Open** *Apr-Oct* 9am-5pm Tue-Sun. **Admission** 60 Kč. No credit cards. **Map** p57 C3 ⑱

From the Bull Staircase is the garden where the Catholic victims of the second and most famous defenestration by Protestants fell to earth, saved by a giant dung heap (an obelisk marks the spot). The gardens, initially laid out in 1562, were redesigned in the 1920s by Josip Plečnik. You can now make the descent to Malá Strana via the terraced slopes of five beautiful Renaissance gardens, which are open, like most gardens in Prague, from April to October only. The pride of the restoration is the lovely Ledebour Gardens (Ledeburská zahrada), featuring a series of fountains, ornate stone stair switchbacks and palace yards, and emptying you out on to the middle of Valdštejnská. Fit hikers might consider ascending to the castle this way as well, though

there is an entrance fee of 60 Kč whichever way that you decide to go.

Plečnik Obelisk
Third Courtyard (224 371 111/old. hrad.cz). Metro Malostranská, then tram 22, 23. **Open** 8am-midnight daily. **Admission** free. **Map** p57 B3 ⑲

After the cathedral, the second most noticeable monument in the third courtyard is this fairly incongruous 17-metre-high (50-foot) granite obelisk, a memorial to the dead of World War I, erected by Josip Plečnik in 1928. The two tapering flagpoles nearby are also the Slovene's work; he was hired by President Tomáš Garrigue Masaryk in the 1920s to create a more uniform look for the seat of the First Republic.

Powder Tower
Prašná věž
Third courtyard, (224 371 111/old.hrad. cz). Metro Malostranská, then tram 22, 23. **Open** *Apr-Oct* 9am-5pm daily. *Nov-Mar* 9am-4pm daily. **Admission** 50-350 Kč; 30-175 Kč reductions; 520 Kč family, for two days. **Map** p57 C2 ⑳

A part of the ticketed Castle tour, the 15th-century Mihulka, as it's also known, was where Rudolf II, King of Bohemia (1576-1612), employed his many alchemists, who were engaged in attempts to distil the Elixir of Life and transmute base metals into gold. Today the tower hosts exhibits (in Czech only) about alchemy and Renaissance life in the castle.

Prague Castle
Picture Gallery

Obrazárna Pražského hradu
Second courtyard (224 371 111/old.hrad.cz). Metro Malostranská, then tram 22, 23. **Open** *Apr-Oct* 9am-6pm daily. *Nov-Mar* 9am-4pm daily; tours Tue-Sun only. **Admission** 150 Kč; 80 Kč reductions; 150 Kč family. No credit cards. **Map** p57 A2 ㉑

On the north side of the courtyard near the Powder Bridge (U Prašného mostu) entrance to Prague Castle is this collection of Renaissance and Baroque works which includes art by Rubens, Tintoretto, Titian and Veronese, as well as lesser-known masters. Though there's no hope of ever piecing together the Emperor's Rudolf II's original collection, which has been scattered to the winds, the Castle has recently bought back on the open market a handful of works from the original cache.

Royal Garden

U Prašného mostu (224 371 111/old.hrad.cz). Metro Malostranská, then tram 22, 23. **Open** *Apr-Oct* 9am-5pm daily. *Nov-Mar* 9am-4pm daily. **Admission** free. **Map** p57 B1 ㉒

Cross over the Powder Bridge (U Prašného mostu) from the castle's second courtyard and you will reach the Royal Garden (Královská zahrada), on the outer side of the Stag Moat (Jelení příkop). Laid out for Emperor Ferdinand I in the 1530s, it once included a maze and a menagerie, but was devastated by Swedish soldiers in the 17th century. In front of the Belvedere palace is the so-called Singing Fountain (Zpívající fontána), created in bronze by Bohemian crafts-

Cable me

The 116-year-old funicular railway up Petřín hill, a true wonder of Czechnology, is now back in action. It's by far the laziest and most thrilling way to get to the top. The system, which rises from Újezd street in Malá Strana, is powered by counterweights, so what hauls you up the hill is the release of another passenger carriage descending from the hilltop. There are three stations: Újezd, Nebozízek in the middle, and the last stop at the top of the hill.

The railway was closed for major repairs for the entire summer of 2006; the surrounding hillside had been made unstable by water erosion over the years and the instability was endangering the belle époque funicular, which had last been renovated in 1985. The European Union chipped in half of the 53 million Kč (roughly £1.3 million) needed for the job after much haggling and many delays, and the smoothly gliding rail cars are now upheld by fine new supporting walls and a drainage system. So fine, in fact, that Prague tourist authorities are hoping to attract more visitors by having the funicular's gears visible for the first time.

As for whether that works, it seems the 1.3 million annual riders of the cable car (regular 20 Kč public transport tickets are all you need) will be the judge. If you go, just be sure to grab a seat facing downhill to catch all of Prague laid out at your feet.

Dalibor Tower p58

men in the 1560s. It used to hum as water splashed into its basin but sings no longer, thanks to overzealous reconstruction.

St George's Basilica
Bazilika sv. Jiří
Jiřské náměstí (224 371 111/old.hrad.cz). Metro Malostranská, then tram 22, 23. **Open** *Apr-Oct* 9am-5pm daily. *Nov-Mar* 9am-4pm daily. **Admission** 50-350 Kč; 30-175 Kč reductions; 520 Kč family, for two days. **Map** p57 C2/D2 ㉓
This basilica, part of the ticketed Prague Castle tour, was built by Italian craftsmen in 1142, building upon the underlying church founded by Prince Vratislav in AD 921. It has burned down and been rebuilt several time over the centuries. Some 50 years after it was originally erected, a Benedictine convent was founded next door. In the original arcades are remnants of 13th-century frescoes and within are the bodies of a saint (Ludmila, strangled by assassins

hired by Prince Wenceslas's mother Drahomira) and a saint-maker (the notorious Boleslav the Cruel, who martyred his brother Wenceslas by having him stabbed to death). The basilica's restored simplicity and clean lines seem far closer to godliness than the mammon-fuelled baroque pomposity of most Prague churches.

St George's Convent
Klášter sv. Jiří
Jiřské náměstí 33 (257 531 644). Metro Malostranská, then tram 22, 23. **Open** 10am-6pm Mon; 9am-5pm Tue-Sun. **Admission** 130 Kč; 180 Kč family. No credit cards. **Map** p57 C2/D2 ㉔
Housing part of the National Gallery's vast collections, the convent features mannerist and baroque art, including paintings from the collections of whimsically whacked-out Rudolf II. A highlight is stylised work of the Antwerp innovator Bartholomaeus Spranger, whose sophisticated colours, elegant eroticism and obscure themes typify mannerism at its best. The baroque canvases of Karel Škréta contrast the feverishly religious work of Michael Leopold Willmann and Jan Krystof Liška. The tendency in baroque painting and sculpture to borrow from each other can be seen in the paintings of Petr Brandl, the most acclaimed Czech artist of the early 18th century. His work is displayed near that of the two great sculptors of the time, Mathias Bernard Braun and Ferdinand Maxmilián Brokof. A workshop offers glimpses of the tools and methods of the masters.

Spanish Hall
Španělský sál
Second courtyard (224 371 111/old. hrad.cz). Metro Malostranská, then tram 22, 23. **Open** Only during concerts. **Admission** Varies. **Map** p57 A2 ㉕
Most Castle visitors don't get the chance to glimpse the inside of this hall, hidden atop a monumental stairway, just visible from inside the passage between the first and second courtyards. The magnificent gold-and-white Baroque hall is a 17th-century ceremonial chamber redone in the 19th century, when the

trompe l'oeil murals were covered with white stucco, and huge mirrors and gilded chandeliers were brought in to transform the space into a glitzy venue for the coronation of Emperor Franz Josef I (who failed to show). In the 1950s the Politburo met here, protected from assassins by a reinforced steel door.

Summer House

U Prašného mostu (224 371 111/old. hrad.cz). Metro Malostranská, then tram 22, 23. **Map** p57 B1 ㉖

Though not open to the public, the quaint, mustard-coloured Dientzenhofer Summer House, to the right of the Royal Gardens entrance, was the presidential residence from 1948 to 1989. Paranoid old Gustav Husák had enormous slabs of concrete installed as defences against possible missile attacks, an addition so ugly that Václav Havel's wife, Olga, refused to let them move in. It's remained empty ever since.

Toy Museum

Jiřská 6 (224 372 294/www.muzeum hracek.cz). Metro Malostranská, then

22, 23 *tram.* **Open** 9.30am-5.30pm daily. **Admission** 60 Kč; 120 Kč family; under-5s free. **Map** p57 E2 ㉗

Part of Czech émigré Ivan Steiger's large collection is displayed on the two floors of this museum in the Castle grounds. Brief texts accompany cases of toys, from teddy bears to an elaborate tin train set. Kitsch fans will love the robots and the enormous collection of Barbie dolls clad in vintage costumes throughout the decades. Good for a rainy day but probably better for the young at heart than the actual young, most of whom greatly prefer playing with toys than looking at them from a historical perspective.

St Vitus's Cathedral

Prague Castle, third courtyard (233 350 788/old.hrad.cz). Metro Malostranská, then tram 22, 23. **Open** *Apr-Oct* 9am-5pm daily. *Nov-Mar* 9am-4pm daily. **Admission** free. **Map** p57 B2/C2 ㉘

Forming the centrepiece of Prague Castle, its oldest and most important site features looming towers, pinnacles and buttresses. Entry is free to the nave and chapels, but a ticket is required for the rest. The cathedral was only completed in 1929, exactly 1,000 years after the murdered St Wenceslas was laid to rest on the site. In pagan times Svatovít, the Slavic god of fertility, was worshipped here, a clue as to why the cathedral was dedicated to his near namesake St Vitus (svatý Vít in Czech). Charles IV, who won an archbishopric for Prague, hired Frenchman Matthew of Arras to build the Gothic wonder, but it was completed by Swabian Peter Parler, hence the Sondergotik or German late Gothic design. It was 19th-century nationalists who completed the work according to Parler's original plans. Inside, the enormous nave is flooded with multicoloured light from the gallery of stained-glass windows created at the beginning of this century. All 21 of them were sponsored during a period of nationalist fervour by finance institutions including, (third on the right) an insurance company whose motto – 'those who sow in sorrow shall reap in joy' – is subtly incorporated into

Sternberg Palace p66

PRAGUE BY AREA

the biblical allegory. The most famous is the third window on the left, in the Archbishop's Chapel, created by Alfons Mucha. It depicts the struggle of Christian Slavonic tribes; appropriately enough, the artwork was paid for by Banka Slavia.

Chapel of St Wenceslas
Svatováclavská kaple
Open 8am-midnight daily.
Admission free. **Map** p57 C2 ㉙
In a public area of St Vitus's, on the right side, is the site of the original tenth-century rotunda where 'Good King' Wenceslas was buried. Built in 1345, the chapel has 1,345 polished amethysts, agates and jaspers incorporated into its design and contains some of the saint's personal paraphernalia, including armour, chain shirt and helmet. The chapel itself is gated off, but you can catch a glint of its treasure trove over the railings. On state anniversaries, the skull of the saint is put on display, covered with a cobweb-fine veil. A door in the corner leads to the chamber that contains the crown jewels. A papal bull of 1346 officially protects the jewels, while legend has it that fate prescribes an early death for anyone who uses them improperly. The curse seemed to work on the Nazis' man in Prague, Reichsprotektor Reinhard Heydrich, who tried on the crown and was assassinated shortly afterward by the resistance. The door to the chamber is locked with seven keys, after the seven seals of Revelations, each looked after by a different Prague state or church official.

Crypt
Open *Apr-Oct* 9am-5pm. *Nov-Mar* 9am-4pm daily. **Admission** 50-350 Kč; 30-175 Kč reductions, 520 Kč family, for two days. **Map** p57 C2 ㉚
Entering from the centre of the cathedral, you descend into the crypt, which is badly in need of restoration and may disappoint. Herein lie the remains of various Czech monarchs, including Rudolf II. Easily the most eye-catching tomb is Charles IV's modern, streamlined metal affair, designed by Kamil

Roškot in the mid 1930s. However, the vault itself, hastily excavated between world wars, has a distinctly cramped, temporary look to it.

Gothic Golden Portal
Zlatá brána
Open 8am-midnight daily. **Admission** free. **Map** p57 C2 ㉛
This grandiose southern entrance to St Vitus's Cathedral, visible from the courtyard sports a recently restored mosaic of multicoloured Venetian glass depicting the Last Judgement. A Getty-funded project returned the original lustre, taking years of work (outdoor mosaics don't do well this far north in Europe for climactic reasons). On either side of the centre arch are sculptures of Charles IV and his wife, Elizabeth of Pomerania, whose talents allegedly included being able to bend a sword with her bare hands.

Great Tower
Open *Apr-Oct* 9am-5pm. *Nov-Mar* 9am-4pm daily. **Admission** 50-350 Kč;

Strahov Library p66

30-175 Kč reductions, 520 Kč family, for two days. **Map** p57 B2 32

Easily the most dominant feature of the cathedral, and accounting for Prague's signature spire, the Gothic and Renaissance tower is topped with a baroque dome. This houses Sigismund, unquestionably the largest bell in Bohemia, made in the middle of the 16th century, weighing in at a hefty 15,120 kilograms (33,333 pounds). The clapper weighs slightly over 400 kilograms (882 pounds). Getting Sigismund into the tower was no mean feat: according to legend it took a rope woven from the hair of the city's noblest virgins to haul it into position. The Prague Castle ticket allows access to the tower from spring to autumn.

Schwarzenberg Palace

Schwarzenberský palác
Hradčanské náměstí 2 (no phone). Metro Malostranská, then tram 22, 23. **Open** *9am-4pm Tue-Sun.* **Map** p51 C2 33

Finally restored after years of building work, this is one of the most imposing Renaissance buildings in Prague. Built between 1545 and 1563, the outside is exquisitely decorated with 'envelope's graffito. For a while it was a pawn in the nationalised property game, but it's been returned to its role since 1945 as the Military Museum, housing a collection of killing instruments and displays on strategy and decisive battles.

Štefánik Observatory

Hvězdárna
Top of Petřín hill (257 320 540/www. observatory.cz). Tram 12, 22, then funicular railway. **Open** *Jan, Feb, Nov-Dec 6-8pm Tue-Fri; 10am-noon, 2-8pm Sat, Sun. Mar 7-9pm Tue-Fri; 10am-noon, 2-6pm, 7-9pm Sat, Sun. Apr-Aug 2-7pm, 9-11pm Tue-Fri; 10am-noon, 2-7pm, 9-11pm Sat Sun. Sept 2-6pm, 8-10pm Tue-Fri; 10am-noon, 2-6pm, 8-10pm Sat, Sun. Oct 7-9pm Tue-Fri; 10am-noon, 2-6pm, 7-9pm Sat, Sun.* **Admission** 40 Kč, 30 Kč reductions; free under-3s. **Map** p51 B5/C5 34

With classic old-regime inconvenient hours, Prague's observatory is nevertheless part of a proud tradition of historical astronomical connections. Both the haughty Dane Tycho Brahe and his protégé Johannes Kepler resided in the city. The duo features in the observatory's stellar displays (which contain some English). Telescopes offer glimpses of sunspots and planets during the day and panoramas of the stars and the moon on clear nights.

Sternberg Palace

Šternberský palác

*Hradčanské náměstí 15 (233 090 570).
Metro Malostranská, then tram 22, 23.*
Open 10am-6pm Tue-Sun. **Admission**
130 Kč; free under-10s. No credit cards.
Map p51 B2 ⊕

Enlightened aristocrats trying to rouse Prague from provincial stupor founded the Sternberg Gallery here in the 1790s. The palace, located just outside the gates of Prague Castle, now houses the National Gallery's European old masters. Not a large or well-balanced collec-

tion, especially since some of its most famous works were returned to their pre-war owners, but some outstanding paintings remain, including a brilliant Frans Hals portrait and Dürer's *Feast of the Rosary*. All in a setting that looks newly redone, although renovations finished over a year ago. There's now space for more paintings from the repositories, and improved ceiling frescoes that had long been covered up.

Strahov Library

*Strahovské nádvoří 1 (233 107 749/
www.strahovskyklaster.cz). Metro
Malostranská, then tram 22, 23.* **Open**
9am-noon, 1-5pm daily. **Admission** 80
Kč. No credit cards. **Map** p51 A3/A4 ⊕

The highlight of the monastery complex is its superb libraries, which appear on posters in universities all over the world. Within the frescoed Theological and Philosophical Halls alone are 130,000 volumes. There are a further 700,000 books in storage and together they form the most important collection in Bohemia. Visitors cannot stroll around them, but are allowed to gawp through the doors. When Joseph II effected a clampdown on religious institutions in 1782, the Premonstratensians managed to outwit him by masquerading as an educational foundation, and their collection was swelled by the libraries. The monks' taste ranged far beyond the standard ecclesiastical tracts, including such highlights as the oldest extant copy of *The Calendar of Minutae* or *Selected Times for Bloodletting*. Nor did they merely confine themselves to books: the 200-year-old curiosity cabinets house a collection of deep-sea monsters that any landlocked country would be proud to possess.

Strahov Monastery

Strahovský klášter
Strahovské nádvoří 1 (233 107 705/ www.strahovskyklaster.cz). Metro Malostranská, then tram 22, 23. **Open** 9am-noon, 1-5pm daily. **Admission** 80 Kč. No credit cards. **Map** p51 A3/A4 ③⑦
The Premonstratensian monks have been meditating here since 1140. Since 1990 several have returned to reclaim the buildings nationalised by the communists in 1948. They can sometimes be seen from Úvoz street walking laps around green fields and meditating, and services are once again being held in the Church of Our Lady, which retained its 12th-century basilica ground plan after remodelling in the early 17th century. One interesting access route to the monastery is from the stairs at Pohořelec No.8, the western-most square in the Hradčany district.

Zrcadlové bludiště

Mirror Maze
Petřín hill (257 315 212). Tram 12, 22, then funicular railway. **Open** *Jan-Mar, Nov, Dec* 10am-5pm Sat, Sun. *Apr, Sept* 10am-7pm daily. *May-Aug* 10am-10pm daily. *Oct* 10am-6pm daily. **Admission** 50 Kč; 40 Kč children. **Map** p51 B5 ③⑧
Housed in a cast-iron mock-Gothic castle, complete with drawbridge and crenellations, is a hall of distorting mirrors that still causes remarkable hilarity among kids and their parents. Alongside is a wax diorama of one of

the proudest historical moments for the citizens of Prague: the defence of Charles Bridge during the Swedish attack of 1648 is a fairground-style hall of wacky reflectors.

Eating & drinking

Malý Buddha

Úvoz 46 (220 513 894). Tram 8, 22. **Open** 1pm-midnight Tue-Sun. **$. Asian**. No credit cards. **Map** p51 A3 ③⑨
The 'Little Buddha' is a teahouse with a difference: great vegetarian spring rolls and noodle dishes go hand in hand with the dozens of teas brewed by the laid-back owner, who's always on hand. Sit in candlelight and inhale whiffs of incense with your eggrolls. Mellow doesn't half describe it. No smoking; shrine at the back.

Nebozízek

Petřín hill, Petřínské sady 411 (257 315 329/www.nebozizek.cz). Metro Malostranská. **Open** 11am-11pm daily. **$$. Czech**. **Map** p51 C5 ④⓪
Conveniently set just next to the top stop of the funicular railway that runs up Petřín hill, this admittedly touristy restaurant can still be worthwhile on a fine, temperate day for its patio view of Old Town across the river.

Petřínské Terasy

Seminářská zahrada 13 (257 320 688/www.petrinsketerasy.cz). Metro Malostranská. **Open** noon-11pm Mon-Fri; 11am-11pm Sat, Sun. **$$. Czech**. **Map** p51 C4 ④①
One of two tourist traps on Petřín hill, the Petřín Terraces offer exquisite views of Prague Castle and the city, unfortnately alongside expensive Krušovice and indifferent service.

U Černého vola

Loretánské náměstí 1 (220 513 481). Tram 22. **Open** 9am-10pm daily. No credit cards. **Pub**. **Map** p51 A3 ④②
One of the best pubs in Prague. The murals make it look like it's been here forever, but in fact the Black Ox was built after World War II. Its superb location, right above the Castle, made

it a prime target for redevelopment in the post-1989 building frenzy, but the rugged regulars bought it to ensure that local bearded artisans would have at least one place where they could afford to drink. The Kozel beer is perfection and, although the snacks are pretty basic, they do their job of lining the stomach for long sessions.

U Císařů

Loretánská 5 (220 518 484/www.u cisaru.cz). Metro Malostranská, then tram 22, 23. **Open** 11am-midnight daily. **$$. Czech. Map** p51 B3 ⓭
Another favoured location for trad Czech within a short walk of Prague Castle, At the Emperor's delivers a nice platter of smoked meats. The potato-thyme soup is excellent and draught beer is as fine as any around.

U Ševce Matouše

Loretánské náměstí 4 (220 514 536). Tram 22. **Open** 11am-11pm daily. **$. Czech. Map** p51 A3 ⓮
The classic steakhouse, Czech style, with done-to-order tenderloins in traditional sauces such as green peppercorns or mushrooms. A short walk east of Prague Castle and in a cosy former shoemaker's workshop (where it was once possible to get your boots repaired while lunching). Reasonable prices given the prime location.

U Zavěšenýho kafe

Úvoz 6 (257 532 868/www.uzavesenyho kafe.com). Metro Malostranská. **Open** 11am-midnight daily. **$. Pub. Map** p51 B3 ⓯
The Hanging Coffee Cup is a mellow, thoroughly Czech spot with plank flooring, trad grub (onion soup and duck with sauerkraut) and a long association with local artists and intellectuals. The name comes from an old tradition of paying for a cup of coffee for someone who may arrive later without funds.

Arts & leisure

Gambra

Černínská 5 (220 514 527). Metro Malostranská, then tram 22, 23.
Open *Mar-Oct* noon-5.30pm Wed-Sun. *Nov-Feb* noon-5.30pm Sat-Sun.
Admission free. **Map** p51 A2 ⓰
A funky gallery specialising in surrealist art, this one happens to be owned by the world-renowned animator Jan Švankmajer, who lives in the attached house. It's a part of the Nový Svět enclave, a collection of brightly coloured cottages restored in the 18th and 19th centuries – all that remains of Hradčany's medieval slums. The rest were destroyed in the great fire of 1541.

Josef Sudek Atelier

Újezd 30 (251 510 760/www.sudek-atelier.cz). Metro Malostranská, then tram 22, 23. **Open** noon-6pm Tue-Sun.
Admission 10 Kč. No credit cards.
Map p51 B3 ⓱
This little gallery, where Josef Sudek long had his photography studio, is accessible through a residential building courtyard. Select shows of quality art photography are held in the intimate exhibition room, while Sudek memorabilia is on view in a separate small room.

Klub 007

Vaníčkova 5, Koleje ČVUT dorm 7 (257 211 439). Metro Dejvická, then bus 143, 149, 217. **Open** 7pm-midnight Mon-Sat. **Admission** 40-100 Kč.
Map p51 A5 ⓲
Student dorm heaven – or hell, depending on how you look at it. If you can find this place (in the concrete basement of dorm, yes, 007), you'll never believe it could be a must on any ska tour of central Europe. But that it is, as you'll soon discover when the bands start up.

Stadium Strahov

Diskařská 100, Břevnov (233 014 111). Metro Karlovo náměstí, then bus 176 or tram 22 to Újezd, then funicular.
Map p51 A5 ⓳
Only open for monster concerts, Strahov is a concrete monstrosity built before World War II without much to offer besides its size to accommodate epic rock shows (capacity 250,000). It's a trek out of the centre, but a special bus service is laid on for big gigs.

Eastern Malá Strana & Smíchov

Malá Strana

Long a holdout against developers, the eastern side Malá Strana features wedding-cake Baroque palaces, churches and a miracle-working wax baby Jesus, along with a local crowd of Bohemians that refuses to give in to modern city life. Still with a true left-bank feel, this traditional warren for artists, craftsmen working for the Castle, and royal retainers continues to host creative idlers at its jazz bars, parks and cafés.

The district as a whole lies between the Vltava river and Prague Castle, skirting the hill that makes up Hradčany. Its eastern backstreets reward exploring, with old-world embassies, rustic old pubs (like Baráčnická rychta) and ornate doors and chapels (St Nicholas, Our Lady Victorious and Our Lady Beneath the Chain); best of all, the once-private formal gardens like the Baroque **Wallenstein Gardens** and **Vrbta Gardens** are now open to strollers.

Founded by the Přemyslid Otakar II in 1287, when he invited merchants from Germany to set up shop on the land beneath the castle walls, the area was transformed into a sparkling Baroque district by the wealthy Catholic aristocracy, who won huge parcels of land in the property redistribution that

Vrtba Gardens p69

followed the Thirty Years' War. Malostranské náměstí now throbs with life deep into the night, with its popular local drinking holes, a few characterful clubs like **U Malého Glena** and **Popocafepetl**, and increasingly swank restaurants like **Palffy Palác** and **U Patrona**.

Kitschy Mostecká street leads from the **Charles Bridge** into the centre of the district, following the **Royal Route**, the path taken by the Bohemian kings to their coronation. **Malostranské náměstí** is a lively square edged by large Baroque palaces and Renaissance gabled townhouses perched on top of Gothic arcades, which inspired the tales of beloved Bohemian writer Jan Neruda, author of *Prague Tales*.

The Smíchov district, upstream to the south, is where Prague shows its new face to the world; the place is full of trendy bars and shops and the style chasers that go with them.

Sights & museums

American Embassy

Tržiště 15. Metro Malostranská.
Map p71 A3 ❶
The 17th-century Schönborn Palace (Schönbornský palác) is now the US Embassy (don't tarry too long unless you want to be searched). It was built by Giovanni Santini-Aichel, who, despite his Mediterranean-sounding name, was in fact a third-generation Praguer and one of the descendants of Italian craftsmen who formed an expat community on Vlašská just up the hill.

British Embassy

Thunovská 14. Metro Malostranská.
Map p71 A2 ❷
Situated at the end of an alleyway, the British Embassy was christened

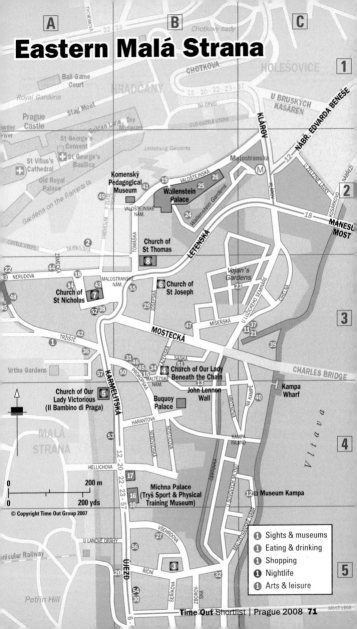

Eastern Malá Strana

A   **B**   **C**

1

2

3

4

5

HOLEŠOVICE

Chotkovy sady

CHOTKOVA

Royal Gardens

Ball Game Court

HRADČANY

U BRUSKÝCH KASÁREN

NA OPYŠI

NÁBŘ. EDVARDA BENEŠE

Prague Castle

Stag Moat

Golden Lane, Toy Museum

OLD CASTLE STEPS

KLÁROV

Powder Tower

St George's Convent

St George's Basilica

Ledeburg Gardens

Malostranská

M

NÁBŘEŽÍ

St Vitus's Cathedral

Old Royal Palace

Gardens on the Ramparts

19 VALDŠTEJNSKÁ 26

Komenský Pedagogical Museum 41

25

Wallenstein Palace

Wallenstein Gardens

MANESŮV MOST

VALDŠTEJNSKÉ NÁM.

24

18

CASTLE STEPS

ŘÍČNÍ

2

TOMÁŠSKÁ

Church of St Thomas

8

LETENSKÁ

NERUDOVA

22

3

44

13

14

MALOSTRANSKÉ NÁM.

43

55

6 Church of St Joseph

Church of St Nicholas

7

52 38

JOSEFSKÁ

Vojan's Gardens

23

U LUŽICKÉHO SEMINÁŘE

48

42

TRŽIŠTĚ

1

36

MOSTECKÁ

47

MÍŠEŇSKÁ

37

21

39

CHARLES BRIDGE

Vrtba Gardens

31 46

34

SASKÁ

Church of Our Lady Beneath the Chain

51

Kampa Wharf

57

50

PROKOPSKÁ

45 15

MALTÉZSKÉ NÁM.

13

NA KAMPĚ

40

KARMELITSKÁ

Church of Our Lady Victorious (Il Bambino di Praga)

5

Buquoy Palace

John Lennon Wall

KAMPA ISLAND

Vltava

MALÁ STRANA

53

HARANTOVA

NOSTICOVA

HELLICHOVA

12 · 20 · 22 · 23 · 57

17

16 10

Michna Palace (Tryš Sport & Physical Training Museum)

12

Museum Kampa

0   200 m

0   200 yds

© Copyright Time Out Group 2007

56

27

VŠEHRDOVA

ÚJEZD

3

32

ŠERÍKOVA

ZBOROV-SKÁ

54 30

uncular Railway

U LANOVÉ DRÁHY

Petřín Hill

6 · 9

MOST LEGIÍ

Key:

- ① Sights & museums
- ① Eating & drinking
- ① Shopping
- ① Nightlife
- ① Arts & leisure

Coming from America

When it comes to winning hearts and minds, the French, British, Germans, Italians and Spanish are all way ahead of the Yanks in Prague. Each of these countries has a thriving cultural centre in the city, offering language courses, exhibitions, concerts, lectures and more, while the US has sponsored the occasional touring jazz singer but not much else. It did, it should be said, help dig out Kampa Island after the devastating floods of 2002 covered it in bacteria-filled mud. But a major player on the arts scene, helping to build a feel-good image?

Yet the new American Center, adjacent to the embassy in the Wratislaw Palace at Tržiště 13, is now helping to change this situation. The Center offers a fresh programme of events that have so far featured such unexpected delights as free film screenings (with Czech subtitles) of indie movies – such as *Enron: The Smartest Guys in the Room* – and a series of documentaries by American folklorist and blues scholar William Ferris.

In what US cultural attaché Michael Feldman praises as a unique offering to local audiences, Film Thursdays show movies you won't find in any Czech multiplex (and probably not at the DVD rental either). Some were first shown at the One World festival of human rights, others are from the US Embassy's own archive.

Ferris's films were screened in collaboration with the hit festival Music on Film-Film on Music (www.moffom.cz), and were an apt early entry for Film Thursdays, helping kick off the new spirit of glasnost with a bang. Shot in the 1960s and '70s, some of the films feature remarkable historical moments, with subjects including a young BB King, while others are approached more from an anthropological angle, like the series of films on communities in the Mississippi delta region, such as *Black Delta Religion* (pictured).
■ The programme for screenings, held at 6pm on Thursdays (at press time) can be found online at prague.usembassy.gov/filmovectvrtky.html.

PRAGUE BY AREA

Church of St Nicholas

'Czechers' by a diplomatic wag. Leading up from here are the New Castle Steps (Nové zámecké schody), one of the most peaceful (and least strenuous) routes up to the castle and a star location in the film *Amadeus*.

Chapel to St John of the Laundry
Kaple sv. Jana Na Prádle
South end of Kampa Park. Metro Malostranská. **Map** p71 B5 **❸**
Washerwomen once rinsed shirts on the banks of the Certovka (near the southern end). Today it's taken up by snoozing office workers and bongo-beating hippies. The river and bridge views are as romantic as they come, while the chestnut trees make shady spots for reading and recharging. In spring the park is filled with pink blossom. Kampa Park the restaurant (p83), one of Prague's classier and pricier places to eat, is at the north end of the island, where the Čertovka runs back into the river by Charles Bridge, offering the finest waterfront view of any dining establishment in town.

Church of Our Lady Beneath the Chain
Kostel Panny Marie pod Řetězem
Maltézské náměstí. Metro Malostranská. **Map** p71 B3 **❹**
The oldest Gothic parts of this church were built by a military-religious order to guard the Judith Bridge, which spanned the Vltava, close to where Charles Bridge sits today. Two heavy towers still stand at the entrance, but they now contain some of the most prized apartments in Prague. The Hussite wars barred the construction of the church and it was never finished.

Church of Our Lady Victorious
Kostel Panny Marie Vítězné
Karmelitská 9 (257 533 646). Tram 12, 22. **Open** 8.30am-7pm Mon-Sat; 8.30am-8pm Sun. **Admission** free. **Map** p71 A4 **❺**
The first Baroque church in Prague (built 1611 to 1613) belongs to the

Barefooted Carmelites, an order that cares for the doll-like, miracle-working 400-year-old Bambino di Praga. The effigy, brought from Spain to Prague in the 17th century, is said to have protected nuns from the plague. A wardrobe of over 60 outfits have been changed by the Order of English Virgins at sunrise on selected days for around 200 years.

Church of St Joseph
Kostel sv. Josefa
Josefská and Letenská streets. Metro Malostranská. **Map** p71 B3 **❻**
This tiny baroque gem, set back from the road, was designed by Jean-Baptiste Mathey. Since 1989, it has been returned to the much-diminished Order of English Virgins, who were also one-time owners of the nearby Vojan's Gardens (Vojanovy sady), one of the most tranquil spots in the city.

Church of St Nicholas
Kostel sv. Mikuláše
Malostranské náměstí (257 534 215). Metro Malostranská. **Open** Nov-Feb 9am-4pm daily. Mar-Oct 9am-5pm daily. **Admission** 60 Kč; 30 Kč reductions. **Map** p71 A3 **❼**
The immense dome and bell tower of St Nicholas dominate Malá Strana, part of the Catholic Church's campaign to fuel the Counter-Reformation. The rich façade by Christoph Dientzenhofer, which was completed around 1710, conceals an interior and dome by his son Kilián Ignaz, dedicated to high Baroque at its most flamboyantly camp – bathroom-suite pinks and greens, swooping golden cherubs, swirling gowns and dramatic gestures; there's even a figure coyly proffering a pair of handcuffs.

Church of St Thomas
Kostel sv. Tomáše
Josefská 8 (257 530 556). Metro Malostranská. **Open** 11am-1pm Mon-Sat; 9am-noon, 4.30-5.30pm Sun. **Admission** free. **Map** p71 B2 **❽**
Walking back down Nerudova, if you continue straight down the tram tracks instead of veering off on to

Josef Sudek Atelier

Malostranské náměstí, you'll see on your left the Church of St Thomas. Its rich baroque façade is easy to miss, tucked into a narrow side street. Based on a Gothic ground plan, the church was rebuilt by Kilián Ignaz Dientzenhofer for the Augustinian monks. St Boniface, a fully dressed skeleton, occupies a glass case in the nave. Rubens painted the altarpiece (now a copy), named *The Martyrdom of St Thomas*.

Galerie Montanelli

Nerudova 13 (257 531 220/www. galeriemontanelli.com). Metro Malostranská. **Open** noon-6pm Mon-Fri. **Admission** free. **Map** p71 A3 ⑨
Located on the main pedestrian route to the Castle, this gallery specialises in established blue-chip Czech artists like Jitka and Květa Válová, and bolsters the younger generation with group shows. It has been co-operating with institutions in places such as Berlin to expose these artists to audiences abroad.

Josef Sudek Atelier

Újezd 30 (251 510 760/www.sudek-atelier.cz). Metro Malostranská. **Open** noon-6pm Tue-Sun. **Admission** 10 Kč; 5 Kč students. **Map** p71 B4 ⑩
This little gallery, where Josef Sudek long had his photography studio, is accessible through a residential building courtyard. Select shows of quality art photography are held in the intimate exhibition room, while Sudek memorabilia is on view in a separate small room.

Kafka Museum

Hergetova cihelna, Cihelná 2b (257 535 507/www.kafkamuseum.cz). Metro Malostranská. **Open** 10am-6pm. **Admission** 120 Kč. **Map** p71 C3 ⑪
The city's first museum to its most celebrated native son author, this collection won raves at the Jewish Museum in New York before settling here. Divided into Existential Space and Imaginary Topography, it's an intelligent look at the man, the city and their unhealthy but eternal effects on each other.

Kampa Museum

U Sovových mlynů 2 (257 286 147/ www.museumkampa.cz). Metro Malostranská. **Open** 10am-6pm daily. **Map** p71 C4 ⑫

On the waterfront of the city's loveliest island, Kampa, this modern art collection, amassed over decades by Jan Mládek, a Czech living in exile during the pre-1989 regime, contains sculpture by Otto Gutfreund and work by Jiří Kolář, among others. It also sets its sights on international stars from Yoko Ono to Christo – and has a gorgeous terrace café on the Vltava.

Lennon Wall

Maltézské náměstí. Metro Malostranská. **Map** p71 B4 ⑬

At the south end of the square, this graffiti-covered wall was a place of pilgrimage during the 1980s for the city's hippies, who dedicated it to their idol and scrawled messages of love, peace and rock 'n' roll across it. The secret police painted over the graffiti, only to have John's smiling face reappear a few days later. This continued until 1989 when the wall was returned to the Knights of Malta as part of a huge restitution package. The John Lennon Peace Club still encourages modest graffiti – preferably in the form of little flowers.

Lichtenstein Palace

Lichtenštejnský palác
Malostranské náměstí 13 (257 534 205). Metro Malostranská. **Open** 10am-7.30pm daily. *Concerts* 7.30pm. **Tickets** 60-150 Kč. **Map** p71 A3 ⑭

The Lichtenstein Palace is the home of the Czech Academy of Music. Regular concerts are given in the Gallery and in the Martinů Hall, although the real star is the summer open-air series of popular operas that take place in the courtyard.

Maltese Square

Maltézské náměstí. Metro Malostranská. **Map** p71 B3 ⑮

The Knights of Malta lived in this quiet square, now lined with mellow cafés and pubs, for centuries until the communists dissolved the order. The Knights regained great swathes of property under the restitution laws, however. Around the corner on Saska ulička are pretty flower shops and boutiques for clubbing clothes.

Michna Palace

Michnův palác
Újezd 40. Metro Malostranská. **Map** p71 B4 ⑯

Built in 1640-50, this fine Baroque pile was intended to rival the Wallenstein Palace (p78), itself built to compete with Prague Castle (p56). With these gargantuan ambitions, Francesco Caratti took Versailles as his model in designing the gardens of Michna. Today they contain little but tennis courts.

Museum of Music

NEW *Karmelitská 2 (257 327 285/ www.nm.cz). Metro Malostranská.* **Open** 10am-6pm Mon, Wed, Sun. **Admission** 60 Kč; 50 Kč reductions. **Map** p71 B4 ⑰

This fresh addition to the dozens of museums in Prague offers the creds of the National Museum plus an impressive palace space in which to encounter part of its incredible collection of instuments, along with exhibits on the greats, from 1920s jazz star Jaroslav Ježek to the *dudy*, or medieval bagpipes.

Nerudova street

Nerudova. Metro Malostranská. **Map** p71 A3 ⑱

The prime walking lane heading up to Prague Castle is a fine place to begin deciphering the ornate signs that decorate many of the city's houses: the Three Fiddles at No.12, for example, or the Devil at No.4. This practice of distinguishing houses continued up until 1770, when that relentless modernist Joseph II spoiled all the fun by introducing numbered addresses. The street is crowded with restaurants, cafés, and shops aimed at the ceaseless flow of tourists to and from the castle.

Paradise Gardens

Rajská zahrada
Valdštejnské náměstí. Metro Malostranská. **Open** *Apr-Oct*

PRAGUE BY AREA

10am-6pm daily. **Admission** 60 Kč; 50 Kč reductions. Map p71 B2 ⑲

An impressive collection of greenery, terraces and baroque arches, that make for one of the most unusual ways to access Prague Castle above. Some will surely find it easier to start from Prague Castle (descend the Bull stairs from the third courtyard) and descend to Malá Strana.

Petřín hill

Petřínské sady
Karmelitska 1. Metro Malostranská.
Map p71 B5 ⑳

The highest, greenest and most peaceful of Prague's seven hills, this area is the largest expanse of greenery in central Prague – a favourite spot for tobogganing children in winter and canoodling couples in summertime. The hill has provided much of the city's Gothic and Romanesque building material. The southern edge of the hill is traversed by the so-called Hunger Wall (Hladová zed), an eight-metre-high (23-ft) stone fortification that was commissioned by Charles IV in 1362 in order to provide some work for the poor of the city.

Prague Jewellery Collection

Pražský kabinet Šperku
Hergetova Cihelna, Cihelná 2b (221 451 400/www.cihelna.info). Metro Malostranská. **Open** 10am-6pm daily.
Admission 60 Kč; 50 Kč reductions.
Map p71 C3 ㉑

Housed in a magnificently reconstructed brickyard on the river, and just a stone's throw from the Charles Bridge, this new museum is the result of a collaboration between the Museum of Decorative Arts and the private COPA company. The collection brings together jewellery and goldsmithing, documenting the evolution of the art from the 17th century to the present, with Tiffany artworks and Fabergé eggs.

Thun-Hohenstein Palace

Thun-Hohenštejnský palác
Nerudova 20. Metro Malostranská.
Map p71 A3 ㉒

Now the Italian embassy, this gem built by Giovanni Santini-Aichel in 1726 is distinguished by the contorted eagles holding up the portal, the heraldic emblem of the Kolowrats for whom the palace was built. The Italians were trumped for a while by the Romanians, who used to inhabit the even more glorious Morzin Palace (Morzinský palác) at No.5, also the work of Santini-Aichel.

Vojanovy sady

U Lužického semináře (no phone). Metro Malostranská. **Open** Apr-Oct 8am-5pm. **Map** p71 B3/C3 ㉓

Not as trafficked nor as precious as the district's nearby Wallenstein Gardens (below), this walled sanctuary of greenery and peacocks is a local secret love and great for a relaxing stroll.

Wallenstein Gardens

Letenská, towards Malostranská metro station. Metro Malostranská.
Map p71 B2 ㉔

A door in a wall leads into the best-kept formal gardens in the city. In the early 17th century they belonged, along with the adjoining Wallenstein Palace (Valdštejnský palác), to General Albrecht von Wallenstein, commander of the Catholic armies in the Thirty Years' War, and known to be a formidable property speculator.

Wallenstein Palace

Valdštejnský palác
Valdštejnská 3 (257 073 136/www.ng prague.cz). Metro Malostranská. **Open** 10am-6pm Tue-Sun. **Admission** 100 Kč; 50 Kč reductions. **Map** p71 B2 ㉕

The palace (which now contains the Czech Parliament) is quite simply enormous. Designed by the Milanese architect Andrea Spezza in the latter half of the 1620s, it once housed a permanent staff of 700 servants along with 1,000 horses. A little-noticed entrance to the palace gardens, just to the right of the Malostranská metro station exit, provides a wonderful way of cutting through the district and leaving the droves of tourists behind.

Kampa Museum p77

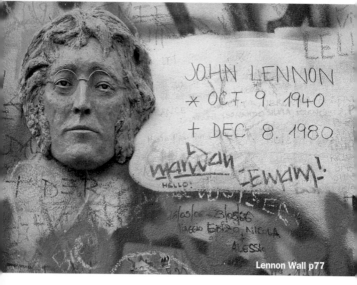

Lennon Wall p77

Wallenstein Riding School

Valdštejnská jízdárna

Valdštejnská 3 (257 073 136/www.ng prague.cz). Metro Malostranská. **Open** 10am-6pm Tue-Sun. **Admission** 100 Kč; 50 Kč reductions. **Map** p71 B2 ㉖

Part of the Wallenstein Palace complex and operated by the National Gallery, this space holds some of Prague's most popular and well-attended exhibitions. These include overviews of Czech artists like National Revival-era patriot František Ženíšek, modernist Václav Špála and symbolist Max Švabinský.

Eating & drinking

Bar Bar

Všehrdova 17 (257 312 246/www. bar-bar.cz). Tram 12, 22. **Open** noon-midnight Mon-Thur, Sun; noon-2am Fri, Sat. **$**. **French**. **Map** p71 B5 ㉗

Usually packed, this unpretentious cellar bar and restaurant on a twisting picturesque Malá Strana backstreet is an old local fave worth finding – which takes some effort. The open sandwiches, salads and grill dishes are standard offerings, but the savoury crêpes really stand out. English-style pancakes with lemon and sugar are priced at a pittance. Waiters are cool and reasonably flexible about substitutions.

Baráčnická rychta

Tržiště 23 (257 532 461/www. baracnickarychta.cz). Metro Malostranská. **Open** noon-11.30pm Mon-Sat; 11am-9pm Sun. **$**. **Czech**. **Map** p71 A3 ㉘

Right out of Jan Neruda's *Prague Tales,* this 19th-century hall is split into two spaces, one small beerhall frequented by hardcore pivo drinkers, both of the student and middle-aged variety, the other a downstairs music hall that often hosts gigs by local rock hopefuls. Obvious tourists may catch the odd scowl, but in general it's a friendly place.

Blue Light

Josefská 1 (257 533 126/www.blue lightbar.cz). Metro Malostranská. **Open** 6pm-3am daily. **Bar**. **Map** p71 B3 ㉙

A cosy bar featuring occasional live jazz music, jazzy sounds on the stereo and jazz posters all over the dilapidated walls. By day Blue Light is a convivial spot to sit with a friend, especially when there's room at the bar. At night it gets more rowdy and conversation becomes nigh impossible but the vibe is certainly infectious. The bar stocks a good selection of malt whiskies.

Bohemia Bagel

Újezd 16 (257 310 694/www.bohemia bagel.cz). Tram 6, 9, 12, 22. **Open** 7am-midnight Mon-Fri; 8am-midnight Sat, Sun. **$**. **Café**. **Map** p71 B5 ㉚

The owners of U Malého Glena, the jazz club, created this place – the republic's first true bagel café – and it's been packed ever since. Free coffee refills, another breakthrough idea in Prague, help wash down the fresh muffins, breakfast bagels and bagel sandwiches. There's also usually something of interest – courses, places to rent, exhibitions – on the bulletin board.

Café El Centro

Maltézské náměstí 9 (257 533 343/ www.elcentro.cz). Metro Malostranská. **Open** noon-midnight daily. **$$**. **Spanish**. **Map** p71 B3 ㉛

An easily overlooked Malá Strana bar just a block off the main square that specialises in mambo soundtracks and tropical cocktails. Efforts to expand into a full restaurant specialising in paella aren't winning over the daiquiri lovers, but the postage-stamp patio at the rear is a boon.

C'est la Vie

Říční 1 (721 158 403/www.cestla vie.cz). Tram 12, 22. **Open** 11.30am-1am daily. **$$**. **Mediterranean**. **Map** p71 B5 ㉜

Self-billed as a 'trendy eaterie for those who want to be in', this improbably upscale place is clearly geared toward Czuppies, but it may be worth cutting through the attitude for a river embankment table, baked butterfish with mushroom risotto or filet mignon with a good cabernet. Service doesn't keep up with the ambitious menu, though.

St Nicholas Café p85

Cowboys

Nerudova 40 (800 152 672/
www.kampagroup.com). Metro
Malostranská. **Open** noon-11pm daily.
$$. Steakhouse. Map p71 A3 ③③
A good deal classier than the previous
incarnation of this labyrinth of brick
cellars (Bazaar Mediteranee) this capa-
ble steakhouse has kept up its theatri-
cal traditions at least, with Stetsons and
kinky leather vests in abundance, hot-
tie servers and live folk rock courtesy
of crooner Jamie Marshall. For the loca-
tion, service and tenderness of the T-
bones, it's incredible value, and topped
by a terrace with the most enviable
views of the city in this district.

Cukrkávalimonáda

Lázeňská 7 (257 530 628). Metro
Malostranská. **Open** 7am-9pm daily.
$. Café. Map p71 B3 ③④
This hip yet homely café is just a block
off the main tourist drag leading from
the Charles Bridge. Look out on to a
quiet corner of Maltézské náměstí while
sipping a Californian chardonnay or

tucking into one of the daily specials of
chicken roulades with heaps of mashed
potato. Expect tall, foamy lattes, a sort
of casually alert service, designer
benches, hanging greenery and slick
magazines for leafing through.

David

Tržiště 21 (257 533 109/
www.restaurant-david.cz). Metro
Malostranská. **Open** 11.30am-11pm
daily. **$$. Continental. Map** p71 A3 ③⑤
Frequented by touring rock stars,
this family-run discreet little dining
room knows how to pamper, old-club
style. The waiters seem more like
butlers as they efficiently whisk roast
boar and port to your table. Definitive
Bohemian classics (roast duck with
sauerkraut, rabbit fillet with spinach
leaves and herb sauce) are strong here.
Booking is essential.

Gitanes

Tržiště 7 (257 530 163). Metro
Malostranská. **Open** noon-midnight
daily. **$. Balkan. Map** p71 A3 ③⑥

ales plus knock-out riverside tables, complete with blankets for when it's chilly, are further draws.

Jo's Bar

Malostranské náměsti 7 (257 531 422/ www.josbar.cz). Metro Malostranská. **Open** 11am-2am daily. **Bar.** **Map** p71 A3 ❸❽

This street-level bar is an adjunct to the rollicking downstairs Jo's Bar & Garáž (p86). It was once renowned for being every backpacker's first stop in Prague and the original source of nachos in the Czech Republic, but founder Glen Emery has since moved on and Jo's is under new ownership. It's still a good place to meet fellow travellers, but it lacks soul these days.

Kampa Park

Na Kampě 8B (296 826 102/ www.kampagroup.com). Metro Malostranská. **Open** 11.30am-1am daily; kitchen closes at 11pm. **$$.** **Seafood. Map** p71 C3 ❸❾

The location's arguably the finest in Prague – in the shadow of Charles Bridge with a beautiful riverside terrace. Al fresco dining on oysters or Thai tuna steak in summer complements a slick bar-room scene inside, which dependably acts as a celeb lightning rod – seems you can't shoot a feature film in Prague without wrapping at Kampa Park.

Na Kampě 15

Na Kampě 15 (257 531 430). Metro Malostranská. **Open** 11am-midnight daily. **$$. Pub. Map** p71 C4 ❹⓿

A rare, if touristy, spot for Bohemian pub grub in all its savoury, greasy glory. In fine weather, grab a spot on the terrace out back or a seat out front and wash down goulash and dumplings or fried mushrooms with well-tapped beer, all for not much more than a real smoke-filled beerhall would charge. Better still, this one's cleaned up for foreigners.

Palffy Palác

Valdštejnská 14 (257 530 522/www. palffy.cz). Metro Malostranská. **Open** 11am-11pm daily. **$$$. Continental. Map** p71 B2 ❹❶

Dalmatian and Montenegren delight: stuffed peppers, sweetcorn proja pastry with Balkan cheese, traditional milk fat spreads, hearty red wines and homely service, all in a hideaway covered with gingham and doilies. It's like coming to your Balkan granny's house, only with much cooler music – emanating from speakers hidden in the birdcages. Don't miss the private table available for curtained-off dalliances and the charming and restful winter garden at the rear.

Hergetova Cihelna

Cihelna 2b (296 826 103, reservations 800 152 692/www.kampagroup.com). Metro Malostranská. **Open** 11.30am-1am daily. **$$. World. Map** p71 C3 ❸❼

Impressive value and creative culinary efforts, both signature qualities of owner Nils Jebens, make this a hot reservation even in winter. The signature obsession with celeb gathering in the upstairs bar is a perfect insight into what makes Prague tick today, but is less intense than at his A-list eaterie Kampa Park next door. Great Belgian

A supper on the terrace of this neglected Baroque palace-cum-classical music academy is something to remember in your old age. The owner, Prague clubbing mogul Roman Řezníček, assures top drawer cuisine like quail confit and roebuck marinated in honey and juniper. The crêpes and salads are generous and delicate affairs.

St Nicholas Café

Tržiště 10 (257 530 204). Metro Malostranská. **Open** noon-2am Mon-Thur, Sun; noon-3am Fri, Sat. **$**. **Café**. **Map** p71 A3 ㊷
An atmospheric vaulted cellar decked out with steamer trunk tables, painted arches and Pilsner Urquell on tap. A mellow but lively crowd gathers in the nooks for late evening conversation about nothing in particular. Also good for giving the brew a rest and taking up a glass of Havana Club rum.

Square

Malostranské náměstí 5 (296 826 114, reservations 800 152 672/ www.kampagroup.com). Metro Malostranská. **Open** 8am-1am daily. **$$**. **Mediterranean**. **Map** p71 A3 ㊸
High-concept Spanish tapas, and nouvelle seafood delights such as tiger prawns and squid fritters, sit aside other Mediterranean treats like pumpkin risotto with Italian sausage and pecorino, all in a celebration of cool, modern design that features running waterfalls and padded cream walls.

U Kocoura

Nerudova 2 (257 530 107). Metro Malostranská. **Open** 11am-midnight daily. **$**. **Pub**. **Map** p71 A3 ㊹
It was briefly owned by the Friends of Beer (a former political party which has morphed into a civic association). Although its manifesto is a bit vague, the staff's ability to pull a good, cheap pint is beyond question.

U Malířů

Maltézské náměstí 11 (257 530 000/ www.umaliru.cz). Tram 12, 22. **Open** 11.30am-midnight daily. **$$$$**. **French**. **Map** p71 B3 ㊺

Still one of Prague's most expensive restaurants – which is saying something these days – this quaint 16th-century house with original painted ceilings specialises in authentic, quality French cuisine and a clientele that dines to impress. Pâté with Sauternes or sea bass, lobster, lamb and squab are typical offerings. Top-end wine is stocked.

U Maltézských rytířů

Prokopská 10 (257 533 666/www. umaltezskychrytiru.cz). Tram 12, 22. **Open** 1pm-11pm daily. **$$**. **Czech**. **Map** p71 B3 ㊻
A candlelit, Gothic cellar once an inn for the eponymous Knights of Malta, this place is justly proud of its venison chateaubriand. Mrs Černíková, whose family runs the place, does a nightly narration on the history of the house, then harasses you to eat the incredible strudel. Booking essential.

U Patrona

Dražického náměstí 4 (257 530 725/ www.upatrona.cz). Metro Malostranská. **Open** 10am-midnight daily. **$$**. **Czech**. **Map** p71 B3 ㊼
An oasis of quality in a stretch of town dominated by naff souvenir shops. Fine dining and delicate conceptions of Czech game classics at just a few tables.

U Sedmi Švábů

Jánský vršek 14 (257 531 455). Metro Malostranská. **Open** 11am-11pm daily; kitchen closes at 10pm. **$$$**. **Czech**. **Map** p71 A3 ㊽
A krčma, or Czech medieval tavern, the Seven Swabians is a trippy, if borderline tacky experience, with occasional live troubadour music, traditional sweet honey liqueur and salty platters of pork knuckle. Only in Prague.

U Zlaté studně

U Zlaté studně 166 (257 533 322/ www.zlatastudna.cz). Metro Malostranská. **Open** 7am-11pm daily. **$$$**. **Map** p71 A2 ㊾
In mild weather, stopping here is the perfect reward for tramping about Prague Castle – you can walk right in from the Castle gardens. Now run by the

PRAGUE BY AREA

management of the standard-setting Aria hotel, At the Golden Well offers spectacular views of the Malá Strana district below, sharp service and a menu that starts off with decadent choices like duck livers marinated in armagnac.

Shopping

Antique Ahasver
Prokopská 3 (257 531 404). Metro Malostranská. **Open** 11am-6pm Tue-Sun. **Map** p71 B3 ⑤⓪
Antique formal gowns, traditional folk clothing, linens, mother-of-pearl hairpins, beaded purses, brooches and trays of charming oddments. English-speaking sales assistants are always ready to supply a story and help you decide.

Květinařství U Červeného Lva
Saská ulička (604 855 286). Metro Malostranská. **Open** 9am-7pm Mon-Sat; 11am-7pm Sun. **Map** p71 B3 ⑤①
This crowded little shop is fairly bursting with colour and variety. Dried flowers hang from the ceiling, plants, cut flowers and wreaths cover every available square centimetre.

Nightlife

Jo's Bar & Garáž
Malostranské náměstí 7 (257 531 422). Metro Malostranská. **Open** 9pm-2am daily. **Admission** 50-100 Kč. **Map** p71 A3 ⑤②
No longer the decadent hub of expat life it was back in the mid 1990s, but still a well-worn, comfortable hangout upstairs with caverns of bars and dance space below.

Popocafepetl
NEW *Újezd 19 (602 277 226/www.popocafepetl.cz). Metro Malostranská.* **Open** 4pm-2am daily. **Admission** free-100 Kč. **Map** p71 A4 ⑤③
This two-level rock and ethno music club has brought new competition to nearby Újezd. With Blues Tuesdays and Gypsy Sundays, the smoky little joint is the place to find great live acts and a host of local characters.

Újezd
Újezd 18 (no phone). Metro Malostranská. **Open** *Bar* 2pm-4am daily. *Café* 6pm-4am daily **Admission** free-100 Kč. **Map** p71 B5 ⑤④
Formerly known as Borat (yes, Sascha Cohen once hung out here and was apparently inspired), this three-level club is still the centre of buzz in Prague's left-bank quarter. With occasional great live rock shows, the bar is always packed with a youthful crowd of local students and artists hanging out beneath the surealist metal decor.

Arts & leisure

Malostranská beseda
Malostranské náměstí 21 (257 532 092). Metro Malostranská. **Open** 5pm-midnight daily. **Admission** 80 Kč. **Map** p71 B3 ⑤⑤
Threadbare it may be, but this unimposing former lecture salon hosts the hottest local live acts in town. It's home to the Sto Zvířat, a popular Czech ska band, among dozens of other acts that play the back room regularly. Battered wood surfaces and windows overlooking Malá Strana's main square add appeal. It also has a well-stocked jazz and alternative CD shop, open 11am-7pm Mon-Sat.

Sport Slivka
Újezd 40 (257 007 231). Metro Malostranská, then tram 12, 20, 22, 23. **Open** 10am-6pm Mon-Fri. **Map** p71 B5 ⑤⑥
Good, reasonable rentals for skiers – a complete package costs 160 Kč per day and snowboards are a bit more. Handy if you're headed off for one of the many Czech ski resorts and don't want any surprises when you get there.

U Malého Glena
Karmelitská 23 (257 531 717/www.malyglen.cz). Metro Malostranská. **Open** 10am-2am daily. **Admission** 100-150 Kč. **Map** p71 A3 ⑤⑦
While this is easily the most crammed club in town, patrons forget about the knee-bashing tables the minute the bands start up in the tiny cellar space.

PRAGUE BY AREA

The freshest jazz players in the country have made Little Glenn's their home for nearly a decade. The sound system has been improved and seats are padded, but get there early if you have a hope of sitting on one for the 9pm show.

Smíchov

Sights & museums

Futura
Holečkova 49 (251 511 804/ www.futuraprojekt.com). Metro Anděl. **Open** noon-7pm Wed-Sun. **Admission** free. **Map** p89 A2 ❺❸
A renovated building houses well-designed exhibition halls: white-cubes, cellar spaces, a labyrinthine series of nooks devoted to video works and a Projekt Room presenting experimental shows by up-and-coming artists like Jiří David and Veronika Bromová but also bright stars of European contemporary art like Annika Larsson.

Staropramen Brewery
Nádražní 84 (257 191 402/www. staropramen.cz). Metro Anděl. **Admission** 100 Kč (tours by appointment only). **Map** p89 B5 ❺❾
The biggest and baddest of Prague's breweries hasn't changed much in over a century and still fills tankers and tankards with the city's signature suds. There's a restaurant on site too.

Eating & drinking

Káva Káva Káva
Lidická 42 (no phone). Metro Anděl. **Open** 7am-10pm Mon-Thur; 7am-midnight Fri, Sat; 9am-10pm Sun. **Café**. **Map** p89 B4 ❻⓪
The newest branch of a successful Old Town café-chain, this place is an LA-style coffee and muffin shop, where they can match your taste from arabica Guatemalan to Sumatra dark roast.

La Cambusa
Klicperova 2 (257 317 949/www.la cambusa.cz). Metro Anděl. **Open** 7pm-midnight Mon-Sat. **$$. Seafood**. **Map** p89 A5 ❻❶

Prague's original premier seafood establishment, much-loved by ex-President Havel, has probably been surpassed for delicate sauces, decor and service but it's a proud neighbourhood institution that's still pretty darn good.

Na Verandách
Nádražní 84 (257 191 111/www. ppivovary.cz). Metro Anděl. **Open** 11am-midnight Mon-Thur; 11am-1am Fri, Sat; 11am-11pm Sun. **$. Czech**. **Map** p89 B5 ❻❷
Ensconced in the mighty Staropramen brewery, this trad Czech restaurant is about the district's best at combining modern, Western-style service with great pub grub like smoked meat dumplings and a brew as well-tapped as you'll find in Bohemia.

Nagoya
Stroupežnického 23 (251 511 724/www. nagoya.cz). Metro Anděl. **Open** 6-11pm Mon-Sat. **$$. Sushi**. **Map** p89 A4 ❻❸
The lastest in the new Japanese craze, Nagoya is a fine addition to the genre, though you'll still pay more for such fare in Prague than in London or New York.

Střelecký ostrov
Střelecký ostrov 336 (224 934 028/ www.streleckyostrov.cz). Metro Národní třída, then tram 18. **Open** 11am-1am. **$. Continental**. **Map** p89 C1 ❻❹
Sitting on a lovely Vltava island in the centre of town, this terraced spot caters to the casual with decent pizzas but also manages good wines and gourmet food.

U Buldoka
Preslova 1 (257 329 154/www.u buldoka.cz). Metro Anděl. **Open** 8pm-4am daily. **Pub**. **Map** p89 B5 ❻❺
A great survivor from the days of old, this darkwood pub is nevertheless a hot ticket for the younger generation, with fleet and friendly service and a bit more adventure on the menu than most pubs.

Nightlife

Big Sister
Nádražní 46 (257 310 043/www.big sister.net). Metro Anděl. **Open** 6pm-3am daily. **Map** p89 C5 ❻❻

The most astounding new wave in Prague's booming sex biz, Big Sister nakedly cashes in on the *Big Brother* phenom by putting live internet cameras inside a brothel. Punters agree to be on the web in exchange for gratis action.

Bluesrock Club

NEW *Nádraží 39 (774 338 310/ www.bluesrockclub.cz). Metro Anděl.* **Open** 5pm-5am daily. **Map** p89 C5 ❻

Founded by the management of the long-closed Bunkr club, this new magnet for local and touring rock and blues bands is a bunker of a sort. Its underground arched brick chambers are unpretentious, affordable and lively.

Drake's

Zborovská 50 (257 326 828/www.drakes. cz). Metro Anděl. **Open** 24hrs daily. **Admission** 190Kč. **Map** p89 B1 ❻

The longest-established gay club this side of the Vltava gets fairly steamy but in a somehow nearly elegant way. Not the spot for a casual beer, though no one will stop you, of course.

Futurum

Zborovská 7 (257 328 571/www. musicbar.cz). Metro Anděl. **Open** 8pm-3am daily. **Admission** 100Kč. **Map** p89 B3 ❻

The district's best sound and lights systems back up progressive programming, excellent local bands and the best non-pop clubbing around, with a proper long bar to boot.

Punto Azul

Kroftova 1 (no phone/www.puntoazul. cz). Metro Anděl. **Open** 6pm-2am Mon-Thur; 7pm-3am Fri, Sat; 7pm-2am Sun. **Admission** free-50 Kč. **Map** p89 A2 ❼

A young local crowd of electronica and techno fans gathers in this trashed, smoky little bar to hear friends spin and to get fairly trashed themselves.

U Bukanýra

NEW *Hořejší nábřeží (no phone). Metro Malostranská.* **Open** 7pm-3am Thur; 9pm-3am Fri, Sat. **Map** p89 C4 ❼

This rollicking house boat hosts dance parties with locally respected DJs like Braun, and other purveyors of acid-jazz, lounge and groove, with refreshing river breezes on deck. It's under the Palackého bridge near the Botel Admirál.

Arts & leisure

Bertramka

Mozartova 169 (257 317 465/www. bertramka.com). Metro Anděl. **Open** 9.30am-5pm daily. **Tickets** 390-450Kč. **Map** p89 A4 ❼

The house where Mozart stayed when in Prague is now a museum devoted to him that puts on regular concerts. Nearly all include at least one work by the Austrian genius.

Delroy's Gym

Zborovská 4 (257 327 042/www. delroys-gym.cz). Metro Anděl. **Open** 7am-10pm Mon-Fri; 9am-10pm Sat, Sun. **Admission** *Gym* 100 Kč/90mins; 1,400 Kč/20 visits. *Taebo* 100 Kč/class. *Thai/kick boxing* 100 Kč/class. *Karate* 150 Kč/class. **Map** p89 C4 ❼

Delroy's specialises in martial arts and boxing but offers courses ranging from aerobics to self-defence. The service and quality, along with English-speaking staff, set it apart.

Squash & Fitness Centrum Arbes

Arbesovo náměstí 15 (257 326 041). Metro Anděl, then tram 6, 9, 12, 20. **Open** 7am-11pm daily. **Rates** 150-340 Kč/hr. **Map** p89 B3 ❼

A smart fitness centre riding the Czech exercise wave with well-managed courts and a reasonably central location.

Švandovo divadlo

Štefánikova 57 (234 651 111/www. svandovodivadlo.cz). Metro Anděl, then tram 6, 9, 12, 20. **Open** *Box office* 10am-6pm Mon-Fri. **Map** p89 A2/A3 ❼

By far the hippest performance space in the district, this historic theatre stages fresh conceptions of Czech and international plays, from *Killer Joe* to modernised Shakespeare. Mishal Lang has directed Havel's *The Beggar's Opera* here, and it's the only theatre to employ English subtitles for Czech performances. Great lobby bar too.

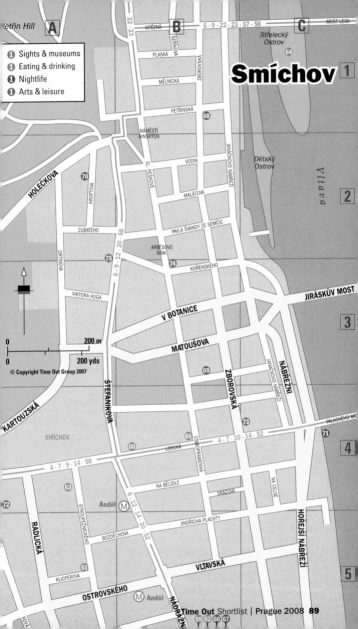

HOTEL *PARIS* PRAGUE

RESTAURANT
SARAH BERNHARDT

LE VIN DE PARIS
VINOTÉKA

Brasserie and Vinotheque
in style of Art Nouveau

Come to enjoy our brand-new vinotheque **Le Vin de Paris** with a wide choice of the best French vines imported directly from Bordeaux and Languedoc chateau vineyards. Our sommelier will be happy to assist you with the right choice. Get the full flavour of the excellent wine with typical French delicacies served on the open buffet bar. And do not forget to take back home with you a piece of remembrance of our hotel – we offer Take Away service!

Brasserie Sarah Bernhardt gently and with attentive effortlessness ties French gourmet cuisine and advanced Czech gastronomy in one outstanding experience. Our Head Chef Mr. Jan Mošna, a student of Mr. Gordon Ramsay, the worldwide famous Head Chef and owner of many fine restaurants awarded with the most Michelin stars all over the world, prepares for you real exquisite dainties. Please let us invite you to a table and show you how enjoyable dining with us might be.

IN STYLE OF ART NOUVEAU

HOTEL PARIS *****
U Obecního domu 1, 110 00 Prague 1, Czech Republic
Phone: +420 222 195 195, fax: +420 224 225 475
fboffice@hotel-paris.cz, www.hotel-paris.cz

Havelský Market p94

Staré Město & northern Nové Město

Prague's Old Town, or Staré Město, district, which retains its tortuous medieval street pattern, yields only grudgingly to modern times and offers much the feel of the walled city it once was. Its cramped, blackened Gothic architecture, though lined with far too many crystal shops on the main thoroughfares, are otherwise incredibly preserved. Because Czechoslovakia fell to the Nazis without resistance, the old centre remained virtually untouched until the 1989 Velvet Revolution, with the exception of creeping damage due to over four decades of communist neglect after 1948. Nowadays, crystal tat aside, the compact heart of the city, and the northern section of Nové Město that borders it to the east, has become newly stylish and

hip, with a plugged-in bar scene along Dlouhá and V Kolkovně streets, and a surprising number of clubbing options, often hidden down dark stairs; only the steady flow of disaffected youth and small signs tip you off to their entrances.

Bounded on the north and west by the Vltava river, the one square-kilometre Staré Město district is also a concentrated dose of the new Bohemia. Two of the country's best symphony halls, the **Rudolfinum** (p117) and **Obecní dům**, home to Prague Spring (p36), are here. It also hosts some of Prague's best cuisine, with definitive Czech, Italian, French, seafood and even Afghan options, plus regular stabs at sushi. The gallery scene is led by the forward-thinking **House at the Golden Ring**, not far from

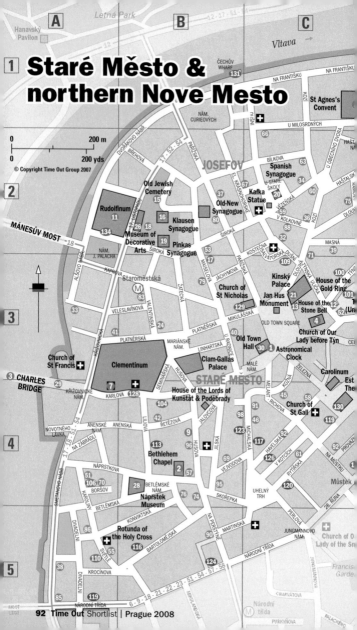

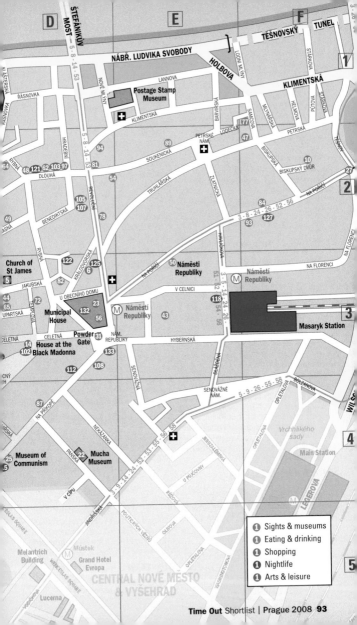

D

ŠTEFÁNIKŮV MOST

5 · 8 · 14 · 53

E

NÁBŘ. LUDVIKA SVOBODY

HOLBOVA

F

TĚSNOVSKÝ

TUNEL

1

KLIMENTSKÁ

ŘÁSNOVKA

NOVÉ MLÝNY

LANNOVA

LODNÍ MLÝNY

ŠTĚPÁNKOVA

HELMOVA

PŮTOVA

STŘELECKÁ

KLIMENTSKÁ

Postage Stamp Museum

BARVÍŘSKÁ

SAMCOVA

MLYNÁŘSKÁ

PETRSKÁ

HRADEBNÍ

5 · 8 · 14 · 53

94

PETRSKÉ NÁM.

LODĚCKÁ

177

47

SOUKENICKÁ

89

BISKUPSKÁ

TĚŠNOV

RYBNÁ

64

48 121 62 103 97

DLOUHÁ

81

54

TRUHLÁŘSKÁ

ZLATNICKÁ

BISKUPSKÝ DVŮR

10

27

2

BENEDIKTSKÁ

105 107

78

HAVLÍČKOVA

3 · 8 · 24 · 26 · 52 · 56

84

93 127

NA POŘÍČÍ

NA FLORENCI

NA FLORENCI

49

ASNÁ

RYBNÁ

122

KRÁLODVORSKÁ

125

6

NA POŘÍČÍ

50 Náměstí Republiky

Náměstí Republiky

Church of St James

5

JAKUBSKÁ

82

U OBECNÍHO DOMU

V CELNICI

51 · 32

3 · 5 · 14 · 24 · 54 · 56

118

M

44

65

UPARTSKÁ

TÝPLOVÁ

Municipal House

132 23

56

M Náměsti Republiky

43

Masaryk Station

3

CELETNÁ

Powder Gate

NÁM. REPUBLIKY

HYBERNSKÁ

14

102

House at the Black Madonna

31

133

CNÝ

112

108

SENOVÁŽNÁ

SENOVÁŽNÉ NÁM.

5 · 9 · 26 · 55 · 58

OPLETALOVA

BOLZANOVA

WILS

4

87

NA PŘÍKOPĚ

NEKÁZANKA

56 58

Vrchlického sady

Main Station

PANSKÁ

56

Mucha Museum

3 · 9 · 14 · 24 · 52 · 53 · 55

LÚČERVA

25

Museum of Communism

5

V CÍPU

JINDŘIŠSKÁ

PUPOŘICH

U PÚJČOVNY

M

Melantrich Building

Můstek

Grand Hotel Evropa

CENTRAL NOVÉ MĚSTO & VYŠEHRAD

OPLETALOVA

OPLETALOVA

Lucerna

❶ Sights & museums
❶ Eating & drinking
❶ Shopping
❶ Nightlife
❶ Arts & leisure

where Franz Kafka grew up and studied. The moody insurance man led a double life, haunted by ghosts of the just-demolished Jewish ghetto, which he remembered from boyhood, where the Josefov area is today. All in all, it's an odd but compelling mix of vitality, trendsetting, frozen time and occasional unrestrained tourist buck making. But that's easy enough to escape on the smaller shadowy lanes all around.

Not that it's not safe, of course; barring the risk of getting tramped on by British stag parties (or pickpocketed at Havelský Market), the area is made for walking, and getting totally but pleasantly lost.

Sights & museums

Astronomical Clock

Orloj
Staroměstské náměstí (724 508 584). Metro Staroměstská. **Open** *Nov-Mar* 11am-5pm Mon; 9am-5pm Tue-Sun; *Apr-Oct* 11am-6pm Mon; 9am-6pm Tue-Sun. **Admission** 50 Kč. **Map** p92 C3 ➊
The orloj has been ticking and pulling in crowds since 1490 – even if its party trick is laughably unspectacular, prompting 'is that it?' looks from bemused spectators. Every hour on the hour, from 8am to 8pm, wooden statuettes of saints appear, with Greed, Vanity, Death and the Turk below. The clock gives Central European, Old Czech and, for some reason, Babylonian Time, all courtesy of Master Hanuš, who was blinded so that he'd never duplicate his masterpiece.

Bethlehem Chapel

Betlémská kaple
Betlémské náměstí 4 (224 248 595). Metro Národní třída or Staroměstská. **Open** *Nov-Mar* 10am-5.30pm Tue-Sun. *Apr-Oct* 10am-6.30pm Tue-Sun. **Admission** 40 Kč; 20 Kč reductions. **Map** p92 B4 ➋
This huge church dating from 1391, was where the proto-Protestant Jan Hus delivered sermons in Czech excoriating the papacy, thus getting himself burned

at the stake in 1415. Neglected for centuries, the chapel was restored by the communists, who saw Hus as a useful working-class revolutionary.

Charles Bridge

Karlův most
East end of Karlova street. **Open** 24 hrs daily. **Admission** free. **Map** p92 A3 ➌
Step into the postcard – the stone bridge was built in 1357, and is still the most popular place to have your pocket picked or to pick up a backpacker, and still delivers that 'I'm really here' thrill. The statues arrived in the 17th century, when Josef Brokof and Matthias Braun were commissioned to inspire the mass conversions of Bohemian Protestants to the Catholicism of the ruling Habsburgs.

Church of Our Lady before Týn

Kostel Matky Boží pod Týnem
Staroměstské náměstí (222 322 801). Metro Náměstí Republiky or Staroměstská. **Open** *Services* 6pm Wed-Fri; 8am Sat; 9.30am, 9pm Sun. **Admission** free. **Map** p92 C3 ➍
A landmark of Staré Město, the church dates from the late 14th century and became a centre of the reforming Hussites' movement in the 15th century, before being commandeered by the Jesuits in the 17th. The southern aisle houses astronomer Tycho Brahe's tomb.

Church of St James

Kostel sv. Jakuba
Malá Štupartská and Jakubská streets (224 828 816). Metro Náměstí Republiky. **Open** 9.30am-noon, 2-4pm Mon-Sat; 2-3.45pm Sun. **Admission** free. **Map** p93 D3 ➎
With 21 altars, fine frescoes and a desiccated human forearm next to the door, St James stands out. The latter item belonged to a 15th-century jewel thief who tried to steal gems from the statue of the Virgin. The Madonna grabbed him and the limb had to be cut off.

City Bike

Královdvorská 5 (776 180 284/ www.pragueonline.cz/citybike).

Shuffle on across

It's survived marauding Swedes, epic flooding and even a VIP party where public access was put on hold while Madonna entertained the swells in private. Far more than a postcard image, the **Charles Bridge** (p94) is synonymous with Prague; it's hard to overestimate the role it plays in generating national pride.

Czechs love to invoke the Golden Age of Charles IV as the high point of Bohemian might and culture, and one of the king's most memorable acts was the founding of this Gothic stone span, the first surviving linkage between the Staré Město district and Malá Strana across the Vtlava.

Thus, tourist agencies had a severe fright early in 2006 when they were told it would be closed for renovations – badly needed to counteract invisible water damage from the 2002 floods – for the entire high season. Renovations were eventually put on hold for a year – but visitors in 2007-08 should be prepared to shuffle across the 14th-century bridge in single file while work goes on.

Though the structure appears as solid as ever, the truth is that seepage, erosion and chemical damage from pollutants in the Vltava have taken their toll. So have partying vandals, who recently broke off pieces of the bridge's famous statues of saints and heaved them into the river (24-hour security cameras have now been installed). Scuba archaeologists looking to recover a Hebrew plaque that was pulled off the stone crucifix in early '06 found other bridge artefacts while down there, including a ceremonial sword and a monstrance from the St Norbert statue. Most of the bridge's 31 statues are now replicas, with the originals housed in Výstaviště's Lapidarium (p153).

Public works projects taking forever are nothing new in Europe, of course, and the bridge's original construction is a prime example. Work started at 5.31am on 9 July 1357 – the time and date that Charles's astrologers and numerologists reckoned to be the most auspicious. The bridge wasn't completed for 23 years.

Astronomical Clock p94

Metro Náměstí Republiky. **Open** 10am-6pm Mon-Fri. **Map** p93 D3 ⑥
If there's anywhere safe to pedal in this town, it's Old Town – though the guys at City Bike also run their two-hour rides (helmet, bike and guide included) along the riverside and citywide. Mongoose Pro mountain bikes depart at 10am, noon and sunset – call to book.

Clementinum

Klementinum
Mariánské náměstí 4 (221 663 111). Metro Staroměstská. **Open** *Library* Jan-Mar 10am-4pm daily; Apr-Oct 10am-8pm daily; Nov, Dec 10am-6pm daily. **Admission** 190 Kč. **Map** p92 A4 ⑦
In the 12th and 13th centuries the Prague headquarters of the Inquisition, the Jesuits moved in during the 16th century, creating the Church of St Saviour (Kostel sv. Salvátora), to reawaken Catholicism in the Protestant populace. At the centre is the Astronomical Tower, where Johannes Kepler once stargazed.

Convent of St Agnes of Bohemia

Klášter sv. Anežky České
U milosrdných 17 (224 810 628). Metro Náměstí Republiky. **Open** 10am-6pm Tue-Sun. **Admission** 100 Kč; 150 Kč family. **Map** p92 C1 ⑧
The first Gothic building in Prague now houses a collection of Bohemian and Central European medieval art from 1200 to 1550. The 14th-century Master of Třeboň defined the distorted 'Beautiful Style' that held sway here till the 16th century.

Czech Museum of Fine Arts

Husova 19-21 (222 220 218/www. cmvu.cz). Metro Staroměstská. **Open** 10am-6pm Tue-Sun. **Admission** 50 Kč; 20 Kč reductions. **Map** p92 B4 ⑨
Ensconced in Renaissance townhouses, this museum exhibits 20th-century Czech art plus foreign artists like Karen LaMonte and international contemporary art on themes of people, nature or technology. Special shows aimed at children are held in the winter holidays.

Galerie Jiří Švestka

Biskupský dvůr 6 (222 311 092/ www.jirisvestka.com). Metro Náměstí Republiky. **Open** noon-6pm Tue-Fri; 11am-6pm Sat. **Admission** free. **Map** p93 F2 ⑩
Returned emigré Jiří Švestka has been specialising since 1995 in bold, internationally recognised Czech artists like Milena Dopitová, Krištof Kintera and Jiří Černický and also exhibits international names like Tony Cragg in this former photography atelier.

Galerie Rudolfinum

Alšovo nábřeží 12 (227 059 309/ www.galerierudolfinum.cz). Metro Staroměstská. **Open** 10am-6pm Tue-Sun. **Admission** 100 Kč; 50 Kč reductions. **Map** p92 A2 ⑪
Prague's only European Kunsthalle model, this gallery is great for catching Czech and international contemporary and modern art, with retrospectives of enigmatic modernists like Alén Diviš and Mikuláš Medek. Major shows by middle-generation local artists like Petr Nikl and František Skála, plus Chinese art, a speciality of the gallery's director. The Rasart series synergizes music, theatre and art.

House at the Golden Ring

Dům U Zlatého prstenu
Týnská 6 (224 827 022). Metro Náměstí Republiky. **Open** 10am-6pm Tue-Sun. **Admission** 80 Kč; 160 Kč family. No credit cards. **Map** p92 C3 ⑫
A broad spectrum of 20th-century Czech works, organised intriguingly by themes rather than by artist or period. A fine basement exhibition space hosts well-curated, fresh and international shows, often exploring digitial media.

House at the Stone Bell

Dům U Kamenného zvonu
Staroměstské Náměstí 13 (224 827 526/www.citygalleryprague.cz). Metro Staroměstská. **Open** 10am-6pm Tue-Sun. **Admission** varies. **Map** p92 C3 ⑬
Prague City Gallery's Gothic sandstone building on Old Town Square features a gorgeous Baroque courtyard and

House of the Black Madonna

three floors of exhibition rooms, some with original vaulting in place. It favours retrospectives of Czech artists such as Toyen and Adolf Hoffmeister and hosts the Zvon biennale of young Czech and Central European artists.

House of the Black Madonna

Dům u Černé Matky Boží
Ovocný trh 19 (224 211 746). Metro Náměstí Republiky. **Open** 10am-6pm Tue-Sun. **Admission** 100 Kč; 150 Kč family. **Map** p93 D3 ⑭
This fantastic cubist building and gallery strives to present a totally plane-defying environment. Worth a visit for the Josef Gočár-designed building alone, it's about the finest example of cubist architecture in Prague but with meager English-language information.

Jewish Museum

Židovské Muzeum
U Staré Školy 1 (221 711 511/www. jewishmuseum.cz). Metro Staroměstská. **Open** *Apr-Oct* 9am-6pm Mon-Fri, Sun.

Nov-Mar 9am-4.30pm Mon-Fri, Sun. Closed Jewish holidays. **Admission** 290 Kč; 190 Kč reductions; under-6s free. *Old-New Synagogue* 200 Kč. No credit cards.
The six sites that make up the Jewish Museum (all listed separately below) have now been expanded and share exhibits with other galleries in the city. Opening hours are the same for all of the venues, but vary according to the season; from April to the end of October, all sites are open from 9am to 6pm daily except Saturdays (when they're closed); from November to the end of March, all are open from 9am to 4.30pm daily except Saturdays. All the sites are closed on Jewish holidays. Together they form a bitter tribute to the third pillar of Czech society that all but disappeared during the Holocaust. Much of museum's contents, now overseen by the thriving Jewish Community organisation, were seized from Jews by the Nazis, who had hoped for a museum dedicated to an extinct race.

Former Ceremonial Hall
Obřadní síň
*U starého hřbitova 3A, Josefov
(222 317 191).* **Map** p92 B2 ⑮
The Romanesque turrets and arches of this building at the exit of the cemetery appear as old as the gravestones but date to just 1906. It hosts fascinating exhibitions on topics like Jewish customs and traditions focusing on illness and death.

Klausen Synagogue
Klausova synagoga
*U starého hřbitova 3A, Josefov
(222 310 302).* **Map** p92 B2 ⑯
The great ghetto fire of 1689 destroyed the original Klausen Synagogue along with 318 houses and ten other synagogues. Hastily rebuilt in 1694, its permanent exhibition explores religion in the lives of the ghetto's former inhabitants. It's topped by two tablets of the Decalogue with a golden inscription, visible from the Jewish Cemetery.

Maisel Synagogue
Maiselova synagoga
Maiselova 10, Josefov (224 819 456). **Map** p92 B3 ⑰
Mordecai Maisel, mayor of the Jewish ghetto under Rudolf II, was one of the richest men in 16th-century Europe from a lucrative trading monopoly, and paid for the construction of the splendid original synagogue. This burned down in 1689 and then was rebuilt in Baroque style. The building was then rebuilt again in the late 19th century, and now houses exhibitions on the Jewish history of Bohemia and Moravia.

Old Jewish Cemetery
Starý Židovský hřbitov
Široká 3, Josefov (no phone). **Map** p92 B2 ⑱
All of Prague's Jews were buried here until the late 1600s, and 12,000 tombstones are crammed into this tiny, tree-shaded patch of ground – a forceful reminder of the cramped ghetto, which remained walled until the late 1700s. Forced to bury the dead on top of one another, an estimated 100,000 bodies lay 12 levels deep. Headstone reliefs indicate the name or occupation of the deceased: scissors, for a tailor, a lion for Rabbi Leow.

Pinkas Synagogue
Pinkasova synagoga
Široká 3, Josefov (222 326 660). **Map** p92 B2 ⑲
Founded in 1479, this temple's walls were inscribed in the 1950s with the names of more than 80,000 Czech Holocaust victims. After the Six Day War, the Czechoslovak government

Jewish Museum

Municipal House Exhibition Hall

blotted them out during 'restoration', but they're all back, a job completed in 1994. Don't miss the powerful exhibition of drawings by children interned in Terezin.

Spanish Synagogue
Španělská synagoga
Vězeňská 1, Josefov (224 819 464).
Map p92 C2 ⓴
Reopened after long neglect in 1998, this temple's domed interior glows with green, red and faux gold leaf, and houses varied and inspired new exhibitions on Jewish history, and a stunning exhibition of synagogue silver. Its predecessor predated the Altneu Synagogue but it was rebuilt in 1868 in the then-fashionable Moorish style.

Kinský Palace
Staroměstské Náměstí 12.
(224 810 758/www.ngprague.cz).
Metro Staroměstská. **Open** 10am-6pm Tue-Sun. **Admission** 100 Kč; 150 Kč family. **Map** p92 C3 ㉑
The National Gallery's renovated Kinský Palace opened with a bang in

2000 with the polemical 'End of the World?' show. It's since toned down its programme with a long-term display of Czech landscape painting from the 17th to the 20th centuries, and photography from the 19th century to the present.

Mucha Museum
Kaunický palác, Panská 7 (221 451 333/www.mucha.cz). Metro Můstek.
Open 10am-6pm daily. **Admission** 120 Kč. **Map** p93 D4 ㉒
The most famous of all Czech visual artists, Alfons Mucha (1860-1939), created mass-produced decorative panels and posters for Sarah Bernhardt in Paris and did much to spread art nouveau throughout Europe. His lithographs, drawings, sketches and notebooks are here, with an engaging video on his life.

Municipal House Exhibition Hall
Obecní dům
Náměstí Republiky 5 (222 002 101/ www.obecni-dum.cz). Metro Náměstí

Republiky. **Open** 10am-6pm daily. **Admission** 100-150 Kč for exhibitions. **Map** p93 D3 ㉓

The exhibition rooms in this art nouveau masterpiece of a building present shows like nowhere-else-seen Josef Čapek paintings or German photojournalist Werner Bischof and Decadent art in the Czech lands. But the best shows harmonise with the stunning space itself, like an overview of Croatian art nouveau.

Municipal Library

Mariánské Náměstí 1 (entrance on Valentinská) (222 310 489/ www.citygalleryprague.cz). Metro Staroměstská. **Open** 10am-6pm Tue-Sun. **Admission** 120 Kč; 60 Kč reductions. **Map** p92 B3 ㉔

The rooms above the Municipal Library run by the Prague City Gallery showcase large-scale exhibitions of historical importance, such as Czech 20th-century photography and finalists for the Jindřich Chalupecký Award – the most prestigious annual Czech art prize.

Museum of Communism

Na Příkopě 10 (224 212 966/www. museumofcommunism.com). Metro Můstek. **Open** 9am-9pm daily. **Admission** 180 Kč. **Map** p93 D4 ㉕

The first of its kind in the country, the Museum of Communism puts the communist era in historical perspective with archive photos and hundreds of relics. Mock-ups of a school-room and interrogation room from the period are eerie indeed.

Museum of Decorative Arts

Uměleckoprůmyslové muzeum Ulice 17 listopadu 2 (251 093 111/ www.upm.cz). Metro Staroměstská. **Open** 10am-7pm Tue; 10am-6pm Wed-Sun. **Admission** 80-130 Kč. **Map** p92 B2 ㉖

This neo-Renaissance museum, a work of art in itself, boasts intricately painted plaster mouldings and crystal windows, plus clever exhibits of objects according to material. Pieces include exquisite furniture, tapestries, pottery, clocks, books, a beautifully preserved collection of clothing and fine displays of ceramics and glass.

Museum of the City of Prague

Muzeum Hlavního města Prahy Na Poříčí 52 (224 816 773/www. muzeumprahy.cz). **Open** 9am-6pm Tue-Sun. **Admission** 80 Kč; 160 Kč family; under-6s free; 1 Kč first Thur of the month reductions. **Map** p93 F2 ㉗

Antonín Langweil spent 11 years of the early 1800s building an incredibly precise room-sized paper model of Prague. This prize exhibit is the only complete depiction of what the city looked like before the Jewish ghetto was ripped down. Other displays follow the city's development from prehistory through to the 17th century.

Náprstek Museum

Náprstkovo muzeum Betlémské náměstí 1 (224 497 500/ www.aconet.cz/npm). Metro Národní třída. **Open** 10am-6pm Tue-Sun. **Admission** 80 Kč. **Map** p92 B4 ㉘

The 19th-century nationalist Vojta Náprstek was fascinated by primitive cultures and gathered ethnographic oddities from Czech travellers in this extension to his house. Native loot from the Americas, Australasia and the Pacific Islands are beautifully arranged.

Old Town Bridge Tower

Staroměstská mostecká věž Křižovnické náměstí (224 220 569). Metro Staroměstská. **Open** *Nov-Feb* 10am-5pm daily. *Mar* 10am-6pm daily. *Apr, May, Oct* 10am-7pm daily. *June-Sept* 10am-10pm daily. **Admission** 60 Kč; 40 Kč reductions. **Map** p92 A4 ㉙

The tower of the 14th-century Gothic gate to Charles Bridge, with Peter Parler's frill visible on the east side, offers a great close-up view of Prague's domes and spires, the wayward line of Charles Bridge, the naff Klub Lávka and the most gigantic addition to Prague clubbing, Karlovy Lázně, all below on the river and beyond.

Old Town Square

Old Town Hall & Astronomical Clock

Staroměstská radnice
*Staroměstské náměstí (724 508 584).
Metro Staroměstská.* **Open** *Town Hall*
Nov-Mar 11am-5pm Mon; 9am-5pm
Tue-Sun. Apr-Oct 11am-6pm Mon;
9am-6pm Tue-Sun. *Tower* May-Sept
10am-10pm. Oct-Apr 10am-7pm.
Admission 60 Kč. **Map** p92 C3 ③⓪

Only half the original Old Town Hall,
built around 1338, remains standing
today. The Nazis blew it up at the
end of World War II but the clock tower
survived and has a viewing platform
definitely worth the climb. The dungeon
was headquarters of the Resistance during the Prague Uprising in 1945, when
enemy supplies were stolen via underground passages. A plaque on the side
of the clock tower thanks the Soviet soldiers who liberated the city afterwards.

Powder Gate

Prašná brána
*U Prašné brány (no phone). Metro
Náměstí Republiky.* **Open** *Apr-Oct*
10am-6pm daily. **Admission** 50 Kč;
40 Kč under-10s. **Map** p93 D3 ③①

This 15th-century relic of the fortifi-
cations that used to ring the town
mouldered until it finally gained a pur-
pose, and a name, when it stored gun-
powder in 1575. Severely damaged by
the Prussians in 1757, it's now a neo-
Gothic star again.

Eating & drinking

Alcohol Bar

*Dušní 6 (224 811 744/www.alcohol
bar.cz). Metro Staroměstská.* **Open**
7pm-3am daily. **Bar. Map** p92 C2 ③②

Clubby, with a wall of single malt
whiskies, plus rums and tequilas from
respected distillers from all over the
Caribbean and Mexico. A New York-
style sophistication pervades, the bar-
men are true gents, and there are
occasional groove DJs.

Allegro

*Veleslavínova 2A (221 426 880/www.
fourseasons.com/prague/dining/dining.*

Municipal Library p101

html). *Metro Staroměstská.* **Open**
Restaurant 6.30am-11pm daily. **$$$$.**
Continental. Map p92 A3 ③③
The Four Seasons flagship is Chef Vito
Mollica's shrine to Tuscan-meets-Czech.
Veal fillet, pan-fried foie gras and truf-
fles or monkfish saltimbocca have won
deserved raves. The terrace looks out on
Prague Castle across the Vltava.

Amici Miei

*Vězeňská 5 (224 816 688/www.amici
miei.cz). Metro Můstek.* **Open** 11.30am-
11pm daily. **$$$. Italian**. Map
p92 C2 ③④
Outstanding cuisine in a slightly over-
lit hall. Veal scallops and simple dish-
es like tagliatelle with parmesan and
rocket are typical dishes, service is
unusually warm and attentive service,
and there's an excellent wine list.

Ariana

*Rámová 6 (222 323 438/ariana.dream
worx.cz). Metro Náměstí Republiky.*
Open 11am-11pm daily. **$. Afghan**.
Map p92 C2 ③⑤

A cosy little Afghan eaterie with excel-
lent tender spiced lamb and sumptuous
vegetarian chalous. Staff are friendly,
and straightback chairs, rugs and brass
lamps make up the decor.

Bakeshop Praha

*Kozí 1 (222 316 823). Metro
Staroměstská.* **Open** 7am-7pm daily.
$. Bakery. Map p92 C2 ③⑥
San Franciscan Anne Feeley launched
this expat mainstay seven years ago
and hasn't looked back since. Zesty
quiches, traditional nut breads, muffins
and peanut butter cookies have every
Westerner in town tucking in.

Barock

*Pařížská 24, Josefov (222 329 221).
Metro Staroměstská.* **Open** 10am-11pm
daily. **$$. Café**. Map p92 B2 ③⑦
A gleaming zinc bar, floor-to-ceiling
windows, and a credible sushi platter
with suitably aesthetic nigiri are some
of the highlights at Barock. The reasonably priced breakfast menu and
powerhouse lattes are further draws.

Duende p106

Bellevue

Smetanovo nábřeží 18 (222 221 443/ www.pfd.cz). Metro Národní třída.
Open noon-3pm, 5.30-11pm daily.
$$$$. Fine dining. Map p92 A5 ③⑧
A rich veal loin in black truffle sauce, and fallow venison in juniper reduction go mighty well with Bellevue's Sunday jazz brunch. The space is formal and traditional but boasts stunning views of Prague Castle. Booking is essential.

Bohemia Bagel

Masná 2 (224 812 560) (257 310 694/www.bohemiabagel.cz). Metro Staroměstská. **Open** 7am-10pm Mon-Fri; 8am-10pm Sat, Sun. **$. Café.**
Map p92 C2 ③⑨
One of the republic's first true bagel cafés (oy!), with complementary coffee refills, fresh muffins, breakfast bagels and bagel sandwiches. Choose from a huge variety, including poppyseed, cinnamon raison, tomato basil and chocolate chip. There's also internet access. What's not to like?

Brasiliero

U Radnice 8 (224 234 474/www. ambi.cz). Metro Staroměstská.
Open 11am-midnight daily. **$$.**
Steakhouse. Map p92 B3 ④⓪
The local Ambiente group's a hit in the city, thanks to branches like Brasiliero, which specialises in heartly Brazilian butchery, with enough chops and fillets to stop any healthy heart.

Café Indigo

Platnéřská 11 (no phone). Metro Staroměstská. **Open** 9am-midnight Mon-Fri; 11am-midnight Sat, Sun.
$. Café. Map p92 A3 ④①
Post-industrial, comfortable art café with a limited menu but cheap wine for students from nearby Charles University and an upbeat and easygoing vibe. Small children's corner in the back.

Café Montmartre

Řetězová 7 (222 221 244). Metro Staroměstská. **Open** 9am-11pm Mon-Fri; noon-11pm Sat, Sun. **$. Café.**
Map p92 B4 ④②

Czech literati like Gustav Meyrink and Franz Werfel all tippled here before it became a Jazz Age hotspot. Creative miscreants still gather around the threadbare settees and battered tables for late-night talk.

Celnice

V Celnici 4 (224 212 240/www.celnice. com). Metro Náměstí Republiky. **Open** 11am-midnight Mon-Thur, Sun; 11am-1.30am Fri, Sat. **$$$. Czech**. Map p93 E3 ⑬

The hippest of the Pilsner-licensed restaurants, Celnice is a mix of classic Czech, with updated fare like kyselo, or sauerkraut soup, pickled Prague ham and pastas, and a sleek, modern sushi bar with DJ dance fare on weekends.

Chateau

Jakubská 2 (222 316 328). Metro Náměstí Republiky. **Open** noon-4am Mon-Thur; noon-6am Fri; 4pm-4am Sat; 4pm-2am Sun. **Bar**. Map p93 D3 ⑭

Wall-to-wall cruising and stoned young Americans but also the most popular bar in town for travelling twentysomethings, which sometimes seems curious.

Čili

NEW *Kožná 8 (777 945 848). Metro Můstek.* **Open** 11am-midnight daily. **Bar**. Map p92 C4 ⑮

A decisive hit on the competitive Prague bar scene, probably for its hidden location on a narrow backstreet off Old Town Square and for its outsize mojitos, G&Ts and comfortably broken in, living room vibe. The overstuffed leather armchairs are the prize real estate.

Country Life

Melantrichova 15 (224 213 366). Metro Národní třída. **Open** 9am-8.30pm Mon-Thur; 9am-5pm Fri; 11am-8.30pm Sun. **$. Vegetarian**. Map p92 C4 ⑯

A Czech neo-hippie fave cafeteria with dirt-cheap vegetarian dishes that are made with organically grown ingredients. Country Life specialises in massive DIY salads, fresh carrot juice,

delectable lentil soup and crunchy wholegrain breads, but it's best to avoid the lunchtime crush.

Credo

Petrská 11 (222 324 634/www. credo-restaurace.cz). Metro Náměstí Republiky. **Open** 10.30am-midnight Mon-Sat. **$$. Café**. Map p93 F2 ⑰

Credo makes for a surprisingly good lunch option, and is situated just two blocks east of Old Town. Starters the likes of gorgonzola-stuffed baked fig and rocket, caper and walnut salad are followed by main courses such as creamy risotto or fillet of sole with Spanish rice.

Dahab

Dlouhá 33 (224 827 375/www.dahab. cz). Metro Náměstí Republiky. **Open** noon-11pm Mon-Thur, Sun; noon-2am Fri, Sat. **$. Middle Eastern**. Map p93 D2 ⑱

A definitive Prague tearoom, resembling a candlelit harem with pistachio cookies, couscous, Turkish coffees and occasional belly dancing. Otherwise, thoroughly calming.

DeBrug

Masná 5 (224 819 283). Metro Náměstí Republiky. **Open** noon-2am daily. **$$. Belgian**. Map p93 D2 ⑲

First it was Stella Artois in Czech beer heaven, now the Belgian bistro trend is spreading throughout the city. Still, DeBrug serves great frites and moules, no getting around that.

Dinitz

Na Poříčí 12 (222 314 071/www.dinitz. cz). **Open** 8am-3am Mon-Fri; 9am-3am Sat, Sun. **$. Café**. Map p93 E3 ⑳

This stylish café is a local secret where the small, quality menus match the classy retro decor. It's a favoured hangout for writers, with light savoury delights plus a short list of well-shaken cocktails, and jazz trios in the corner. Note that at the time this guide went to press, a new owner was planning to change the café's name to 'Bissli', and bring in more Middle Eastern fare.

Duende

Karoliny Světlé 30 (775 486 077/ www.duende.cz). Metro Národní třída. **Open** 1pm-1am Mon-Fri; 3pm-1am Sat; 4pm-1am Sun. **$**. **Café**. **Map** p92 A4 ❺❶

New Bohemian in a nutshell, with fringed lampshades, boozy regulars and low-budget Prague intellectuals from the publishing and film scenes. Stay late and try the potato soup.

Ebel Coffee House

Týn 2 (224 895 788/www.ebelcoffee.cz). Metro Náměstí Republiky. **Open** 9am-10pm daily. **$**. **Café**. **Map** p92 C3 ❺❷

Serious coffees (more than 30 prime arabica varieties), courtesy of journalist and designer Malgorzata Ebel, plus passable quiches, bagels and brownies, served in a lovely cobbled courtyard.

Franz Kafka Café

Široká 12, Josefov (222 318 945). Metro Staroměstská. **Open** 10am-8pm daily. **$**. **Café**. **Map** p92 B2 ❺❸

This dark wood, old-world coffeehouse features intimate booths, old engravings of the Jewish Quarter and, naturally, lots of Kafka portraits. Tables on the street are convenient when touring Josefov.

Himalaya

NEW *Soukenická 2 (739 035 371). Metro Náměstí Republiky.* **Open** 11am-11pm Mon-Fri; noon-11pm Sat, Sun. **$**. **Indian**. **Map** p93 D2/E2 ❺❹

Easily the most affordable, credible Indian option for a relaxed dinner in the Old Town area, this cosy little place is good for the soul of many an expat who feels starved of spice. Samosas, vindaloo, rogan and korma feature in the well-thumbed menu.

Kabul

NEW *Karoliny Světle 14 (224 235 452/ www.aa.cz/kabulrestaurant). Metro Národní třída.* **Open** 11am-11pm daily. **$**. **Afghan**. **Map** p92 A5 ❺❺

Hasib Saleh's cosy little eaterie, done up in Persian rugs and hanging lanterns, is a local fave, serving up fine specialities like ashak pastry pockets and bamya okra fingers, all with fresh flatbreads.

Kavárna Obecní dům

Náměstí Republiky 5 (222 002 763/ www.vysehrad2000.cz). Metro Náměstí Republiky. **Open** 7.30am-11pm daily. **$**. **Café**. **Map** p93 D3 ❺❻

The Vienna-style coffeehouse component to the multifaceted, magnificently restored Municipal House. Replete with secessionist brass chandeliers, balconies, a pianist and always a few grand dames, there's no more memorable venue for an espresso.

Klub Architektů

Betlémské náměstí 5A (224 401 214/ www.klubarchitektu.com). Metro Národní třída. **Open** 11.30am-midnight daily. **$**. **Continental**. **Map** p92 B4 ❺❼

This dim designer cellar of an architecture and design gallery is a great value with credible, creative Euro cuisine and a fine, quiet summer patio next door to the Bethlehem Chapel.

Kogo Pizzeria & Caffeteria

Havelská 27 (224 214 543/www. kogo.cz). Metro Můstek. **Open** 8am-11pm Mon-Fri; 9am-11pm Sat, Sun. **$$**. **Italian**. **Map** p93 D3 ❺❽

Scampi, bruschetta, bean soup and focaccia done quickly, stylishly and surprisingly affordably, all served up on white linen tables by foxy Yugoslavian waitress but it manages never to be stuffy. Nicely topped pizzas and tiramisu are further draws.

Kolkovna

V kolkovně 8 (224 819 701/www. kolkovna.cz). Metro Staroměstská. **Open** 11am-midnight daily. **$**. **Czech**. **Map** p92 C2 ❺❾

Crowds of post-1989-generation locals pack this pretty re-creation of old Prague, which is licensed by the brewery Pilsner Urquell, The art-nouveau interior and trad pub grub like potato pancakes and beer-basted goulash attract bright and beautiful patrons.

Kozička

Kozí 1 (224 818 308/www.kozicka.cz). Metro Náměstí Republiky. **Open** noon-

4am Mon-Fri; 6pm-4am Sat; 6pm-3am
Sun. **Bar**. Map p92 C2 ⑥⑩
A popular, unpretentious local scene
can be found here. The place has homely nooks and crannies throughout,
mighty steaks are served until 11pm
and Krušovice is available on tap.

KU Bar Café
NEW *Rytířská 13 (221 181 081).*
Metro Můstek. **Open** 5pm-3am
Mon-Fri; 5pm-4am Sat, Sun. **Bar**.
Map p92 C4 ⑥①
Natalie Portman shook it up here all
night in 2006, but anyone more interested in good DJ tracks, drink-mixing
and atmosphere will find this place
heavy on pretense, if possibly fun for
one overpriced shot.

La Casa Argentina
NEW *Dlouhá 35 (222 311 512).*
Metro Náměstí Republiky. **Open**
10am-2am daily. **$$$**. **Argentine**.
Map p93 D2 ⑥②
Serving up some of the finest cuts, ribs
and filet mignon in Prague, this new
South American eatery knows its stuff
and offers fleet service. *Empanadas*
and grilled corn go along with mouth-
watering tenderloin.

La Casa Blů
*Kozí 15 (224 818 270/www.lacasablu.
cz).* Metro Staroměstská. **Open** 11am-
11pm Mon-Sat; 2-11pm Sun. **$**.
Mexican. Map p92 C2 ⑥③
Rugs draped over hard-back chairs,
street signs and tequila specials
evoke Latin culture in Prague, with
an authentic Mexican menu. Try the
buzzer even if the door is locked – peo-
ple routinely wheedle their way in past
closing time.

La Degustation
NEW *Haštalská 18 (222 311 234/
www.ladegustation.cz).* **Open** 5pm-
midnight Mon-Sat. **$$$$**. **Fine
dining**. Map p93 D3 ⑥④
The latest venture of the respected
Ambiente group has set the new stan-
dard for gourmet cuisine in Prague
with its phenomenal 12-course fixed-
price meals featuring Wagju beef,
squab, sweetbreads, tongue, truffles

and montbriac cheese. Try the modern
or trad Bohemian or continental menu
and set aside two-plus hours.

La Provence
*Štupartská 9 (826 826 155/
reservations 800 152 672/www.
kampagroup.com).* Metro Náměstí
Republiky. **Open** noon-11pm daily.
$$$. **French**. Map p92 C2 ⑥⑤
Run capably by the Czech Republic's
answer to Terrence Conran, Nils
Jebens, this French eaterie does fine
foie gras, tiger prawns, roast duck and
monkfish in a setting that's rustic,
classy and comfortable, something
most unusual for a location close to
Old Town Square.

La Scene
U Milosrdných 6 (222 312 677).
Metro Staroměstská. **Open** noon-
midnight Mon-Fri; 7pm-midnight
Sat. **$$**. **Wine bar**. Map p92 B2/C2 ⑥⑥
A quiet, sleek lounge wine bar with
pan-fried foie gras and rhubarb purée
and some of the best lamb in town,
served with gingerbread crust. The
modern interior complements the 13th-
century convent and hall of the
National Gallery.

La Veranda
*Elišky Krásnohorské 2 (224 814 733/
www.laveranda.cz).* Metro Staroměstská/
tram 17, 18. **Open** noon-midnight
Mon-Sat; noon-10pm Sun. **$$$**.
Fusion. Map p92 B2/B3 ⑥⑦
This *très moderne* gustatory sanctuary for the newly rich lays on garlic
foam fish ragoût soup along with
classic Czech dishes such as roast
duck with thyme. It's also still affordable, if a bit OTT.

Le Café Colonial
*Široká 6, Josefov (224 818 322/
www.lecafecolonial.cz).* Metro
Staroměstská. **Open** 10am-midnight
daily. **$$**. **French**. Map p93 D2 ⑥⑧
Airy, with teak accents, miniature
quiches, delicate pork and delightful
salads. More formal dining's on the
other side where there's a veranda and
designer furniture in Matisse-inspired
tones. Resolutely French.

Le Terroir

Vejvodova 1 (602 889 118). Metro Můstek. **Open** 11am-11pm daily. **$$$. Wine bar.** Map p92 B4 ⑥⑨

Just a few warm starters on the menu, but a killer foie gras terrine in an ancient cellar space that's grand for sipping wine when the sun goes down.

Lehká Hlava

NEW *Boršov 2 (222 220 665/ www.lehkahlava.cz). Metro Náměstí Republiky.* **Open** daily 11.30am-11.30pm. **$$. Vegetarian.** Map p92 A4 ⑦⓪

With a trippy interior and servers who speak in whispers, this New Age vegetarian eatery and gallery is a soothing hideout. The place offers wholewheat ragoût, goat's cheese dishes and an amazing range of teas and juices. The entrance is in a quiet courtyard.

Mama Lucy

NEW *Dlouhá 1 (222 327 207). Metro Staroměstská.* **Open** 11am-midnight daily. **$$. Mexican.** Map p92 C2 ⑦①

Just a block off Old Town Square, this definitive Czech-Mex establishment does fajitas, burritos, enchiladas and quesadillas, all served with a smile but at rates that reflect its location.

Marquis de Sade

Templová 8 (no phone). Metro Náměstí Republiky. **Open** 4pm-3am. **Bar.** Map p93 D3 ⑦②

JB Shoemaker – the legendary former owner – has now gone, but little else has changed at this infamous expat drinking hole (except for the beer prices), where bad behaviour is ever-encouraged, and way too much absinthe is sampled nightly.

Metamorphis

Malá Štupartská 5 (221 771 068/ www.metamorphis.cz). Metro Náměstí Republiky. **Open** 9am-1am daily. **$$. Pasta.** Map p92 C3 ⑦③

Sedate and capable, this family-run pasta café and pension has just one disadvantage: it's directly on a main tourist route to Old Town Square. The cellar restaurant within is enhanced by live jazz at night.

Monarch

Na Perštýně 15 (224 239 602/www. monarch.cz). Metro Národní třída. **Open** 11am-11pm Mon-Sat. **$. Wine bar.** Map p92 B4 ⑦④

A great wine shop and bar with more than 25 varieties of cheese and a good selection of regional sausages. The place for South American or California imports, plus the best local vintages.

Orange Moon

Rámová 5 (222 325 119/www. orangemoon.cz). Metro Náměstí Republiky. **Open** 11.30am-11.30pm daily. **$. Southeast Asian/Indian.** Map p92 C2 ⑦⑤

Thai, Burmese and Indian food served in a warm, unpretentious, well-lit cellar space. Eager servers bring over the curries and Czech beer, a divine combination as it turns out. The entrance is easy to miss, so just follow the voices of customers regaling.

Papas

Betlémské náměstí 8 (222 222 229/ www.papasbar.cz). Metro Vltavská. **Open** 11am-midnight daily. **$. Café.** Map p92 B4 ⑦⑥

A lively cocktail specialist with deep maroon red interiors, Papas is no shrinking flower and a fave of expat students and Czuppies alike. Caipirinha's are mixed with gusto by the energetic staff and the bar food is colourful and varied enough to do well for lunch.

Perpetuum

Lodecká 4 (224 810 401/www. cervenatabulka.cz). Metro Náměstí Republiky. **Open** 11.30am-11pm daily. **$$. Continental.** Map p93 F1 ⑦⑦

Whimsical playschool decor and lava-grilled lamb, plus poultry comfort foods are offered here. Baked duck-leg with bacon dumplings, apple and sauerkraut are cheerily served up alongside rabbit skewer with cream and lime sauce.

Picante

Revoluční 4 (222 322 022/www. picante.cz). Metro Náměstí. **Open** 24 hrs daily. **$$. Mexican.** Map p93 D2 ⑦⑧

PRAGUE BY AREA

This overlit, all-night, fast food counter actually does the finest homemade salsas, steamed pork carnitas and soft maize tacos in town, something heaven-sent for American expats.

Pivnice u Pivrnce

Maiselova 3, Josefov (222 329 404). Metro Náměstí Republiky. **Open** 11am-midnight daily. **$. Czech.** **Map** p92 B3 79

Pivnice u Pivrnce offers old-fashioned Czech cooking and above-average presentation. Svíčková (beef in lemon cream sauce), duck with sauerkraut and walls covered with crude cartoons guaranteed to offend are key features here. The Radegast beer is well tapped and nicely priced too.

Pravda

Pařížská 17, Josefov (222 326 203/pravdarestaurant.cz). Metro Staroměstská. **Open** noon-midnight daily. **$$$. World. Map** p92 B2 80

Owner Tommy Sjoo, who helped bring fine dining to post-1989 Prague, runs this airy, elegant spot. Chicken in Senegal peanut sauce vies against Vietnamese nem spring rolls and borscht, all done credibly. Service is cool and graceful.

Řecká Taverna

Revoluční 16 (222 317 762/www.reckataverna.cz). Metro Náměstí Republiky. **Open** 11am-midnight daily. **$. Greek. Map** p93 D2 81

Affordable, authentic Greek food in a cheerfully tacky tavern, across the street from Old Town. Stuffed vine leaves in tzatziki, spinach pie and saganaki cheese stand alongside savoury souvlaki and kebabs. Ouzo, retsina and cold frappé are on-hand to wash it all down.

Red Hot & Blues

Jakubská 12 (222 323 364). Metro Náměstí Republiky. **Open** 9am-11pm daily. **$. Mexican. Map** p93 D3 82

Expat blues player on a stool, fresh house salsa for the Mexican food, Cajun chicken recipes and American-style brunch served on the patio, conveniently heated for winter.

Siam-I-San

Valentinská 11 (224 814 099). Metro Staroměstská. **Open** 10am-midnight daily. **$$. Thai/Japanese.** **Map** p90 B3 83

Chic Thai, unexpectedly above a designer glassware shop, with the biggest selection of fiery Southeast Asian appetisers in town – a favourite among well-heeled expats.

Siam Orchid

Na Poříčí 21 (222 319 410/www.siamorchid.cz). Metro Náměstí Republiky. **Open** 10am-10pm daily. **$$. Thai. Map** p93 F2 84

This easy-to-miss family joint up some stairs leading off a shopping passage has the most authentic, unpretentious Thai in town: chicken satay and delish mains of fried tofu with mung beans and fiery chicken and cod curries are some of the highlights, plus there's Thai beer.

Slavia

Smetanovo nábřeží 2 (224 218 493/www.cafeslavia.cz). Metro Národní třída. **Open** 8am-11pm daily. **$. Café. Map** p92 A5 85

The mother of all Prague cafés, where Karel Tiege and a struggling Václav Havel once tippled and plotted the overthrow of communism, the Slavia would hardly be recognised by its former customers today. Still, it has stunning Castle views and a decent salmon toast – plus some very accomplished pickpockets.

Století

Karolíny Světlé 21 (222 220 008/www.stoleti.cz). Metro Národní třída. **Open** noon-midnight daily. **$. Continental. Map** p90 A5 86

A blue cheese, pear and almond salad named after Valentino, or a spinach soufflé or tender steak go with the old world decor and swift service.

SushiPoint

Na Příkopě 19 (608 643 923/www.sushipoint.cz). Metro Můstek. **Open** 11am-11pm daily. **Japanese. Map** p93 D4 87

The latest place to be seen tossing back raw tuna and pickled ginger, with a crowd of spendy new, young Czech consumers fresh from the shopping malls all around.

Tretter's

V kolkovně 3 (224 811 165/www. tretters.cz). Metro Staroměstská. **Open** 7pm-3am Mon-Sat; 11am-2am Sun. **Bar. Map** p92 C2 ⑥⑧

The beautiful, competent staff and incredible selection of cocktails are Mike Tretter's points of pride, and there's often a singer or someone else lounging on top of the bar.

U Govindy Vegetarian Club

Soukenická 27 (224 816 631). Metro Náměstí Republiky. **Open** 11am-5pm Mon-Fri. **$. Vegetarian. Map** p93 E2 ⑥⑨

Cheap but not so cheerful, this Krishna restaurant offers a basic self-service vegetarian Indian meal for a mere 85 Kč. At least it's a clean spot for sharing a table while seated on floor cushions (there are real tables and chairs too).

U medvídků

Na Perštýně 7 (224 211 916/www. umedvidku.cz). Metro Národní třída. **Open** 11.30am-11pm daily. **$$. Czech. Map** p92 B5 ⑨⓪

Five centuries of cred as a beerhall make the Little Bears a mecca for Budvar drinkers. Elevated pub grub includes the likes of pork in plum sauce and fillets in dark beer reduction.

U modré kachničky

Michalská 16 (224 213 418/ www.umodrekachnicky.cz). Metro Staroměstská. **Open** 11.30am-11.30pm daily. **$$. Czech. Map** p92 C4 ⑨①

One of the most successful little dining rooms since the Velvet Revolution in a granny's furniture setting on a narrow side street, with slightly modernised classics, such as roast duck with pears and boar steak with mushrooms.

U Provaznice

Provaznická 3, Nové Město (224 232 528). Metro Můstek. **Open** 11am-midnight daily. **Pub. Map** p92 C4 ⑨②

Incredibly enough, this classic pub, with all the Bohemian trad fare (duck, smoked meat and dumplings) is friendly, buzzy, reasonably priced and spitting distance from the Můstek metro and tourist throngs.

U Rozvařilů

Na Poříčí 26 (224 219 357). Metro Náměstí Republiky. **Open** 11am-11pm Mon-Fri; 11am-8pm Sat, Sun. **$. Map** p93 F2 ⑨③

A chrome-covered, mirrored version of that old pre-revolutionary classic, the workers' cafeteria. Servers in worn white aprons, harassed-looking customers in white socks and sandals, and soups, guláš, dumplings and chlebíčky (open-faced mayonnaise and meat sandwiches) are all features.

U Sádlů

Klimentská 2 (224 813 874/www. usadlu.cz). Metro Náměstí Republiky/ tram 5, 14, 26. **Open** 11am-1am Mon-Sat; noon-midnight Sun. **$. Czech. Map** p93 D2 ⑨④

OK, it's medieval kitsch – but efficient, tasty, fun and affordable medieval kitsch. Enjoy a mead accompanied with pepper steak or boar. Nice armour is on display in the bar area.

U Vejvodů

Jilská 4 (224 219 999/ww.restaurace uvejvodu.cz). Metro Můstek. **Open** 10am-4am Mon-Sat; 11am-3am Sun. **$$. Czech. Map** p90 B4 ⑨⑤

Unfortunately, popular with German tour buses, but still an iconic vast beerhall with quick service and old-style wood interiors, accented by the obligatory huge copper beer vat lids.

U Zlatého tygra

Husova 17 (222 221 111/ www.uzlatehotygra.cz). Metro Staroměstská. **Open** 11 am-11pm daily. **Pub. Map** p92 B4 ⑨⑥

The former haunt of beloved Czech novelist Bohumil Hrabal, who died in 1997, is still filled with his cranky contemporaries but it does serve some of the finest Pilsner Urquell in Old Town if you're willing to suffer their stares.

PRAGUE BY AREA

¡Viva Czech-Mex!

Why Mexican food is chilli-hot – or not.

Most visitors to the Czech Republic are surprised when they hear that one of the country's top radio stations broadcasts American country and western hits – and not just to Prague. Listeners nationwide have been tapping their cowboy boots to Waylon and Willie tunes since well before 1989. What's more, President Václav Klaus actually mounted a horse and put on a Stetson during his last run for office – and made a rodeo appearance in Texas a high priority on a recent US diplomatic tour (during which he again donned a ten-gallon hat).

It shouldn't be too much of a stretch of the imagination, then, to hear that Czechs fancy themselves as being pretty accomplished at cooking Mexican food. Serving up what they imagine would fit right in in a scene from *Limonádový Joe*, the classic Czech-language Western parody musical, places like Mama Lucy (p108; pictured), Sonora (p148) and, to a lesser extent, Radost FX (p130), glory in their creative use of tortillas, peppers and sometimes beans.

Which is all fine and in fact goes down quite a treat with most of the clientele. It's only when an expat comes along, very likely one raised on the Californian conception of Mexican food, that the trouble starts.

The comments are usually hushed but slip out almost as soon as the food is served: 'I can't believe these beans are crunchy – doesn't the chef cook them all day?' Perhaps most inevitable is the clincher: 'You call this hot?' Many a relationship, and likely a few marriages, has ended over this international minefield of passionate opinions.

Certain expats, in fact, found the Czech-Mex offerings so meagre, they took to setting up their own Mexican joints – usually festooned with warnings to the locals that hot means *hot*. Red Hot & Blues (p109) was one of the first, and an expat sanctuary for years, followed by the Latino-run La Casa Blů (p107), and American-owned Banditos (p126) and Picante (p108).

All, interestingly, have proven big hits with Czechs – who are perhaps eager to demonstrate that they can stand their habanero chillies just as well as the next guy.

¡Buen provecho!

Antique v Douhé

NEW *Dlouhá 37 (224 826 347).
Metro Staroměstská.* **Open** 10am-
7pm Mon-Fri; noon-6pm Sat, Sun.
Map p93 D2 **97**

A gold mine of Bohemian goodies
from yesteryear, ranging from handmade toys to lovely art deco table
lamps. Tin advertising signs and lovely pins, brooches and rings, some
quite affordable and all thoroughly
unique, are stocked. The friendly staff
speak English too.

Art Deco

*Michalská 21 (224 223 076). Metro
Staroměstská or Národní třída.* **Open**
2pm-7pm Mon-Fri; 10am-5pm Sat.
Map p92 B4 **98**

Dress-up fun! Vintage clothing and lots
of jewellery, as well as an eclectic mix
of other random goodies. Prices are
retro as well.

Big Ben Bookshop

*Malá Štupartská 5 (224 826 565/
www.bigbenbookshop.com). Metro
Náměstí Republiky.* **Open** 9am-6.30pm
Mon-Fri; 10am-5pm Sat; noon-5pm Sun.
Map p93 D3 **99**

Excellent children's section, tons of
English-language newspapers and
magazines, and a friendly staff that
knows its stock. Fiction, non-fiction,
best sellers and old faves.

Bric a Brac

*Týnská 7 (222 326 484). Metro
Staroměstská or Náměstí Republiky.*
Open 11am-7pm daily. **Map** p92
D3 **100**

This shop is tiny, but so crammed full
of treasures that you could lose yourself, or at least an hour. Street signs,
jewellery and old cameras are only a
few of the finds.

Dr Stuart's Botanicus

*Týnský Dvůr 3 (224 895 446/
www.botanicus.cz). Metro Náměstí
Republiky.* **Open** 10am-6.30pm daily.
Map p92 C3 **101**

Handmade soaps, lotions and bathing
salts and gels, plus herbal oils, teas,
honey and other food stuffs. All products

are 100% Czech, made with local
ingredients grown outside of Prague.

Kubista

*Dům u Černý Matky Boží, Celetná 34
(224 236 378/www.kubista.cz). Metro
Náměstí Republiky.* **Open** 10am-6pm
Tue-Sun. **Map** p93 D3 **102**

Fans of cubism, or anyone looking for
something original, may be seduced by
unique porcelain, lovingly wrought re-
creations and art books from this shop
of the excellent museum at the House
of the Black Madonna.

La Casa del Habano

NEW *Dlouhá 35 (222 312 305/
www.lacasadelhabano.com). Metro
Staroměstská.* **Open** 10am-10pm
daily. **Map** p93 D2 **103**

A franchise of the Cancun-based chain
of luxe cigar emporiums cum bars,
this darkwood, clubby room is bound
to attract the Czech nouveaux riches
with its 40-year-old single malts,
humidors and impressive selection of
Cuban stogies.

Manufaktura

*Karlova 26 (221 110 079). Metro
Staroměstská.* **Open** 10am-6pm daily.
Map p92 B4 **104**

A treasure trove of Czech-made goods,
especially blue print items, which is a
fabric dyeing technique used in
Bohemia in the late 18th century.
Placemats, tablecloths, handkerchiefs
make great gifts.

Modes Robes

*Benediktská 5 (224 826 016/
www.cabbage.cz/modes-robes). Metro
Náměstí Republiky/tram 5, 8, 14.*
Open 10am-6pm Mon-Fri; 10am-4pm
Sat. **Map** p93 D2 **105**

Designed by local artists, this decade-
old collective creates clothing, accessories and art with a wide range of
dresses for every body and every age.

Pavla & Olga

NEW *Karolíny Světlé 30 (no phone).
Metro Národní třída.* **Open** 10am-
7pm daily. **Map** p92 A4 **106**

The boutique run by two hip Czech
sisters is just one small room but

Antique v Douhé

manages to get in all the glossy magazines with its creations for local celebrities, which incorporate fresh, sophisticated designs and quality materials – alas, nothing for guys, though.

Pohodlí

Benediktská 7 (224 827 026/www. etno.cz). Metro Náměstí Republiky. **Open** 11am-7pm Mon-Fri; 10am-4pm Sat. **Map** p93 D2 107
We are the world, and we have the music from all corners to prove it. Indian and African music, plus some local Czech and Moravian folk and world as well.

Slovanský Dům

Na Příkopě 22, (221 451 400/www. slovanskydum.cz). Metro Můstek. **Open** 10am-8pm daily. **Map** p93 D3 108
Prague's slickest downtown mall is to be found on Na Příkopě, and contains the city's most popular multiplex cinema, a decent Italian café, plus a nice sushi restaurant. Jewellery and fashion shops fills out the rest. And once you're all shopped out, revive your weary muscles with a Thai massage.

Tatiana

Dušní 1 (224 813 723/www.tatiana. cz). Metro Staroměstská. **Open** 10am-7pm Mon-Fri; 11am-4pm Sat. **Map** p92 C3 109
Designer fashions, designed to be worn, that mix elegance and practicality. Clothes are perfectly cut and beautifully styled, with small details that make each piece striking, yet functional.

Toalette

NEW *Karolíny Světle 9 (777 128 729). Metro Národní třída.* **Open** 10am-7pm daily. **Map** p92 A5 110
Monika Burdová's second-hand-clothes-shop-cum-designer-boutique is a great find on one of Old Town's most appealing little lanes. Quirky streetwear meets affordable fashions by local artists.

Trafika Můstek

Václavské náměstí (no phone). Metro Můstek. **Open** 8am-10pm daily. **Map** p92 C4 111
If it's an English-language periodical you're looking for, this kiosk at the bottom of Wenceslas Square should be your first port-of-call. If they don't

PRAGUE BY AREA

Marquis de Sade p108

have what you're looking for, you probably won't find it in the city.

Nightlife

Banco Casino

Na Příkopě 27 (221 967 380/ www.bancocasino.cz). Metro Náměstí Republiky. **Open** 24 hrs daily. **Map** p93 D3 ⓬

Classy enough to serve as a set in Prague-shot Bond flick *Casino Royale*, the Banco is a reputable, plush establishment with private salons and high-tech slots for those not into green felt.

Blues Sklep

NEW *Liliová 10 (774 277 060). Metro Můstek.* **Open** 7pm-1am daily. **Map** p92 B4 ⓭

Find the entrance in a passage off a quiet street and descend into an arched cellar bar that books capable young jazz and blues acts in a relaxed space. The sofa's tempting but this cool venue can also get a bit dank so wooden chairs may win out.

Cabaret Captain Nemo

Ovocný trh 13 (224 211 868/www. escort.cz). Metro Můstek. **Open** 8pm-5am daily. **Map** p93 D3 ⓮

This busy strip club adds water to the usual array of nude dancers and private rooms, apparently to some effect.

Casino Palais Savarin

Na Příkopě 10 (224 221 636/www. czechcasinos.cz). Metro Náměstí Republiky. **Open** 1pm-4am daily. **Map** p93 D4 ⓯

Old-school Mitteleuropa gambling with hushed, well-groomed croupiers, and with an old, grand palace stairway to sweep you in. The vibe is professional and assured, so wear a jacket and expect complementary drinks.

Friends

Bartolomějská 11 (226 211 920/ www.friends-prague.cz). Metro Národní třída. **Open** 6pm-4am daily. **Map** p92 B5 ⓰

A welcoming, sociable gay bar with a sizeable dancefloor and amusingly kitsch tunes rolling out over a good

sound system all night long. A grown-up break from the more predatory bars featuring rent boys and German businessmen.

Meloun

NEW *Michalská 12 (224 230 126). Metro Můstek.* **Open** 8pm-5am daily. **Map** p92 C4 ⓱

A slice of small-town Czech Republic in the centre of Prague, this collection of cellar rooms blasts loud local rock through the cigarette haze to young patrons too blitzed to notice. The terrace restaurant provides a welcome break, at least.

Millennium Casino

V Celnici 10 (221 033 401/www. millenniumcasino.cz). Metro Náměstí Republiky. **Open** 3pm-4am daily. **Map** p93 E3 ⓲

Roulette, poker and blackjack in a classy setting with professional, unintimidating croupiers. Millennium offers a good, clean bet in a city where many casinos can be dodgy.

N11

Národní třída 11, Nové Město (222 075 705/www.n11.cz). Metro Národní třída. **Open** 8pm-4am Tue-Thur; 7pm-5am Fri, Sat. Call for Sun opening hrs. **Map** p92 A5 ⓳

A crisp sound system makes this small, clean club a good pick for taking in pop rock. Sunday blues acts like Stan the Man keep the crowd on its feet, with decent bar food on tap.

Petrovič

NEW *Rytířská 8 (224 210 635). Metro Můstek.* **Open** 6pm-midnight daily. **Map** p92 C4 ⓴

Not just a handy downtown Russian restaurant with authentic cuisine and staff, but also a rising venue for jazz and rock acts with an appreciative local audience that enjoys lurking in the deep club cellar.

Roxy

Dlouhá 33 (224 826 296/www.roxy.cz). Metro Náměstí Republiky. **Open** 7pm-2am Mon-Thur; 7pm-4am Fri, Sat. **Map** p93 D2 ㉑

PRAGUE BY AREA

Estates Theatre

Dominated by digital dance tracks, but this crumbling former movie house is also a hot live venue for folks like Eric Ni of Living Colour or local and Euro tribal and electronica acts.

Tropison cocktail bar
Náměstí Republiky 8 (224 801 276).
Metro Náměstí Republiky. **Open**
8pm-3am Mon-Wed; 8pm-5am Thur,
Fri; 7pm-5am Sat; 6pm-3am Sun.
Map p93 D3 **122**
Come for the stunning terrace views atop what was once a communist department store, and the silly Latin dance parties, not for the service or uninspiring menus.

U staré paní
Michalská 9 (224 228 090/www.
ustarepani.cz). Metro Můstek/Národní
třída. **Open** 7pm-2am daily. **Map**
p92 B4 **123**
With cheap wine and grub, the Old Lady features hot Czech jazz players with late, unscheduled jams sometimes rounding out Fridays and Saturdays.

Vagon
Národní třída 25 (221 085 599/
www.vagon.cz). Metro Národní třída.
Open 6pm-5am Mon-Sat; 6pm-1am
Sun. **Map** p92 B4 **124**
A smoky little cellar with a long history that attracts students, young DJs and bands covering rock and reggae. The entrance is in the shopping passage.

Velmý Jemný Klub Limonádový Joe
NEW *Revoluční 1 (221 803 304).*
Metro Náměstí Republiky. **Open**
7pm-1am daily. **Map** p93 D3 **125**
Limonádový Joe was a beloved Czech singing cowboy from the movies and this eclectic, highly local club next to the Kotva department store has a bit of a western theme but mostly it's known for a retractable roof, cheap drinks and amusing local rock bands.

Vertigo
Havelská 4 (774 744 256/www.vertigo-
club.cz). Metro Můstek. **Open** 9pm-4am
daily. **Map** p92 C4 **126**

Three levels of capable café and clubbing space, with decent DJs, decor, lights and sound. Despite all that, the atmosphere is at times far from lively.

Arts & leisure

Archa Theatre

Divadlo Archa
Na Poříčí 26 (221 716 333/www. archatheatre.cz). Metro Náměstí Republiky or Florenc. **Open** *Box office* 10am-6pm Mon-Fri & 2 hrs before show time. **Tickets** 100-300 Kč. **Map** p93 F2 **127**

Prague's hippest and most daring theatre brings international avant-garde luminaries of dance, theatre and music to its versatile and well-equipped space. Also the cream of Czech avant-garde – Filip Topol, Petr Nikl and Agon orchestr – perform here, as well as international acts like Min Tanaka and Einstürzende Neubauten.

Chapel of Mirrors

Zrcadlová kaple
Klementinum, Mariánské náměstí (221 663 111/212). Metro Staroměstská. **Open** *Box office* 2hrs before the concert. Concerts usually start 5pm & 8pm. **Map** p92 B4 **128**

Mozart used to perform in this pink marble chapel in the vast Clementinum complex and his artistic chamber music descendants carry on today, often during afternoons.

Church of St Nicholas

Chrám sv. Mikuláše
Staroměstské náměstí (224 190 994). Metro Staroměstská. **Open** Concerts usually start at 5pm or 8pm. **Map** p92 B3/C3 **129**

This is one of Prague's most celebrated churches, with a stunning Baroque interior. Irregular choral concerts and organ recitals are just as grand as the setting.

Estates Theatre

Stavovské divadlo
Ovocný trh 1 (224 901 448/www. nd.cz). Metro Můstek/Staroměstská. **Open** *Box office* 10am-6pm daily. **Map** p92 C4 **130**

The theatre in which Mozart premièred *Don Giovanni* and *La Clemenza di Tito* was built by Count Nostitz in 1784. It has since become the German opera house, with Carl Maria von Weber as director. Some of the dance performances sometimes use taped music (!).

Jazz Boat

Čechův most (603 551 680/www. jazzboat.cz). Metro Staroměstská.
Open 8.30pm-11pm Tue-Sun.
Map p92 B1 **131**

Find the EVD pier just down from the Čechův bridge and board the most tuneful cruise in town, where top jazz players serenade your dinner of shnitzel and beer (not included in the 590 Kč entry).

Municipal House

Obecní dům
Náměstí Republiky 5 (222 002 336/ 101/www.obecni-dum.cz). Metro Náměstí Republiky. **Open** *Box office* 10am-6pm daily. **Map** p93 D3 **132**

The highest form of Czech art nouveau, built around the Smetana Hall, home to the Prague Symphony Orchestra. The Prague Spring Festival kicks off here every year, in a setting of ceiling mosaics of old Czech myths.

Palace Cinemas Slovanský dům

Na Příkopě 22 (257 181 212/www. palacecinemas.cz). Metro Náměstí Republiky. **Map** p93 D3 **133**

Prague's most central multiplex shows recent Czech films with English subtitles and international ones in their original language. It also boasts a high-tech digital projector that can simulcast live concerts or show digital films. There's a 30% ticket discount on Wednesdays.

Rudolfinum

Alšovo nábřeží 12 (227 059 352/www. rudolfinum.cz). Metro Staroměstská. **Open** *Box office* mid Aug-mid July 10am-6pm Mon-Fri. **Map** p92 A2 **134**

A gorgeous neo-classical cream and blue concert venue with two halls: the Dvořák for orchestral works, the Suk for chamber and vocal music. An evening here cuts to the heart of old Europa.

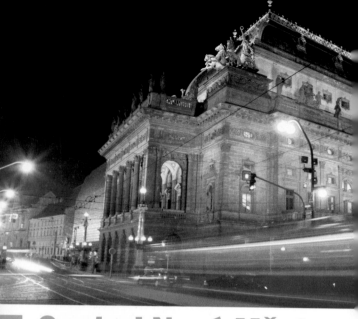

Central Nové Město & Vyšehrad

Central Nové Město

Laid out on an uncharacteristically rational street plan, the core section of Prague's 'New Town' has grown from a collection of horse markets six centuries ago to the commercial boulevards surrounding Wenceslas Square today and bordering Staré Město, the Old Town. Alas, it's also the city's least charming quarter, where sleaze and traffic interrupt the hunt for exceptional bars, restaurants and galleries.

They are here, though, provided you look hard enough, with new additions like **Il Conte Deminka**

(p128) and the unpretentious **Himalaya** tucked away in small back streets. Nightlife is another of this neighbourhood's fortes, with **Radost FX Café**, **Nebe** and the **Lucerna Music Bar** leading the way.

Aside from being the hub of Prague's burgeoning consumer culture, central Nové Město is where modern influences ripple through the art world. Plugged-in galleries like the **Prague House of Photography** and **Gallery Art Factory** are the places to catch the wave.

And, though increasingly darkened by car exhaust fumes, these streets are nevertheless full

National Theatre p137

Antonín Dvořák Museum
Muzeum Antonína Dvořáka
*Villa Amerika, Ke Karlovu 20
(224 918 013/www.dm.cz). Metro
IP Pavlova.* **Open** *Apr-Sept* 10am-
1.30pm, 2-5.30pm Tue-Sun; *Oct-Mar*
9.30am-1.30pm, 2-5.30pm Tue-Sun.
Admission 50 Kč. **Map** p121 D4 ❷
Catching a chamber recital of Dvořák's
music in the villa where he worked and
composed is a thrill, especially seeing
as Czech musicians perform him like
no one else on earth. The lovely sum-
merhouse was designed by Kilian
Ignaz Dientzenhofer. Sadly, these days
it's surrounded by incongruous modern concrete blocks.

Dancing Building
Tančící dům
*Masarykovo nábřeží and Resslova
streets. Metro Karlovo náměstí.*
Map p120 A4 ❸
A collaboration between Croatian architect Vlado Milunič and the American
Frank Gehry, and completed in 1996,
this whimsical glass tower is also
known locally as the 'Fred and Ginger'
building. According to Gehry, the original inspiration for the pinch in the middle of the tower came from the desire to
protect a neighbour's panoramic views
of Prague Castle.

Emmaus Monastery
Emauzy
*Vyšehradská 49 (221 979 219/
www.emauzy.cz). Metro Karlovo
náměstí.* **Open** 9am-4pm Mon-Fri.
Map p120 B5 ❹
If the two modern spires of this 14th-
century church, founded by Charles IV,
seem incongruous, that's because they
were added after the baroque versions
were destroyed by a stray Allied bomb
during World War II – the flight crew
thought they were over Dresden.

Faust House
Faustův dům
*Karlovo náměstí 40. Metro Karlovo
náměstí.* **Map** p120 B4 ❺
This highly ornate 17th-century villa
is where Edward Kelly, the earless
English alchemist, once lived, as, they

of architectural wonders, not least
boulevard-like Wenceslas Square.

The area is bounded roughly
to the north by Národní, which
forms the border with Staré Město,
and to the east by Legerova, which
forms the border with Vinohrady.
The arterial Vinslavoya, with its
heavy traffic, forms a natural
barrier in the south. Following
the central streets Žitná or Ječná
west takes you past some of the
more historic buildings in Nové
Město to the Vltava river.

Sights & museums

Adria Palace
*Jungmannovo náměstí 28.
Metro Můstek.* **Map** p120 C1 ❶
Constructed between 1923 to 1925, this
building is a hymn to Rondocubism
– though, apart from the terrace café on
the second floor, which does offer a great
view over busy Národní street, there's
not much here these days to detain you.

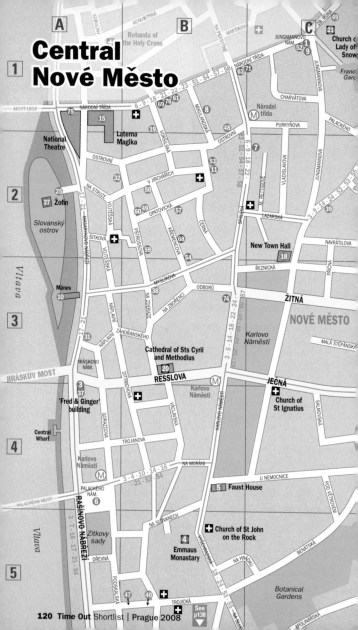

Central
Nové Město

A
Rotunda of
the Holy Cross

B

C
Jungmannovo
Nám.
Church of
Lady of
Snow

1

52
61
9

Franc
Garc

MOST LEGII

NÁRODNÍ TŘÍDA

63
71

75 NÁRODNÍ TŘÍDA

6 · 9 · 18 · 21 · 22 · 23

69 76 61

NÁRODNÍ TŘÍDA

CHARVÁTOVA

15

MIKULANDSKA

8

PALACKÉHO

Laterna
Magika

19

VORŠILSKÁ

48

Národní
třída
M

PURKYŇOVA

7

OSTROVNÍ

2

National
Theatre

OSTROVNÍ

25
27 Žofín

NA STRUZE

32

V JIRCHÁŘÍCH

53
11

6 · 51 · 54 · 18 · 22 · 57 · 58

VLADISLAVOVA

JUNGMANNOVA

3 · 9 · 24 · 52 · 53 · 55

39

50

V. RETTIGOVÉ

LAZARSKÁ

Slovanský
ostrov

60 49

OPATOVICKÁ

57

ŠITKOVÁ

VOJTĚŠSKÁ

59

KŘEMENCOVA

68

ČERNÁ

SPÁLENÁ

NAVRÁTILOVA

New Town Hall
18

54

MYSLÍKOVA

ŘEZNICKÁ

PŘÍČNÁ

Mánes
10

NA ZDERAZE

38

ODBORŮ

74

ŽITNÁ

Vltava

NÁPLAVNÍ

ZÁHOŘANSKÉHO

3 · 6 · 14 · 18 · 22 · 24

3 · 6 · 14 · 18 · 22 · 55 · 57

NOVÉ MĚSTO

3

17 · 21

31

NÁPLAVNÍ

Karlovo
Náměstí

MALÁ ŠTĚPÁNSKÁ

JIRÁSKŮV MOST

JIRÁSKOVO
NÁM.

DITTRICHOVA

**Cathedral of Sts Cyril
and Methodius**
20

RESSLOVA
M

Karlovo
Náměstí

JEČNÁ

SALMOVSKÁ

3
37

'Fred & Ginger'
building

GORAZDOVA

VÁCLAVSKÁ

**Church of
St Ignatius**

Central
Wharf

TROJANOVA

4

Karlovo
Náměstí
M

NA MORÁNI

U NEMOCNICE

POD VĚTROVEM

PALACKÉHO
NÁM.

6

3 · 4 · 10 · 14 · 16
3 · 21 · 52 · 54

5 **Faust House**

PALACKÉHO MOST

RAŠÍNOVO NÁBŘEŽÍ

Zítkovy
sady

NA SLOVANECH

**Church of St John
on the Rock**

Vltava

3 · 7 · 16 · 17 · 21 · 54

4
**Emmaus
Monastary**

18 · 24 · 53 · 55

BENÁTSKÁ

5

DŘEVNÁ

PODSKALSKÁ

47   40

TROJICKÁ

Botanical
Gardens

See
p138

NA HRÁDKU

APOLINÁŘSKÁ

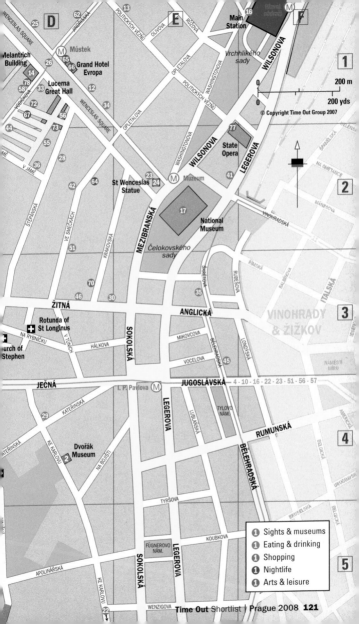

D 25 62 **13** POLITICKÝCH VĚZŇŮ OLIVOVA RŮŽOVÁ **E** 16 Main Station **M** **F**

Wenceslas Square

Melantrich Building **M** Můstek **65** Grand Hotel Evropa Vrchlického sady WILSONOVA **1**

14 26 66 OPLETALOVA POLITICKÝCH VĚZŇŮ WASHINGTONOVA

78 33 Lucerna Great Hall 12 0 200 m
58 © Copyright Time Out Group 2007
72 WENCESLAS SQUARE 34 0 200 yds

67 56 OPLETALOVA 17

44 73 WILSONOVA State Opera LEGEROVA

55 WASHINGTONOVA

36 28 **M** Muzeum 41 **2**
V JÁMĚ 23

ŠTĚPÁNSKÁ 42 64 St Wenceslas Statue 24

VE SMEČKÁCH 51 MEZIBRANSKÁ 17 National Museum VINOHRADSKÁ

KRAKOVSKÁ Čelokovského sady ŘÍMSKÁ BALBÍNOVA ITALSKÁ

70 35 RUBEŠOVA

46 30 SOKOLSKÁ ANGLICKÁ **3**
ŽITNÁ VINOHRADY & ŽIŽKOV

Rotunda of St Longinus MIKOVCOVA LONDÝNSKÁ NÁMĚSTÍ MÍRU
NA RYBNÍČKU BĚLEHRADSKÁ

urch of Stephen V TŮNÍCH HÁLKOVA VOCELOVA 45

JEČNÁ **M** I. P. Pavlova JUGOSLÁVSKÁ 4 - 10 - 16 - 22 - 23 - 51 - 56 - 57

29 KATEŘINSKÁ LEGEROVA TYLOVO NÁM. **4**
LUBLAŇSKÁ AMERICKÁ

KATEŘINSKÁ KE KARLOVU Dvořák Museum 2 NA BOJIŠTI RUMUNSKÁ BĚLEHRADSKÁ

TYRŠOVA

KOUBKOVA BRUSELSKÁ

FÜGNEROVO NÁM. **5**
SOKOLSKÁ LEGEROVA

APOLINÁŘSKÁ KE KARLOVU WENZIGOVA

1 Sights & museums
1 Eating & drinking
1 Shopping
1 Nightlife
1 Arts & leisure

National Museum p124

say, did a poor student who was lured into a pact with the Prince of Darkness: incredible riches in exchange for his soul, which Satan then snatched through a hole in the roof.

František Palacký statue

Palackého náměstí. Metro Karlovo náměstí. **Map** p120 A4 ❻

This huge bronze tribute to the 19th-century historian who took 46 years to write the first history of the Czech people in Czech was created by Stanislav Sucharda. The solemn Palacký sits on a giant pedestal, oblivious to the beauties and demons flying around him.

Galerie České pojišťovny

Spálená 14 (224 054 368/www. galeriecpoj.cz). Metro Národní Třída. **Open** 10am-6pm daily. **Admission** 10Kč. **Map** p120 C2 ❼

Follow one of three passages (from Spálená, Purkyňova or Vladislavova streets) through a courtyard to this gallery in an art nouveau building by Osvald Polívka. Shows present contemporary Czech photography and painting by artists of the middle generation, such as Tomáš Císařovský, Jaroslav Rona and Richard Konvička.

Galerie Gambit

Mikulandská 6 (602 277 210/ www.gambit.cz). Metro Národní třída. **Open** noon-6pm Tue-Fri. **Admission** free. **Map** p120 B1 ❽

This pocket-sized gallery concentrates on small shows of new works by leading Czech postmodernists – Michael Rittstein, Petr Nikl and Bedřich Dlouhý – while also presenting fresh young artists. Foreign artists also show hereand there are displays of contemporary design too.

Galerie Kritiků

Jungmannova 31 (224 494 205/ www.galeriekritiku.com). Metro Národní Třída. **Open** 10am-6pm Tue-Sun. **Admission** 40 Kč; 20 Kč concessions. **Map** p120 C1 ❾

This elegant space in the Adria Palace, with its grand pyramid skylight, has

proved itself to be a class act. It is particularly strong on group shows, and its offerings of international art often come from Japan.

Galerie Mánes

Masarykovo nábřeží 250 (224 930 754/www.galeriemanes.cz). Metro Karlovo náměstí. **Open** 10am-6pm Tue-Sun. **Admission** varies; free children. **Map** p120 A3 ❿

The largest of the Czech Fund for Art Foundation's network of galleries, Mánes is also a beautiful, if run-down, piece of 1930s functionalist architecture by Otakar Novotný. This riverside gallery typically hosts anything from international travelling shows to exhibitions of contemporary Czech artists like Lukáš Rittstein.

Galerie Velryba

Opatovická 24 (224 931 444). Metro Národní třída. **Open** noon-9pm Mon-Fri; 11am-9pm Sat. **Admission** free. **Map** p120 B2 ⓫

Located in the basement of the trendy Velryba café, this gallery is the showcase for students in the photography department of the Czech film academy FAMU and, increasingly, photo departments at other schools.

Gallery Art Factory

Václavské náměstí 15 (224 217 585/ www.galleryartfactory.cz). Metro Můstek. **Open** 10am-6pm Mon-Fri. **Admission** 50 Kč. **Map** p121 D1 ⓬

The interior of the former printing house of the main communist-era newspaper retains the factory feel with painted concrete floors and old industrial hardware as part of the interior. Specialising in shows by Slovak artists, the gallery also organises the annual Sculpture Grande outdoor exhibition of large-scale sculptures up and down Wenceslas Square and Na Příkopě.

Gestapo Headquarters

Politických vězňů 20 (no phone). Metro Můstek. **Map** p121 E1 ⓭

This street, whose name means 'Political prisoners', still has very bad karma (a block north lies the home of the Communist Party of Bohemia and Moravia). No organised museum has been planned.

Langhans Galerie

Vodičkova 37 (222 929 333/ www.langhansgalerie.cz). Metro Můstek. **Open** noon-6pm Tue-Sun. **Admission** 60 Kč; 30 Kč concessions. **Map** p121 D1 ⑭

Once home to the Jan Langhans Atelier, where anyone who was anyone in interwar Prague had their portrait made. Now the emphasis is on historical shows, mixed in with work by established and emerging photographers. The recurring theme of memory here has made for some rather haunting exhibitions.

Laterna Magika

Národní třída 4 (224 931 482/ www.laterna.cz). Metro Národní třída. **Map** p120 A1/A2 ⑮

The Magic Lantern, a frosted-glass monstrosity, was built between 1977 and 1981 as a communist showpiece, the interior filled with imported marble and leather, now well-worn and patched. The black light shows that play here aren't worth the admission, perhaps in keeping with an unintentionally ironic socialist relic.

Main Station

Hlavní nádraží
Wilsonova (972 241 883). Metro Hlavní nádraží. **Map** p121 F1 ⑯

The city's main train station – also known as Wilsonovo nádraží, or Wilson Station – was scheduled for renovation as went to press, but its lower levels are typical of 1970s communist architecture. A glimpse of its art nouveau former self is visible in the Fanta Kavárna, a sometimes seedy upstairs café overlooking the main passenger corridor to the platforms.

National Museum

Národní muzeum
Václavské náměstí 68 (224 497 111/ www.nm.cz). Metro Muzeum. **Open** *May-Sept* 10am-6pm daily. *Oct-Apr* 9am-5pm daily. **Admission** 110 Kč; 130 Kč family; free under-6s. **Map** p121 E2 ⑰

The iconic neo-Renaissance museum at the top of Wenceslas Square has done more than take Soviet bullets in 1968; its displays have finally been modernised, with interactive exhibitions on new media now running alongside the older cases of fossils, geodes and stuffed animals. There's still a lack of labels in English but an audio guide is available for an extra 200 Kč.

New Town Hall

Novoměstská radnice
Karlovo náměstí 23 (224 948 229). Metro Karlovo náměstí. **Map** p120 C2 ⑱

Dating back to the 14th century, this tower established the uniquely Czech form of civil protest known as defenestration when local burghers tossed occupying Habsburg officials to their deaths from a high window in 1419.

Le Patio p135

PRAGUE BY AREA

The Town Hall's current incarnation was built during the 19th and early 20th centuries.

Nová síň

Voršilská 3 (224 930 255). Metro Národní třída. **Open** 11am-6pm Tue-Sun. **Admission** 10-20 Kč. **Map** p120 B1 ⑲

A skylit white cube in which many artists rent space and curate their own shows. It's a draw for artists like Otto Placht, who selected it for a month-long project which involved painting a floor-to-ceiling mural in situ.

Orthodox Cathedral of Sts Cyril & Methodius

Kostel sv. Cyrila a Metoděje *Resslova 9 (224 920 686). Metro Karlovo náměstí.* **Open** Oct-Apr 10am-4pm Tue-Sun. May-Sept 10am-5pm Tue-Sun. **Admission** 50 Kč adults; 20 Kč concessions. **Map** p120 B3 ⑳

This baroque 1730s church, scarred by shelling, is where two Czech paratroopers trained in England, Josef Gabčík and Jan Kubiš, met their end. Dropped into Bohemia in late 1941 to assassinate Reinhard Heydrich, Reichsprotektor of Bohemia and Moravia, they succeeded but were discovered here by the SS and Gestapo, who bombarded the church until the assassins took their own lives.

Our Lady of the Snows

Kostel Panny Marie Sněžné *Jirmanovo náměstí. Metro Můstek.* **Map** p120 C1 ㉑

The towering black-and-gold baroque altarpiece is awe-inspiring. Also worth seeking out is the church's side chapel (accessible via a door on the right in the rear), where you can gawp at the trio of gruesome crucifixes. Outside is the world's only cubist lamp post.

Police Museum

Muzeum policie ČR *Ke Karlovu 1 (974 824 855/www.mvcr.cz/ministerstvo/muzeum.htm). Metro IP Pavlova.* **Open** 10am-5pm Tue-Sun. **Admission** 20 Kč; 40 Kč family. **Map** p121 D5 ㉒

Sadly Brek, the stuffed wonder dog responsible for thwarting the defection of several hundred dissidents, has been given a decent burial, but there are still plenty of gruesome exhibits here to delight the morbid, including killer lighters and pens.

Real Tour

Václavské náměstí (602 459 481/ www.walkingtoursprague.com).
Metro Muzeum. **Open** Tours 12.30pm Mon, Wed, Thur, Sat. **Map** p121 E2 ㉓
Three-hour walking tours leading to Prague Castle depart from the equestrian statue of St Wenceslas daily, led by the clever and entertaining Paul and Michal, who charge 300 Kč a head for their historical/pop culture schtick. Pub breaks fill out the sights.

St Wenceslas

Top of Václavske náměstí.
Metro Muzeum. **Map** p121 E2 ㉔
The Czech patron saint, sitting astride his mount, is still the most popular meeting spot in Prague (as in 'meet me at the horse'), surrounded by Saints Agnes, Adelbert, Procopius and Ludmila, Wenceslas's grandmother. A few steps below is a headstone with the images of Jan Palach and Jan Zajíc, who burned themselves alive here to protest the Soviet-led occupation of 1968.

Slovanský Island

Masarykovo nábřeží. Metro Národní třída. **Map** p120 A2 ㉕
In the days before slacking became an art form, Berlioz was appalled at the 'idlers, wasters and ne'er-do-wells' who congregated on this little Vltava River landfall. It's still hard to resist the outdoor café or the rowing-boats available for hire.

Wenceslas Square

Václavské náměstí. Metro Můstek. **Map** p121 D1 ㉖
The modern hub of Nové Město (and indeed the entire city), this broad, one-kilometre boulevard has been the backdrop to every major event of the city's recent history, from the founding of the Czechoslovak Republic in 1918 to the 1989 Velvet Revolution.

Žofín

Slovanský ostrov (224 934 400, www.zofin.cz). Metro Národní třída.
Map p120 A2 ㉗
A newly restored cultural centre on an island in the Vltava River, this large yellow building dating from the 1880s hosted tea dances and concerts until just before World War II. Today you're more likely to find lectures and concerts here, along with one of the sweetest riverside beer gardens in Prague.

Eating & drinking

Alcron

Štěpánská 40 (222 820 038). Metro Můstek. **Open** 6.30-11pm & 5.30pm-11pm Mon-Sat. **$$$$**. **Seafood**.
Map p121 D2 ㉘
This historic hotel dining room, with just seven tables, is a serious seafood star. Chef Jiří Štift is master of the pike-perch and the savoury sauce. It's ensconsed in the SAS Radisson, formerly known as the Alcron.

Banditos

Melounova 2 (224 941 096). Metro IP Pavlova. **Open** 9am-12.30am Mon-Sat; 9am-midnight Sun. **$$**. **Mexican**.
Map p121 D4 ㉙
A Mexican/Latin/Tex-Mex joint serving decent southwest American favourites and good burgers in an expat-friendly atmosphere. Recommended dishes include spicy chicken sandwich, Caesar salad and cheeseburgers.

Cicala

Žitná 43 (222 210 375/www. trattoria.cicala.cz). Metro IP Pavlova.
Open 11.30am-10.30pm Mon-Sat. **$**. **Italian**. **Map** p121 D3 ㉚
The owner brings in fresh Italian wonders weekly, whether it's calamari or figs, presented like a work of art. This easily missed subterranean two-room eatery on an otherwise unappealing street is worth seeking out, as it's a bastion of Prague's Italian community.

Wenceslas Square

Don Pedro

Masarykovo nábřeží 2 (224 923 505/
www.donpedro.cz). Metro Karlovo
Náměsti **Open** 11.30am-11pm daily.
$$. Columbian. Map p120 A3 ③①
A true rarity in Prague, this homely,
bright Columbian eaterie serves up
authentic zesty empanadas, spicy beef
and potato soup and gorgeously grilled
meats. Oxtail cola guisada with yuca
root is a fave, and well worth the South
American-speed service.

Dynamo

Pštrossova 29 (224 932 020/
www.dynamorestaurace.cz).
Metro Národní třida. **Open** 11.30am-
midnight daily. **$$$. Continental.**
Map p120 A2 ②②
This sleek designer diner typifies the
renaissance sweeping through the
area south of the National Theatre.
Steaks and pasta just about keep up
with the decor; don't miss the wall of
single-malt Scotches.

Fuzion

NEW *Vodičková 38 (224 215 156/*
www.fuzion.cz). Metro Můstek.
Open 7am-8pm Mon-Fri; 8am-5pm
Sat, Sun. **$. Café. Map** p121 D1 ③③
The best coffees, fresh fruit smoothies,
fresh cookies and baguette sandwiches in the Wenceslas Square area, as
scores of students have found out.
They're also hip to the free Wi-Fi and
comfy sofa upstairs.

Hot

Václavské náměsti 45 (222 247 240).
Metro Muzeum. **Open** 9am-midnight
daily. **Steakhouse. Map** p121 D1 ③④
Trendy, retro steakhouse, in the lobby
of the trendy, retro Hotel Jalta, occupying prime real estate on Wenceslas
Square, which the cafe tables overlook.

Il Conte Deminka

NEW *Skřetova 1 (224 224 915).*
Metro IP Pavlova. **Open** 11am-11pm
Mon-Fri; noon-11pm Sat, Sun. **$.**
Indian. Map p121 E3 ③⑤
This renowned café, 115 years old in
2008, has wall-to-wall atmosphere,
obviously, and has now added gourmet
Italian cuisine, hence the name. Not to

be confused with the next-door classic
Czech place that also uses the hallowed
Deminka moniker, it's now a graceful
and cuisine-competent incarnation.

Jáma

V Jámě 7 (224 222 383/www.jamapub.
cz). Metro Můstek. **Open** 11am-1am
daily. **$. Czech-Mex. Map** p121 D2 ③⑥
American-owned and with patio space
out back, Jáma still has the loud college vibe that made its name. Czech
scenesters are here too and lunch specials and happy-hour deals are a big
draw, as is the Czech-Mex menu.

La Perle de Prague

Corner of Rašínovo nábřeží & Resslova,
(221 984 160). Metro Karlovo náměsti.
Open 7-10.30pm Mon; noon-2pm,
7-10.30pm Tue-Sat. **$$$. French.**
Map p120 A4 ③⑦
This eyrie atop Frank Gehry's 'Fred
and Ginger' building was once king of
the hill. Patrons are from expense-
account territory and French cuisine is
indeed fly, but worth it? Even the views
through the smallish recessed win-
dows are a bit disappointing.

Lemon Leaf

Na Zderaze 14 (224 919 056/www.
lemon.cz). Metro Karlovo náměsti.
Open 11am-11pm Mon-Thur; 11am-
12.30am Fri; 1pm-12.30am Sat; 1-11
pm Sun. **$$$. Thai. Map** p120 B3 ③⑧
Well-done Thai in a warm, yellow and
dark wood setting with bargain lunch
specials have kept Lemon Leaf close to
capacity since opening. No compromises
for spice-phobic Czechs have been made
with the tom ka kai or prawn curries.

Novoměstský Pivovar

Vodičkova 20 (222 232 448/www.
npivovar.cz). Metro Můstek. **Open**
10am-11.30pm Mon-Fri; 11.30am-
11.30pm Sat; noon-10pm Sun. **$$.**
Czech. Map p120 C2 ③⑨
One of a surprisingly small number of
brew pubs in Prague, Novoměstský is
a vast underground warren with great
beer and pub grub. Unfortunately, how-
ever, it also has the busloads of tourists,
slack service and dodgy maths that
more often than not go with them.

The beer pioneers

The captains of industry in the Czech Republic are no longer interested in factories (that was the old regime). These days, they prefer to promote the country's intellectual assets, courting software companies instead of steelmakers.

The exception is the **Beer Factory** (pictured), which recently opened on Wenceslas Square (No. 58, 736 630 868). The welcome new venture does something bold, embracing a dangerous but time-honoured tradition: making a game of drinking.

Every table at the Beer Factory contains four beer taps that customers operate themselves, to refill their mugs as often as they like. A computer tracks the usage, posting the score of each table on a huge screen that everyone can see. At 39 Kč a pour, it's a bargain for this location, even with your own labour factored in.

What's more, taps dispense the excellent sour-ish Pilsner Urquell, a much-favoured Czech beer, which is supplied from a massive underground tank – a system that guarantees the highest quality.

Just a handful of pubs in the city feature such a facility – the genteel **Pivovarský dům** (p130), just south of Wenceslas Square on Žitna street, being one of them. Though Czechs annually consume the largest amount of beer per capita in the world, they're generally happy to stick with Pilsner, Gambrinus, Staropramen and Budvar, and most Czech pubs normally serve lager from just a handful of producers. Pivovarský dům's manager, Aleš Dočekal, pushes the envelope, stocking a greater variety of beer than virtually all other bars in Prague, including varieties from the bar's own microbrewery, wheat beer and even beers flavoured with champagne and coffee.

Nové Město has in fact always been *pivo* (typical Czech beer) heaven, with more space for big beer halls than Old Town. But for something more sophisticated than tourist-filled **Novoměstský Pivovar** (p128) – a cavernous space that attracts busloads of Germans – head just south of the National Theatre (p137), where you'll find a mean cluster of bars.

Oliva

NEW *Plavecka 4 (222 520 288).*
Metro Můstek. **Open** 11.30am
-3pm, 6pm-midnight Mon-Sat. **$$$.**
Mediterranean. Map p120 B5 ㊾
Chef Rudolf Doležal's cool little green
silk-adorned eaterie has created a
buzz with its tomato tarte tatin, saffron
tagliatelle, and grilled duck with
polenta. Service is excellent too, making
this worth the hike a bit south from
the city centre.

Opera Garden

Zahrada v opeře
Legerova 75 (224 239 685/www.
zahradavopere.cz). Metro Muzeum.
Open 11.30am-midnight daily. **$$.**
Fusion. Map p121 E2 ㊶
The entrance to the Opera Garden
is hard to find (at the back of the office
building) but sumptuous feasts
at this Czech and international dining
room make it worth the effort. Tuna
steak in filo is a delight, and is in keeping
with the airy minimalist decor and
gliding waiters.

Pack

Ve Smečkách 21 (222 210 280/www.
thepack.cz). Metro Muzeum. **Open**
9am-2am Mon, Fri; noon-2am Tue-
Thur; 6.30am-2am Sat, Sun. **Sports**
pub. Map p121 D2 ㊷
Perhaps named after the mobs of yobs
who were anticipated as customers, the
Prague version of Hooters offers buffalo
wings and hangover breakfasts
served by charming girls.

Pivovarský Dům

NEW *Vodičkova 20 (222 232 448/*
www.npivovar.cz). Metro Můstek.
Open 10am-11.30pm Mon-Fri;
11.30am-11.30pm Sat; noon-10pm
Sun. **$$. Czech**. Map p120 C3 ㊸
This microbrewery has had a loyal
local following since opening its doors
in 2000. It combines the best of old
Czech beerhalls, including the classics
like pork knee, smoked meat
dumplings and fresh sauerkraut, with
Western-style spick-and-span cleanliness
and ingratiating service. The
five-litre table-top beer tanks and the

wheat beer and other variations are
(surprisingly) rare innovations in the
traditional, slightly hidebound world
of pubbing in Prague.

Pizza Coloseum

Vodičkova 32 (224 214 914/www.
pizzacoloseum.cz). Metro Můstek.
Open 11am-11.30pm daily. **$.**
Italian. Map p121 D1/D2 ㊹
Just off Wenceslas Square, this cellar's
a top Prague pizzeria. Excellent
bruschetta, flame-baked pizza and big,
saucy pastas complement well-stocked
wine racks and a familiar range of
steak and fish.

Radost FX Café

Bělehradská 120 (224 254 776/www.
radostfx.cz). Metro IP Pavlova. **Open**
Restaurant 11.30am-3am daily. *Club*
10pm-4am Thur-Sat. **$. Vegetarian**.
Map p121 E3 ㊺
Prague's first vegetarian restaurant
still has the latest opening hours
around, plus all-night pastas, couscous
and meatless Mexican food. It's of
variable quality and the ornamental
tables do bash your knees but it's as
popular as ever – not least because of
the seriously groovy, tassled backroom
lounge area.

Ridgeback

Žitná 41 (no phone). Metro IP
Pavlova. **Open** 4pm-4am daily.
Bar. Map p121 D3 ㊻
A popular bar for young locals, who
are often seen toting skateboards and
are fond of carrying on until the sun
comes up in a sweet-smelling haze.

Soho Restaurant
& Garden

Podolské nábřeží 1 (244 463 772/
www.sohorestaurant.cz). Tram 18.
Open 11.30am-1am daily. **$$.**
Fusion. Map p120 B5 ㊼
A short trek south of the centre, and
not ideal if you're wearing jeans, but
worth it for a modernist terrace and
mussels au gratin with parmesan,
or Chilean salmon sashimi starters.
Gracious staff and a thoughtful, reasonable
wine list as well.

Globe Bookstore & Coffeehouse p133

Thanh Long

Ostrovní 23 (224 933 537). Metro Národní třída. **Open** 11.30am-11pm daily. **$$. Chinese**. Map p120 B1 ⓭
Notable principally for its central location and blissfully over-the-top trappings, such as the revolving 'Lazy Susan' tables, pagoda lanterns and the huge moving-light painting in the back. The cuisine, by contrast, is blanded down to suit rather conservative Czech tastes.

Tulip Café

Opatovická 3 (224 930 019). Metro Národní třída. **Open** 11am-2am Mon-Thur, Sun; 11am-7am Fri, Sat. **$. Diner**. Map p120 B2 ⓭
Amazingly popular across the Czech and expat scenes, this groovy café with back patio offers imaginative American diner variations, but has serious service issues. The packs of American students don't seem to mind, though.

Universal

V Jirchářích (224 934 416). Metro Národní třída. **Open** 11.30am-midnight Mon-Sat; 11am-11.30pm Sun. **$. Continental**. Map p120 B2 ⓾
Old French advertisements, servers who know their stuff, and daily specials (cod in white sauce, flank steak and rolled veggie lasagne), come with delectable sides of fresh spinach or roasted gratin potatoes.

Zlatá Hvězda

Ve Smečkách 12 (296 222 292/ www.sportbar.cz). Metro Muzeum. **Open** 11am-midnight Mon; noon-2am Tue, Wed, Thur; 11am-4.30am Fri; noon-4.30am Sat; noon-midnight Sun. **Sports bar**. Map p121 D2 ⓾
Scuffed interior, crap service and just-edible pizzas have done nothing to chase off the sports fans who gather here to watch all the games on the battered big-screens.

Shopping

Antikvariát Galerie Můstek

Národní 40 (224 949 587). Metro Národní třída. **Open** 10am-7pm

Radost FX Café p130

Mon-Fri; noon-4pm Sat; 2pm-6pm Sun. Map p120 C1 ⓾
A discriminating antikvariát with fine antiquarian books and a reliable stock of major works on Czech art.

Antikvariát Kant

Opatovická 26 (224 934 219/ www.antik-kant.cz). Metro Národní třída. **Open** 10am-6pm Mon-Fri. Map p120 B2 ⓾
An eclectic mix of prints and dust-encrusted tomes are to be found here. There's quite a large, although strange, section of English books, and an extensive and very organised post-card collection. The prints on the walls are varied, and the cheap books in the entryway are worth more than a passing glance.

Bazar Antik Zajímavosti

Křemencova 4 (no phone). Metro Národní třída. **Open** 9am-6pm Mon-Fri. Map p120 B2/B3 ⓾
Heavy on the glass, this is your typical Czech bazaar. Tea cup fans will think they've found nirvana, but other

shoppers can appreciate the linens and the small collection of paintings, plus the unique lamps.

Beruška

Vodičkova 30 (no phone). Metro Můstek. **Open** 9am-6pm Mon-Fri. **Map** p121 D2 ⑤⑤

A small shop filled with toys for both younger and older children. Stuffed animals, cleverly designed wooden toys and puzzles, and board games are all sold here.

Cellarius

Lucerna Passage, Štěpánská 61 (224 210 979/www.cellarius.cz). Metro Můstek. **Open** 9.30am-9pm Mon-Sat; 3-8pm Sun. **Map** p121 D1 ⑤⑥

A huge selection of wines is crammed into the small space that is Cellarius. It's maze-like, so be sure to look both to the left and the right so that you don't miss anything. The owner stocks wine from local vineyards as well as some well-selected imports, including French, Bulgarian and Chilean varieties.

Fashion Galerie No.14

Opatovická 14 (no phone). Metro Národní třída. **Open** noon-7pm Mon-Sat. **Map** p120 B2 ⑤⑦

Not for the budget conscious, but definitely for the fashion plate. Each item here is an original, and the quality and design is beautiful. Mainly dresses, but there are some casual items too.

Foto Škoda

Palác Langhans, Vodičkova 37 (222 929 029/www.fotoskoda.cz). Metro Můstek. **Open** 8.30am-8pm Mon-Fri; 9am-6pm Sat. **Map** p121 D1 ⑤⑧

Sales, repairs, developing, supplies: this photography shop has everything you could possibly want. It's excellent for the professional, but amateurs will be able to find what they need as well.

Globe Bookstore & Coffeehouse

Pštrossova 6 (224 934 203/www. globebookstore.cz). Metro Národní třída. **Open** 9.30am-midnight daily. **Map** p120 B2 ⑤⑨

Jamming with J.A.R.

Prague pop bands have a remarkable staying power, or at least the small club of them that includes the band J.A.R. (pictured). Known for its funky, bluesy jazz rock and what it self-bills as party music, the 12-year-old band clearly possesses more sophistication and brassiness than a flavour-of-the-week boy or girl band, and that's surely one reason why it's survived and thrived. But it also stands out for its incredible level of musicianship (a quality that's obviously no prerequisite to having hordes of fans in Prague or anywhere else). J.A.R. provides its fans not only with regular shows at venues such as Nové Město's Lucerna Music

Bar (p135), a wonderfully worn-in underground concert space – but also with technical skills and lyrics that justify the successful solo careers of several members of the band.

Singer Dan Barta, whose own albums *Illustratosphere* and *Entropicture* sold phenomenally well locally, blends intensity with spontaneous, tender, high-register crooning. His shows are rare, sold-out affairs. (He can be seen with J.A.R. far more often.) A former X-ray technician and recovering heroin addict, Barta changed direction from pop rock to jazz-based stuff of much greater complexity in the late 1990s and has won much critical acclaim and a new, more mature fan-base. (And, because this is Prague, he also paid the rent for a while by playing both Jesus and Judas in the smash-hit Czech-language adaptation of *Jesus Christ Superstar*, which ran for years.)

J.A.R.'s sax man František Kopp, meanwhile, is one of the top jazz horn talents in the Czech Republic, with a handful of solo albums that blend world music, originals and classic standards, while bassist Robert Balzar is another Czech jazz king with his own calendar, recording deals and a string of appearances with the likes of Iva Bittová, the avant-garde singer sensation, and Slovak hipster rocker Richard Müller.

Roman Holý, the vocalist and keyboard man, is the fourth pillar. He's run his own show for years while also headlining with popular funk band Monkey Business.

Check J.A.R.'s gig dates and sample sounds at www.rap.cz.

Probably the best-known expat hang-out in Prague, the Globe should cover your all your anglophone reading needs and more. There's a simple restaurant at the back of the store, internet access and lots of new and used books.

Hamparadi Antik Bazar
Pštrossova 22 (224 931 162). Metro Národní třída. **Open** 10.30am-6pm daily. **Map** p120 B2 ⑥⓪
Quirky treasures are scattered among the typical bazaar offerings of porcelain and glass. Be sure to browse carefully, as it's easy to overlook something fun. Toys and old advertisements add to the nostalgic motif.

Le Patio
Národní 22 (224 934 853). Metro Národní třída. **Open** 10am-7pm Mon-Sat; 11am-7pm Sun. **Map** p120 B1 ⑥①
Le Patio brings the world to Prague with an eclectic mixture of imported home furnishings.

Svara's Hexenladen
Jindřišska 7 (224 228 418). Metro Můstek. **Open** 9am-6pm Mon-Fri. **Map** p121 D1 ⑥②
For the practising Wiccan back home, a wide selection of oils, candles, stones and herbs representing Celtic, Egyptian and New Age traditions. Nearly all your Wicca and occult supplies are here, along with jewellery and books.

Tesco
Národní třída 26 (222 003 111). Metro Můstek or Národní třída. **Open** *Department store* 8am-9pm Mon-Fri; 9am-8pm Sat; 10am-8pm Sun. *Supermarket* 7am-10pm Mon-Fri; 8am-8pm Sat; 9am-8pm Sun. **Map** p120 B1 ⑥③
Always packed, the big international chain covers all your expat needs: from peanut butter to taco shells downstairs, plus pharmacist's supplies, to souvenirs, clothes and electronics upstairs.

Nightlife

Darling Club Cabaret
Ve Smečkách 32 (www.kabaret.cz). Metro Muzeum. **Open** noon-5am Mon,

Tue, Thur, Sun; 8pm-5am Wed; noon-6am Fri, Sat. **Map** p121 D2 ⑥④
Prague's most epic strip and sex club brings in high-rollers from all over with up to 100 working girls per night, all out of a Las Vegas fantasy.

Duplex
Václavske náměstí 21 (224 232 319/ www.duplexduplex.cz). Metro Můstek. **Open** 9.30pm-2am Tue-Thur. **Admission** 150 Kč. **Map** p121 D1 ⑥⑤
A pop disco located atop Wenceslas Square, where mobs of Italian teens meet local cruisers, laser beams and expensive cocktails.

Hot Pepper's
NEW *Václavské náměstí 21 (224 232 319/www.hotpeppersprague.cz). Metro Můstek.* **Open** 9pm-5am daily. **Map** p121 D1 ⑥⑥
The latest up-and-coming strip club on Wenceslas Square is competing with the more established competition by offering changing shows nightly, including the enthusiastic Army of Pepper's. There's a decent menu available as well, although the place's free entry policy is soon eclipsed by the high drink and food prices.

Lucerna Music Bar
Vodičkova 36 (224 217 108/ www.musicbar.cz). Metro Můstek. **Open** 8pm-3am daily. *Concerts* 9pm. **Map** p121 D1 ⑥⑦
Incredible rock, jazz and blues talents roll through this neglected old cellar concert space, from Sean Lennon to Hiram Bullock. Lucerna has in fact always hosted the greats, including the likes of Satchmo and Josephine Baker in times past.

Nebe
NEW *Křemencova 10 (224 932 052). Metro Národní třída.* **Open** 6pm-3am Mon-Sat; 5pm-1am Sun. **Map** p120 B2 ⑥⑧
A cellar bar-club where English voices can be heard nightly, along with the break beats. Well-worn and a magnet for US college students taking a semester in Prague, Nebe does at least know how to rock.

Vyšehrad p138

Radost FX Café

See p130.

Rock Café

Národní třída 20 (224 933 947/ www.rockcafe.cz). Metro Národní třída. **Open** 10am-3am Mon-Fri; 5pm-3am Sat; 5pm-1am Sun. *Concerts* 9pm. **Map** p120 B1 69

Rising local stars, but also the backpacker crowd. Once a post-revolution rock pioneer, these days it's only occasionally a hot ticket and features endless rockumentary screenings and Czech 'revival' bands.

Arts & leisure

AghaRTA

Krakovská 5 (222 211 275/www. agharta.cz). Metro Muzeum or IP Pavlova. **Open** *Club* 7pm-midnight daily. *Concerts* 9pm. *Jazz shop* 5pm-midnight Mon-Fri; 7pm-midnight Sat, Sun. **Admission** 100 Kč. **Map** p121 D3 70

This club off Wenceslas Square is one of the best for modern jazz. An even mix of Czechs and foreigners mingles in the relatively small but comfortable space. The CD shop sells local recordings for 150-400 Kč. Look for releases on the club's own ARTA label.

Evald

Národní třída 28 (221 105 225/ www.evald.cinemart.cz). Metro Národní třída. **Map** p120 B1/C1 71

The best downtown arthouse cinema is tiny but has exclusive bookings on some European art, independent American and Czech films, which they sometimes show with English subtitles. Advance booking recommended for new films.

Lucerna

Vodičkova 36 (224 216 972/www. lucerna.cz). Metro Můstek. **Map** p121 D1 72

Still holding on to quickly fading glory, this art-nouveau masterpiece is a reminder of cinema-going's glory days. The elevated lobby bar has large windows that let you watch the

1920s-era shopping arcade, and somebody still occasionally tickles the ivories on the piano.

Lucerna Great Hall

Vodičkova 36 (224 225 440/www. lucpra.com). Metro Můstek. **Open** Concerts start 7pm-8pm. **Admission** 200-900 Kč. **Map** p121 D1/D2 73

Run independently from the Lucerna Music Bar (see p135), this vast, pillared underground performance hall hosts big-time acts from the likes of Maceo Parker to the Cardigans. There are no regular box office hours so book ahead through an agent like Ticketpro (see p216).

MAT Studio

Karlovo náměstí 19 (224 915 765/ www.mat.cz). Metro Karlovo náměstí. **Map** p120 B3 74

Definitely the smallest theater in town. The intimate screening room shows a fair mix of offbeat films, Czech classics with English subtitles and rare selections from the Czech TV vaults.

National Theatre

Národní divadlo Národní 2 (info 224 901 448/ box office 224 901 377/www.nd.cz). Metro Národní třída. **Open** *Box office* Sept-June 10am-6pm daily. **Map** p120 A1 75

This symbol of Czech nationalism concentrates on Czech opera, the core of the repertoire being Smetana and Dvořák, together with some Janáček. Non-Czech operas and impressive ballets are also performed.

Reduta

Národní třída 20 (224 933 487/ www.redutajazzclub.cz). Metro Národní třída. **Open** *Box office* 5pm-9pm daily. *Club* 9pm-12.30am daily. *Concerts* 9pm. **Admission** 200 Kč. **Map** p120 B1 76

Virtually unchanged since the Velvet Revolution, this old chestnut of a club steadfastly hangs on to its cramped, awkward seating and overpriced beer. Admittedly, some of the best musicians in town often sit in with the evening's band, though.

State Opera

Státní Opera

Wilsonova 4 (224 227 266/www.opera. cz). Metro Muzeum. **Open** *Box office* 10am-5.30pm Mon-Fri; 10am-noon, 1-5.30pm Sat, Sun. **Map** p121 E2/F2 ⑦

Once the German Theatre, opened in 1887, where Mahler conducted, it's now the second house of the National Theatre with consistently bold contemporary opera alongside standards from the Italian, German, French and Russian repertoires.

Světozor

Vodičkova 39 (224 946 824/www. kinosvetozor.cz). Metro Můstek. **Map** p121 D1 ⑦

Part of the repertory house association Osa 9, this veteran movie house has proven its credentials by hosting film fests as well as a great repertoire of indies, usually with original soundtracks and most often with English subtitles (worth checking in advance though – look for *angl. titulky*).

Vyšehrad

Sights & museums

Vyšehrad

Soběslavova 1 (www.praha-vysehrad.cz). Metro Vyšehrad. **Map** below A2 ⑦

These 10th-century hilltop castle ruins feature a cemetery that holds a dozen of the greats of Czech culture and the neo-Gothic Saints Peter and Paul, whose spires dominate this side of the river's skyline.

Eating & drinking

Rio's

Štulcova 2 (224 922 156/www. riorestaurant.cz). Metro Vyšehrad. **Open** 11am-midnight daily. **Map** below A2 ⑥

The cuisine and service are unexceptional here – the main draw is the view from Prague's oldest hilltop castle ruins, located a 12-minute metro ride south of the centre.

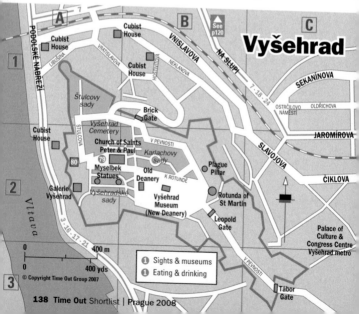

Vinohrady & Žižkov

Vinohrady

Vinohrady, once a separate (and wealthy) town, is named for the wine grapes once grown here. These days it blossoms with smart cafés, posh hotels and other real estate, and a flourishing gay scene. The heart of the neighbourhood is Náměstí Miru, a round 'square' spiked by the twin spires of St Ludmila. Its main artery, Vinohradská, formerly called Stalinova třída, is lined with art-nouveau apartment blocks.

Sights & museums

Church of St Ludmila
Kostel sv. Ludmily

Náměstí Miru (no phone). Metro Náměstí Miru. **Map** p141 A2 ❶
Spooky and opulent, this neo-Gothic church marks a hub of the Vinohrady district, the point from which protesters started the march that brought down communism in 1989.

Eating & drinking

Artyčok
Londýnská 29 (222 524 110/ www.artycok.cz). Metro IP Pavlova. **Open** 11am-1am daily. **$$**. **World**. **Map** p141 A2 ❷
Passable Czech-Mex, Thai and tapas are to hand, but the main attraction is the terrace on a lovely street. That and the affordability – although it's not for those in a hurry.

Café Medúza

Belgická 17 (222 515 107). Metro Náměstí Míru. **Open** 11am-1am Mon-Fri; noon-1am Sat, Sun. **$**. **Café**. **Map** p141 A4 ❸

On quiet Belgická street, this is one of the city's cosiest, if threadbare, winter hideout spots, run by two sisters who serve warming soups and mulled wine to bookish regular patrons.

Café Sahara

NEW *Ibsenova 1 (222 514 987). Metro Náměstí Míru.* **Open** 8am-midnight daily. **$**. **Mediterranean**. **Map** p141 A2 ❹

A well located labyrinth of stylish, elegant furnishings in earthy tones, accented by cool fountains and a lovely terrace out back. Serious coffees, classy pasta dinners and lingering lunches are all covered.

Efes

Vinohradská 63 (222 250 015). Metro Náměstí Míru. **Open** 11am-11pm Mon-Sat. **$**. **Turkish**. **Map** p141 C2 ❺

Friday night belly dancing aside, this simple little cellar is about prime Anatolian cuisine, with exotic, warming tastes like *ayvar*, a red pepper, chilli and garlic paste you spread on fresh sourdough, the tsatsiki-like *cacic* and great vegetarian fare. *Sonbahar kisiri* is a cracked-wheat mix of walnuts and olives, and the *kizartma* of caramelized eggplant and peppers seduces fast – quite a bit faster than the relaxed service. Kebabs, meanwhile, are juicy and tender, and fine minced meat and Turkish spices feature in the mezes.

Kaaba

Mánesova 20 (222 254 021). Tram 11. **Open** 8am-10pm Mon-Fri; 10am-10pm Sat, Sun. **$**. **Café**. **Map** p141 A1 ❻

Catch a buzz: celebrated coffees from around the globe, cult wines from well-known domestic producers and cool international modern decor. Excellent for lazy mornings of page turning and refills.

La Lavande

Záhřebská 24 (222 517 406). Metro Náměstí Míru. **Open** noon-3pm, 7-11pm Mon-Fri. **$$$**. **Continental**. **Map** p141 B4 ❼

This new arrival at the high end of Prague's culinary scene offers quality cooking and service in a semi-casual French farmhouse atmosphere. Recommended dishes include fresh gazpacho, goat's cheese millefeuille, fried anchovies with coriander and sour cream, beef Rossini, crunchy salad with English bacon and grated Parmesan.

Park Café

Riegrovy sady 28 (no phone). Metro Jiřího z Poděbrad. **Open** 11am-11pm daily. **$**. **Café**. **Map** p141 B1 ❽

One of the liveliest beer gardens in the district, this one's always crowded with old-timers, kids, dogs and expats. The beer is cheap and copious, though, and rock bands liven it up for summer. Just watch where you step.

Pastička

Blanická 25 (222 253 228/www.pasticka.cz). Metro Náměstí Míru. **Open** 11am-1am Mon-Fri; 5pm-1am Sat, Sun. **Map** p141 B1 ❾

The Little Mousetrap is a beloved neighbourhood hang-out spot that's always jumping with an eclectic crowd – especially on the summer terrace out back. They go in for gab, pub grub, beer and cigarettes. Lots of 'em.

Popocafepetl

Italská 2 (777 944 672/www.popocafepetl.cz). Metro Náměstí Míru. **Open** 9am-1am Mon-Fri; 4pm-1am Sat, Sun. **$**. **Café**. **Map** p141 A2 ❿

A sister café to the one in Malá Strana, this is the quieter, gentler Popo, but not by much. The regulars throng here till the wee hours. They're not here for the fine service or beers, but somehow it's always got that buzz, with its mix of local bohemians and decadent expats.

Roca

Vinohradská 32 (222 520 060). Metro Náměstí Míru. **Open** 11am-11pm daily. **$$**. **Italian**. **Map** p141 B2 ⓫

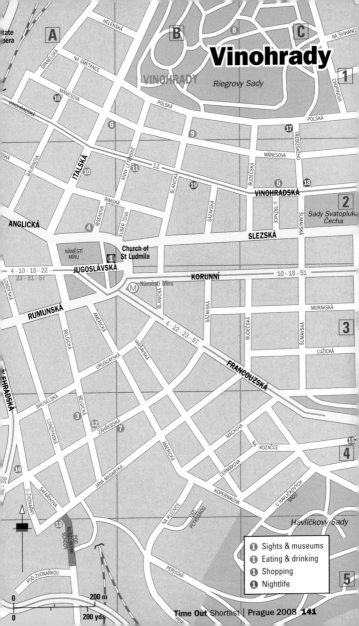

Vinohrady

A **B** **C**

HELÉNSKÁ

8

NA ŠVIHAN

1

ŠPANĚLSKÁ

NA SMETANCE

VINOHRADY

Riegrovy Sady

CHOPINOVA

MÁNESOVA

16

POLSKÁ

VINOHRADSKÁ

POLSKÁ

BALBÍNOVA

6

9

17

TŘEBÍZSKÉHO

ŠKA

ITALSKÁ

10

11 11

ANNY LETENSKÉ

BLANICKÁ

MÁNESOVA

BUDEČSKÁ

5

18

19

VINOHRADSKÁ

RÍMSKÁ

SÁZAVSKÁ

2

IBSENOVA

4

SLÉ... TOVÁ

U TRŽNICE

ŠUMAVSKÁ

Sady Svatopluka Čecha

ANGLICKÁ

SLEZSKÁ

NÁMĚSTÍ MÍRU

Church of St Ludmila

4 · 10 · 16 · 22
23 · 51 · 57

JUGOSLÁVSKÁ

KORUNNÍ

10 · 16 · 51

LONDÝNSKÁ

Náměstí Míru
Ⓜ

BLANICKÁ

SÁZAVSKÁ

BUDEČSKÁ

ŠUMAVSKÁ

MORAVSKÁ

RUMUNSKÁ

BELGICKÁ

AMERICKÁ

4 · 22 · 23 · 57

3

LUŽICKÁ

HRADSKÁ

URUGUAYSKÁ

VARŠAVSKÁ

FRANCOUZSKÁ

BRUSELSKÁ

LONDÝNSKÁ

BELGICKÁ

3

12

ZÁHŘEBSKÁ

7

AMERICKÁ

MÁCHOVA

NA KOZAČCE

15

4

ŠAFAŘÍKOVA

JANA MASARYKA

ČERMÁKOVA

KOPERNIKOVA

U MIKULÁŠKÝCH SADŮ

14

U ZVONAŘKY

13

POD NUSELSKÝM SCHODY

NA KLEOVCE

NAD PETRUŠKOU

Havlíčkovy Sady

PERUCKÁ

POD ZVONAŘKOU

5

❶ Sights & museums
❶ Eating & drinking
❶ Shopping
❶ Nightlife

0 ———— 200 m
0 ———— 200 yds

Roca p140

Good, downhome Italian, courtesy of the owners Roberta and Camilla, whose names each lend a syllable to the name of this local favourite hideout. Tortellini pork soup starts things off nicely, with hearty pastas in creamy sauces on offer as other primi. The tender chicken scallopini with dreamy mushroom and nutmeg sauce follows. Service is fleet and decor rustic and casual.

Žlutá pumpa

Belgická 12 (no phone). Metro Náměstí Míru. **Open** noon-1am Mon-Fri; 4pm-1am Sat, Sun. **$$$**. **Continental**. **Map** p141 A4 ⑫
The Yellow Pump is a buzzy local pub with reasonably priced Czech-Mex food, the latest trend, it seems, in trying to find new angles on trad pubbing. A colorful, lively joint, but don't expect great service or chow.

Zvonařka

Šafaříkova 1 (224 251 990). Metro IP Pavlova. **Open** 11am-midnight daily. **Bar**. **Map** p141 A5 ⑬

Stylish new bar in a graceful old building that's been turned into one of the swankest hotels in town. A fine view of the Nusle valley rewards those sitting outside.

Shopping

Fra

Šafaříkova 15 (274 817 126/www. fra.cz). Metro Náměstí Míru. **Open** 9am-11pm Mon-Fri; 1-11pm Sat, Sun. **Map** p141 A4 ⑭
A bookshop and café specialising in small-press volumes and works in translation by Czech and Central European writers, with a studious crowd of characters who stage readings and occasional poetry nights.

Shakespeare & Sons

Krymská 12 (271 740 839/www. shakes.cz). Metro Náměstí Míru. **Open** noon-midnight daily. **Map** p141 C4 ⑮
Patterned on Paris's Shakespeare & Co, Prague's conception is considerably scaled down but features walls of well-chosen new and used books, as well as a calendar of publishing-related events and readings and Bernard beer on tap. Cosy, low-key and comfortable if you can find the backstreet it's on.

Nightlife

Le Clan

Balbínova 23 (222 251 226). Metro Náměstí Míru. **Open** 10pm-3am Tue-Fri, Sun; 10pm-6am Sat. **Map** p141 A1 ⑯
With a dimly lit entrance (hit the bell to be buzzed in) and none of the downstairs decadence visible from without, this bar and club feels secretive and nefarious – which, of course, it is. Red plush interiors, sofas, passable basic cocktails and a lower-level dancefloor that's sometimes open all add up to a great hideout.

Saints

Polská 32 (222 250 326/www.prague saints.cz). Metro Náměstí Míru. **Open** 7pm-4am daily. **Map** p141 C1 ⑰

Shakespeare & Sons

successful it took over the old Gejzeer club on this spot and expanded it massively. Giddy atmosphere and highly danceable DJ and theme nights.

Žižkov

Down the hill to the north and east of Vinohrady is Žižkov, which balances Vinohrady's charms with a concentration of pubs said to be the world's greatest per capita. Notorious for its artists, indulgers and large Romany population, the district is loved for its quirky outlandishness. Always a working-class district, it's also home to the greatest monument to working-class hero Jan Žižka, the one-eyed Hussite fighter, and an impressive former signal-jamming tower.

Karlín, which stands on reclaimed land that was inundated in the floods of 2002, has blossomed from the mud into a booming district with new apartments, shops, bars and an art scene centered on the Karlín Studios, a massive former industrial hall that hosts the third Prague Biennale (www.praguebiennale.org) in 2007 – an appealingly rebellious event. No longer sponsored by the National Gallery, which has attempted to launch its own biennale, the original has only grown and improved with its independence, becoming the art event of the year.

A friendly, casual gay bar and dance club that doubles as an information hub for the community in Prague (the website offers loads of gay accommodation and entertainment listings), run by British owners who excel at cocktails.

Termix

Třebízského 4a (222 710 462/www. club-termix.cz). Metro Jiřího z Poděbrad. **Open** 10pm-5am daily. **Map** p141 C2 ⑱
A crammed, jammed little bar and dance club with a mixed local and foreign crowd, a bar that's better at beer than anything elaborate and a decorator who likes old car parts. It does swing all night long, however.

Valentino

NEW *Vinohradská 40 (222 513 491/www.club-valentino.cz). Metro Náměstí Míru.* **Open** 2pm-5am daily. **Admission** varies; free except Fri & Sat. **Map** p141 B2 ⑲
Prague's biggest and most popular gay disco on the district's main drag with three floors of fun, two dancefloors, multiple bars and the odd darkroom. So

Sights & museums

Church of the Sacred Heart

Nejsvětější Srdce Páně
Náměstí Jiřího z Poděbrad (no phone). Metro Jiřího z Poděbrad. **Map** p144 B4/B5 ⑳
Ecclesiastical modernism reaches new heights in this fantastic (for 1928-32, of course) church, whose rose window features an unbroken ramp you could ascend on a bicycle. In one of the most inspiring structures in the city, by Josip

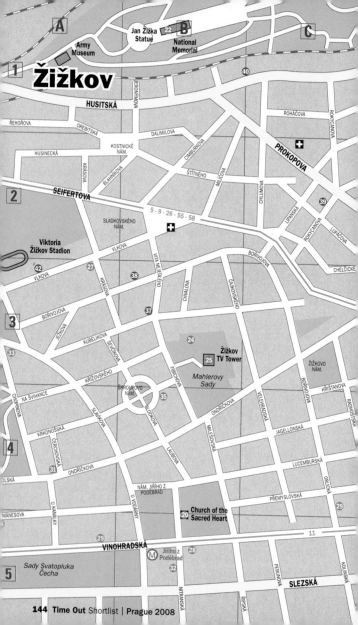

A

B

C

Jan Žižka
Statue 22

National
Memorial

Army
Museum

40

1

Žižkov

HUSITSKÁ

JERONÝMOVA

ROHÁČOVA

ŘEHOŘOVA

OREBITSKÁ

DALIMILOVA

PROKOPOVA

ROKYCANOVA

HUSINECKÁ

KOSTNICKÉ
NÁM.

CIMBUROVA

ŠTÍTNÉHO

MILÍČOVA

CHLUMOVA

LIPANSKÁ

39

LUPÁČOVA

KRÁSOVA

BLAHNÍKOVA

2

SEIFERTOVA

ROKYCANOVA

5 · 9 · 26 · 55 · 58

SLADKOVSKÉHO
NÁM.

CHELČICKÉ

Viktoria
Žižkov Stadion

VLKOVA

BOŘIVOJOVA

VÍTA NEJEDLÉHO

42

VLKOVA

27

38

CHVALOVA

ČAJKOVSKÉHO

3

BOŘIVOJOVA

37

JESENIOVA

KUBELÍKOVA

SEIFERTOVA

24

Žižkov
TV Tower

33

KŘIŽÍKOVA

25

FIBICHOVA

Mahlerovy
Sady

BOŘIVOJOVA

Žižkovo
NÁM.

KŘÍŠŤANOVA

RADHOŠŤSKÁ

NA ŠVIHANCE

ŠKROUPOVO
NÁM.

BLODKOVA

35

SLAVÍKOVA

ONDŘÍČKOVA

VELEHRADSKÁ

JAGELLONSKÁ

CHLUMOVA

KRKONOŠSKÁ

ČERHOVSKÁ

MILEŠOVSKÁ

LAUBOVA

4

31

ONDŘÍČKOVA

LUCEMBURSKÁ

ORLICKÁ

NÁM. JIŘÍHO Z
PODĚBRAD

Church of the
Sacred Heart

PŘEMYSLOVSKÁ

29

U KANÁLKY

20

11

MÁNESOVA

U VODÁRNY

29

VINOHRADSKÁ

28

PERUNOVA

KOLÍNSKÁ

5

Sady Svatopluka
Čecha

Jiřího z
Poděbrad

32

NITRANSKÁ

ŘÍPSKÁ

SLEZSKÁ

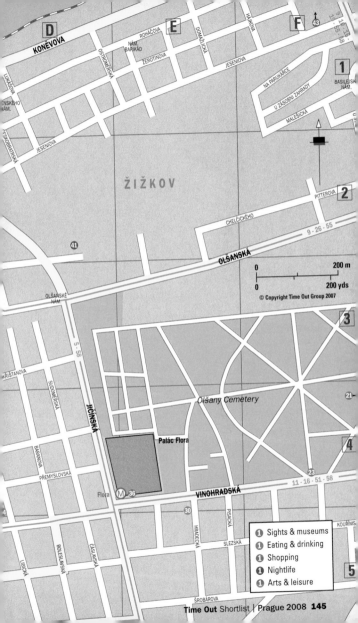

Žižkov Tower

National Memorial

Plečnik, the pioneering Slovenian architect who also redid Prague Castle to make the mark of the First Republic.

Jewish Cemetery

Židovské hřbitovy
Vinohradská and Jičínská (no phone).
Metro Želivského. **Open** 9am-4pm
Mon-Thur, Sun. **Admission** 20 Kč.
Map p145 F4 ㉑
Not to be confused with the Old Jewish Cemetery (p99) in Staré Město, this neglected posthumous home to Franz Kafka, founded in 1890, has ivy-covered graves mainly thanks to the Holocaust – few family members remain to care for the graves, while those across the street are lovingly weeded with fresh flowers. For Kafka's grave, follow the sign by the Želivského metro entrance; it's approximately 200m (660ft) down the row by the southern cemetery wall.

National Memorial

Národní památník
U památníku 1900 (222 781 676).
Metro Florenc. **Open** times vary (booking required). **Admission** Varies. **Map** p144 B1 ㉒

Unless you've got 19 friends to book a party inside, you'll be relegated to the exteriors of this monumental mausoleum for communist big-wigs, where Klement Gottwald was encased in glass for a time. Its façades feature Soviet war heroes and it's topped by the largest equestrian statue in the world, a 16.5-ton (16,764-kg) effigy of Hussite hero Jan Žižka. The view from the top of Vítkov hill's impressive too.

Olšany Cemetery

Olšanské hřbitovy
Vinohradská 153/Jana Želivského (272 739 364). Metro Flora or Želivského. **Open** dawn-dusk daily.
Map p145 F4 ㉓
The Garden of Rest honours Red Army soldiers who died in Czechoslovakia. To the right of the entrance, is the grave of anti-communist martyr Jan Palach, the student who set fire to himself in Wenceslas Square in 1969.

Žižkov Jewish Cemetery

Fibichova (no phone). Metro Jiřího z Poděbrad. **Open** 9.30am-1pm
Tue, Thur. **Admission** 20 Kč.
Map p144 B3 ㉔

All that remains of the cemetery that once covered this square, displaced by the communist regime to make way for its Western signal-jamming transmitter, Žižkov Tower (below). A poignant reminder of the not-too-distant past.

Žižkov Tower

Máhlerovy sady (242 418 784). Metro Jiřího z Poděbrad. **Open** 11am-11pm daily. **Admission** 60 Kč; free under-5s. **Map** p144 B3

The huge, thrusting, three-pillared television tower in Žižkov has long been dubbed the Pražský pták, or Prague Prick, by locals. Completed early in 1989 as a foreign signal-jamming transmitter, it now broadcasts reality TV shows to eager Czechs. A lift flies up to the eighth-floor viewing platform; alternatively, take a drink in the fifth-floor café of this 216m (709ft) monstrosity. The intriguing, rather disturbing babies on the side are the work of Czech bad-boy artist and satirist David Černý.

Eating & drinking

Aromi

Mánesova 78 (222 713 222). Metro Jiřího z Poděbrad. **Open** 11am-10pm Mon-Thur, Sun; 11am-11pm Fri, Sat. **$$$. Italian. Map** p144 A5

One of Prague's best new Italian restaurants is thankfully located off the tourist radar. Authoritative kitchen mastery meets low-key rough wood and brick interiors and homey presentation of everything from the six-seafood antipasti platter to veal on saffron risotto with thyme. Excellent wines, fairly priced, from around the boot.

Blind Eye

NEW *Vlkova 26 (no phone/www.blindeye.cz). Metro Jiřího z Poděbrad.* **Open** 7pm-4am daily. **$. Bar. Map** p144 A3

Until recently run as a speakeasy, this thoroughly local bar is now legal again but still features dark corners and well worn interiors, making for a rough and ready late night meet-up spot.

Černá kočka Bílý kocour

NEW *Vinohradská 62 (222 519 773). Metro Jiřího z Poděbrad.* **Open** 11am-3am daily. **$. Grill bar. Map** p144 B5

A whimsical cellar bar that's become a late night scene among the district's hip (but not obnoxious) set. Rib tips, chicken wings and burgers go well with the warm yet fleeting staff – these two qualities rarely meet in Prague restos. Fortunately, Black Cat White Cat's the exception.

Hapu p148

Hapu

Orlická 8 (222 720 158). Metro Jiřího z Poděbrad. **Open** 6pm-2am Mon-Sat. **$**. **Bar**. Map p144 C4 ㉙

A one-room cellar with beaten-up sofas and a small bar – but it mixes the best cocktails in the district and attracts a fun crowd of international raconteurs.

Infinity

NEW *Chrudimská 7 (272 176 580/www. infinity.cz). Metro Flora.* **Open** 6pm-2am daily. **$**. **Bar**. Map p145 E4/E5 ㉚

The long bar in this cellar hideout attracts a stylish local set, as does the light menu of salads, lamb carpaccio and suchlike. Brick and red-washed interiors make for mellow sipping, with DJ action (of varying quality) after 10pm.

James Bond Café

Polská 7 (222 733 871). Metro Jiřího z Poděbrad. **Open** 6pm-2am daily. **$**. **Café**. Map p144 A4 ㉛

This 007-inspired café didn't hold back when it came to mod seating and bar surfaces, but its cocktails don't quite live up to 'licensed to kill' – although service is a notch up from many a bar around.

Mozaika

Nitranská 13 (224 253 011). Metro Jiřího z Poděbrad. **Open** 11.30am-midnight Mon-Fri; 4pm-midnight Sat, Sun. **$**. **World**. Map p144 B5 ㉜

A friendly local place for solid value and decent comfort food like the hamburger with fresh mushrooms, served on a homemade spinach roll, the hearty daily soup special and pork chops with baked potato and cherry sauce.

Rossini

NEW *Chopinova 26 (222 729 041). Metro Náměstí Míru.* **Open** 11am-11pm daily. **$$**. **Italian**. Map p144 A3 ㉝

This rustic, wood-panelled room serves up gorgeously done pastas, carpaccio, mortadella and well chosen regional Italian wines. Book well ahead for one of the sought after, but surprisingly affordable tables on any weekend. On a quiet side street well worth scouting out.

Sonora

Radhošťská 5 (222 711 029). Metro Flora. **Open** 11am-midnight daily. **$**. **Mexican**. Map p145 D4 ㉞

Some of the city's closest approximations to Mexican food, complete with mole sauce, salsa, taco salad, beef burritos and tasty quesadillas. All complemented perfectly by cheap Czech beer.

U Sadu

Škroupovo náměstí 5 (222 727 072). Metro Jiřího z Poděbrad. **Open** 10am-2am daily. **$**. **Czech**. Map p144 B4 ㉟

Bustling with students and locals, also cheap and Czech, with well-located

Rossini

The lush life

In the Czech lit classic *Good Soldier Švejk*, Jaroslav Hašek describes the work habits of the wily conscript to the Imperial army: on the way to a simple errand, he would stop for one beer in every pub along the way, ending up a good day behind.

Czechs still smile warmly at the thought and, though private enterprise calls for a bit more efficiency, would rather give up a limb than drop pubs from their lunch-hour or after-work ritual. The Žižkov district, with more pubs per capita than anywhere else in the world, is where such beer fans go to die.

When the weather is mild, venues in verdant settings, such as Parukářka, beckon convincingly. Indeed, watching the twinkling lights of Prague as you sip a *pivo* on this hill overlooking the city, you may well decide to stay on in Prague forever. Drinkers in the **Park Café** (p140) in Reigrovy sady, a pub to the east in Vinohrady,

enjoy an even more dramatic view, with Prague Castle in the distance.

Those already too wobbly to make it up such hills, or who want to be in closer proximity to the football on the big-screen TV, can still get a breath of reasonably fresh air on the benches outside **U Sadu** (p148), which are generally in place from April to October.

For bars rather than beerhalls, the district offers lots more options, all demanding a visit to determine the true champion. **Černá kočka Bílý kocour** (p147) is a new, fun trendsetter with tasty bar food, **Hapu** (p148) a laid-back cocktail king, while **Bukowski's** (p151) is a return to the fold of Prague barmaster Glen Emery. **Žižkov Tower** (p147) offers a sci-fi experience to be savoured, though you probably won't be impressed by the drinks or the service.

All in all, then, probably best to keep a taxi phone number handy and cancel all of tomorrow's appointments. Let the crawl begin!

Akropolis

outside seating in the summer and a friendly, smokey, packed interior the rest of the year.

Shopping

Palác Flóra

Vinohradská 151 (255 741 700/www. palacflora.cz). Metro Flóra. **Open** 8am-midnight daily. **Map** p145 E4 ㊱

The latest and greatest in the tidal wave of Czech malls, those monuments to the new consumerism that locals love so dearly they have dates here and hang out all day in the mall cafés and bars. Handy if you need a clean shirt, too.

Nightlife

Akropolis

Kubelíkova 27 (296 330 911/www. palacakropolis.cz). Metro Jiřího z Poděbrad. **Open** *Divadelní Bar* 7pm-5am daily. *Malá Scená Bar* 7pm-3am daily. *Concerts* 7.30pm. **Admission** from 90 Kč. **Map** p144 B3 ㊲

The heart of indie rock and world music in Prague, this club hosts series such as United Colours of Akropolis and Jazz Meets World to promote a rich array of artists and avant-garde acts, from throat-singing monks to Berlin klezmer. The downstairs bars offer nightly DJs and MCs free of charge and the attached restaurant serves until late.

Bukowski's

NEW *Bořivojova 86 (222 212 676). Metro Jiřího z Poděbrad.* **Open** 6pm-midnight daily. **Map** p144 B3 ㊳

Thank heavens, longtime expat barman and former lumberjack Glen Emery has opened another drinking hole, this time with a Swedish chef, an American sound engineer and a Slovak downhill skier as cohorts. Fine Pilsner and a ready-made crowd of amusing miscreants.

Klub XT3

NEW *Rokycanova 29 (222 783 463/ www.xt3.cz). Metro Jiřího z Poděbrad.* **Open** 6pm-5am daily. **Admission** from 30Kč for live acts. **Map** p144 C2 ㊴

Difficult to find but worth it when it's hot – Klub XT3's been host to wild acts

like Gogol Bordello – but if you hit it on a skate punk night, you may find yourself moving on sooner rather than later.

Matrix

Koněvova 13 (608 706 791/www. matrixklub.cz). Metro Florenc. **Open** 8pm-4am Tue-Sat. **Map** p144 B1/C1 ㊵

This former meat refrigerating facility is a rough and ready techno dance hole these days with a young, dreadlocked, sweet-smelling crowd who probably shouldn't be here on a school night.

Parukářka

NEW *Olšanská & Prokopova (no phone/www.parukarka.cz). Metro Flora.* **Open** *Pub* 7pm-2am daily. *Club* varies. **Map** p145 D2 ㊶

This rustic old pub atop a grassy hill is an attraction indeed, with occasional live bands and a dedicated crowd of characters, but it's the club in the old bunker deep inside the hill that's the real attraction. Normally open at weekends, you descend down spiral stairs once you find the curved lead-filled fallout shelter door above Prokopská street.

Sedm Vlků

Vlkova 7 (222 711 725/www.sedm vlku.cz). Metro Jiřího z Poděbrad. **Open** 5pm-3am Mon-Sat. **Map** p144 A3 ㊷

For such a tiny little club, this one is right out front in terms of DJ action, with some of the city's powerhouse acts on the decks and a dedicated local crowd of techno cognoscenti. Cruisy as hell with a distinct lack of inhibitions.

Arts & leisure

Karlín Studios

Divadlo Na Vinohradech *Křižíkova 34 (no phone). Metro Křižíkova.* **Open** *Public gallery* noon-6pm Tue-Sun. **Map** p145 F1 ㊸

A vast complex in a former factory, this public gallery also contains two private exhibition spaces, Entrance and Behémot. It also provides studio space for a select group of artists, and holds two open days for these studios twice a year. It hosted the Prague Biennale 3 in 2007.

Letná park

Holešovice

PRAGUE BY AREA

Holešovice, situated across the Vltava river to the north of Old Town, is decidedly on the rise. Downtown prices have driven apartment buyers, companies, artists and expats to this former industrial zone. The grime and neglected façades still give it character, but it also features great green spaces. Its former factories are becoming gallery and living space and one of Prague's two international train stations, Nádraží Holešovice, links to the wider world. Meanwhile, families and in-line skaters inhabit **Stromovka park** and **Letná** and the cafés and pubs all around.

Holešovice's main drag, Dukelských hrdinů, features a sleek constructivist building, **Veletržní palác**, a modern art mecca of the National Gallery. Výstaviště, up the street, is an appealingly run-down exhibition ground with a lapidarium that houses the original saints from Charles Bridge and a funfair, Lunapark, behind its glorious main hall. Stromovka, a park to the west, laid out by Rudolf II in the 16th century, provides green space, as does Letná to the south. Lifestyling lies in between at places like Fraktal and La Bodega Flamenca. Mecca, on the eastern side of the district, is a top Prague club with a fresh thirtysomething crowd.

A ten-minute walk north of Stromovka by bridge (or bus No.112 from Metro Nádraží Holešovice) brings you to **Zoo Praha**, which is still enjoying the new facilities put in after the epic flood of 2002.

Sights & museums

Lapidárium

*Výstaviště (233 375 636/www.nm.cz).
Metro Nádraží Holešovice.* **Open** noon-
5pm Tue-Fri; 10am-5pm Sat, Sun.
Map p155 D1 ①

Don't go looking for the original stone
saints from Charles Bridge on the
bridge itself. They're all resting peace-
fully here, along with outstanding
Czech stone sculptures from 11th to
19th centuries.

National Gallery
Collection of 19th-,
20th- & 21st-Century Art

Sbírka moderního a současného umění
*Veletržní palác, Dukelských hrdinů 47
(224 301 122/www.ngprague.cz). Metro
Vltavská.* **Open** 10am-6pm Tue-Sun.
Admission 1 floor 100 Kč; 2 floors
150 Kč; 3 floors 200 Kč; all four floors
250 Kč. Temporary exhibitions 50 Kč;
free under-10s. **Map** p155 D2/D3 ②

This functionalist building, designed
by Oldřich Tyl and Josef Fuchs and
opened in 1929, houses the National
Gallery's collections of modern and
contemporary art, including paintings
by Karel Purkyně and 19th-century
symbolists like Max Švabinský and
František Bílek. The groundbreaking
abstract artist František Kupka is
well represented here as well, along
with Czech cubists.

Výstaviště

*Za Elektárnou 49 (220 103 111/
www.incheba.cz). Metro Nádraží
Holešovice.* **Open** 2-9pm Tue-Fri;
10am-9pm Sat, Sun. **Admission** free
Tue-Fri; 20 Kč Sat, Sun; free under-6s.
Map p154 C1 ③

Built out of curvaceous expanses of
wrought iron to house the Jubilee
Exhibition of 1891, Výstaviště signalled
the birth of the new architectural form
in Prague. The best view of the exterior
is from the back, where a monumental
modern fountain gushes kitschily at
night, in time to popular classics and a
light show. The grounds host the
Lapidárium and the delightfully dilapidated funfair Lunapark.

Zoo Praha

*U Trojského zámku (296 112 111/
www.zoopraha.cz). Metro Nádraží
Holešovice.* **Open** 9am-4pm daily.
Admission 80 Kč. **Map** p154 A1 ④

Having tragically lost a baby elephant
in the floods of 2002 because of its low-
lying location, the zoo is back in fight-
ing shape with new exhibition grounds
and enclosures, having received massive donations and funding.

Eating & drinking

Fraktal

Šmeralova 1 (no phone). Metro Vltavská.
Open 11am-midnight daily. **$**. **Café**.
Map p154 B3 ⑤

An intense out-of-centre bar scene phenomenon, this cosy little drinking hole
with occasional live music and/or book
launches has friendly owners. They
have settled on a trashy convivial place
where anything goes. With an improved
menu of the inevitable Czech-Mex, a few
cocktails are also worth noting: Mojitos
and tequila gold with orange and cinnamon are a treat.

La Bodega Flamenca

*Šmeralova 5 (233 374 075). Metro
Vltavská.* **Open** 4pm-1am Mon-Thur,
Sun; 4pm-3am Fri, Sat. **$**. **Spanish**.
Map p154 B3 ⑥

The easily missed entrance to this cellar tapas bar, two doors north of
Fraktal, conceals a perpetual sangria
party. Owner Ilona oversees the bar,
serving up tapas such as marinated
olives and garlic mushrooms. Bench-
style seats line the walls and fill up fast
and, in true Spanish style, things only
really start hotting up after 1am.

La Creperie

*Janovského 4 (220 878 040). Metro
Vltavská.* **Open** 9am-11pm Mon-Sat;
9am-10pm Sun. **$**. **Crêperie**. **Map**
p155 E3 ⑦

This French-owned niche serves large
crêpes, both sweet and savoury, for a
pittance. Seating here is in a comfortable
but closet-sized basement, so it's probably not ideal for office parties. Above
average wine list, and fresh croissants.

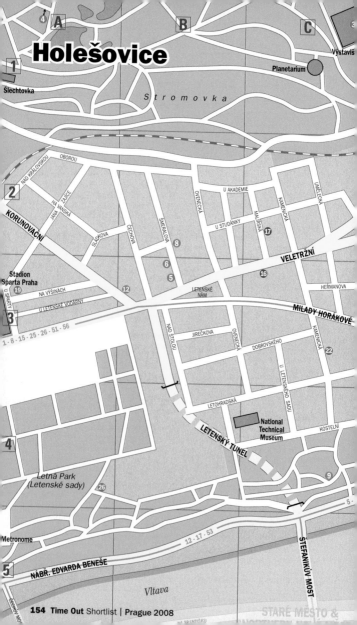

Holešovice

A B C

1

Šlechtovka

Výstaviš

Planetarium

S t r o m o v k a

OBOROU

NAD KRÁLOVSKOU

U AKADEMIE

OVENECKÁ

UMĚLECKÁ

2

HA VANSKÁ

JANA ZAJÍCE

KORUNOVAČNÍ

SLOKOVA

ČECHOVA

ŠMERALOVA

U STUDÁNKY

MALÍRSKÁ

KAMENICKÁ

17

8

VELETRŽNÍ

6

16

5

HERMANOVA

Stadion
Sparta Praha

NA VÝŠINÁCH

12

LETENSKÉ
NÁM.

19

U SPARTY

U LETENSKÉ VODÁRNY

MILADY HORÁKOVÉ

3

1 · 8 · 15 · 25 · 26 · 51 · 56

JIREČKOVA

NAD ŠTOLOU

OVENECKÁ

DOBROVSKÉHO

KAMENICKÁ

22

U LETENSKÉHO SADU

LETOHRADSKÁ

KOSTELNÍ

National
Technical
Museum

LETENSKÝ TUNEL

4

9

Letná Park
(Letenské sady)

26

Metronome

12 · 17 · 53

5 ·

ŠTEFÁNIKŮV MOST

5

NÁBŘ. EDVARDA BENEŠE

Vltava

STARÉ MĚSTO &

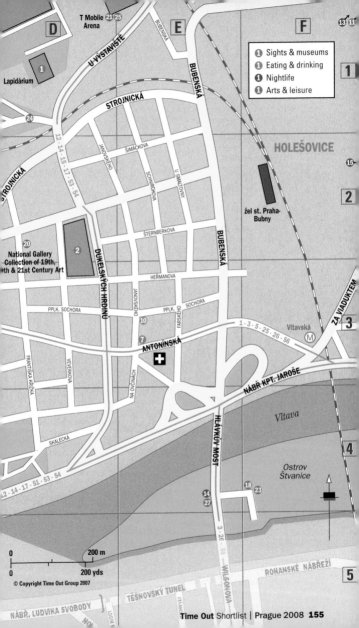

D

T Mobile Arena 21 25

U VÝSTAVIŠTĚ

E

BUBENSKA

BUBENSKÁ

F

13 11

1

Lapidárium

1

24

STROJNICKÁ

❶ Sights & museums
❶ Eating & drinking
❶ Nightlife
❶ Arts & leisure

STROJNICKÁ

12 · 14 · 15 · 17 · 53 · 54

JANOVSKÉHO

ŠIMÁČKOVA

SCHNIRCHOVA

U SMALTOVNY

HOLEŠOVICE

15

2

žel st. Praha-Bubny

20

ŠTERNBERKOVA

National Gallery Collection of 19th, th & 21st Century Art

2

DUKELSKÝCH HRDINŮ

BUBENSKÁ

HEŘMANOVA

JANOVSKÉHO

PPLK. SOCHORA

PPLK. SOCHORA

FARSKÉHO

SOCHORA

1 · 3 · 5 · 25 · 26 · 56

Vltavská

Ⓜ

ZA VIADUKTEM

3

10

7

ANTONÍNSKÁ

✚

FRANTIŠKA KŘÍŽKA

VEVERKOVA

NA OVČÍNÁCH

NÁBŘ. KPT. JAROŠE

SKALECKÁ

Vltava

2 · 14 · 17 · 51 · 53 · 54

HLÁVKŮV MOST

4

Ostrov Štvanice

14
27

18 23

3 · 26

200 m
0

0   200 yds

© Copyright Time Out Group 2007

WILSONOVA

ROHANSKÉ NÁBŘEŽÍ

5

TĚŠNOVSKÝ TUNEL

NÁBŘ. LUDVÍKA SVOBODY

Le Tram

Šmeralova 12 (233 370 359). Metro Vltavská. **Open** 8pm-6am daily. **$.** **Bar.** Map p154 B2 **8**

A French-owned hole-in-the wall made up of old (you guessed it) tram parts. Other than that, it's the same cheap beer and Cuba libres as everywhere else.

Letenský zámeček

Letenské sady 341 (in Letná Park) (233 375 604/www.letenskyzamecek. cz). Metro Hradčanská. **Open** *Beer garden* 11am-11pm daily. *Restaurants* 11am-11.30pm daily. **$$. Czech.** Map p154 C4 **9**

This leafy enclave on the hill above the Vltava is arguably the city's finest summer beer garden. A local crowd gathers under the chestnut trees for cheap beer in plastic cups late into the evening, every evening. The adjoining Brasserie Ullman and Restaurant Belcredi have gone upmarket with modern designer interiors, a dressy crowd, and excellent Bernard beer on tap.

Ouky Douky

NEW *Janovského 14 (266 711 531/ www.oukydouky.cz). Metro Vltavská.* **Open** 8am-midnight daily. **$. Café.** Map p155 E3 **10**

A bookstore café without much to read for English speakers, this place is the original location of the Globe Bookstore and Coffeehouse. Owners tried to copy its formula, but not very successfully.

Pivovar U Bulovky

Bulovka 17, Libeň (284 840 650). Metro Palmovka, then tram 10, 15, 24, 25. **Open** 10am-midnight daily. **Pub.** Map p155 F1 **11**

František Richter's pub, though well beyond the Holešovice district borders, is known to beer afficionados far and wide for its excellent microbrew beers, home-made sausage and his unique flavouring inspirations. The Friday night blues bands don't hurt either.

Un Chien Andalou

Korunovační 4 (731 221 167). Metro Hradčanská, then tram 1, 8, 15. **Open** 7pm-5am daily. **Bar.** Map p154 B3 **12**

Cool, dark and sofa-filled, this plush little place is a local secret, where live bands occasionally perform, usually as iconoclastic as the bar staff. Decent cocktails and with a wall-to-wall decadent atmosphere.

Nightlife

Cross Club

NEW *Plynární 23 (736 535 053/www. crossclub.cz). Metro Nádraží Holešovice.* **Open** 2pm-3am Mon-Fri; 4pm-5am Sat, Sun. Map p155 F1 **13**

This centre for music, film, dance and drink is a colourful, graffiti-filled space for just about anything. Tough to find, but worth it for roots value and the Bohemian company it keeps.

Face to Face

Ostrov Štvanice 1125 (no phone). Metro Náměstí Republiky. **Open** 8pm-6am Thur-Sat. **Admission** 100 Kč. Map p155 E4 **14**

In an ugly exhibition hall you have to reach by foot, this place can have fun parties for grown-ups in an only-in-Prague setting but it's generally for teens looking to get wasted and score.

Mecca

U Průhonu 3 (283 870 522/www. mecca.cz). Metro Vltavská. **Open** *Club* 8pm-2am Mon-Thur, Sun; 8pm-6am Fri, Sat. *Restaurant* 10am-11pm Mon-Thur; 10am-6am Fri; 8pm-6am Sat. *Concerts* 9pm. **Admission** 100-300 Kč. Map p155 F2 **15**

A comfortably cool space in semi-industrial Holešovice, Mecca has two levels, three bars and hundreds of loyal house and techno fans who turn out in style to catch their fave DJs. Founder Roman Řezníček always puts on a class act, lending longevity and character to this club that many others lack.

Misch Masch

Veletržní 61 (603 222 227/www. mischmasch.cz). Metro Vltavská. **Open** 8pm-4am Thur-Sat; 10pm-4am Fri, Sat. Map p154 C3 **16**

The district's biggest and brashest disco, but much changed since the

National Gallery p153

days when it was Disco Letná; there's a buzzy scene here that goes in for all-night dancing and drinking to excess amid arty surrounds and pseudo-intellectual conversation (shouted).

Wakata

Malířská 14 (233 370 518/www.wakata. cz). Metro Vltavská. **Open** 5pm-3am Mon-Thur; 5pm-5am Fri, Sat. **Map** p154 C2 ⑰

Bar stools are made of motorcycle seats, and a stoned crew of servers and DJs comprise the staff, but Wakata is open late and has a truly anarchic neighbourhood feel.

Arts & leisure

I. ČLTK

Ostrov Štvanice 38 (222 316 317/ www.cltk.cz). Metro Florenc or Vltavská. **Open** 7am-midnight daily. **Rates** 300-600 Kč/hr. **Map** p155 F4 ⑱

Ten outdoor clay courts, three of which are floodlit, plus sparkling indoor facilities (four hard courts, two clay courts), newly reconstructed since 2002's floods. Booking essential.

AC Sparta Praha

Toyota Arena, Milady Horákové 98, (220 570 323/www.sparta.cz). Metro Hradčanská. **Admission** *European games* 400-900 Kč. *League games* 60-160 Kč. **Map** p154 A3 ⑲

Sparta is the team to beat in Czech football. It's comparatively poor in Europe, but this hasn't stopped it from pulling off some mighty upsets against wealthier opponents. Their 18,500-capacity stadium, aka Letná, is the country's best.

Divadlo Alfred ve Dvoře

Františka Křížka 36 (233 376 997/ www.alfredvedvore.cz). Metro Vltavská. **Open** *Box office* 1hr before performance or buy tickets from Celetná Theatre box office. **Tickets** 130 Kč; 80 Kč students. **Map** p155 D2 ⑳

A small, modern building constructed in a residential courtyard. Physical, non-verbal and experimental theatre as well as some dance and mime artists.

HC Sparta Praha

T-Mobile Arena, Za Elektárnou 419 (266 727 443/www.hcsparta.cz). Tram 5, 12, 14, 15, 17. **Open** *Box*

Fraktal p153

The new cultural quarter

Cross Club

To anyone picking their way through what looks like industrial wasteland in the Holešovice district, in order to find the Cross Club (on the west side of the thoroughfare Plynarni, two blocks east of the Nadrazi Holesovice metro station's south exit; see p156), one thing's apparent: this area has an edgy, arty vibe that can't be matched by any other quarter. You'll spot the said club by the incredible array of car parts welded together to form canopies. Whole teams of welders have scoured salvage yards for months to come up with the steel rebar and engine blocks used to create the weirdest pub garden in town. You wouldn't be surprised to find the Terminator sitting here, just waiting to blast someone away for saying the wrong thing.

For all that, it's a remarkably friendly, inclusive kind of art bar, as you discover when you venture inside. The only way to get a drink (generally cheap beer or wine in a plastic cup) is to wander through the dark corridors within. Some rooms look like submarine interiors, complete with frames forming two levels of seating in a narrow passage. Others have perforated walls, the holes formed by truck wheels, through which you can glimpse a DJ or chatting couples in the next area.

And Holešovice's art collections are as impressive as its bars these days. The National Gallery's modern art space at Veletržní palac (p153) – the former trade fair building, and a wonder of functionalist design – features a newly organised floor of Czech industrial designs from the previous century, from chic little typewriters and cocktail siphons to designs for planes and bridges. Czech typography, which is admired worldwide, is also on display here.

Private galleries are blooming too, with places like Hunt Kastner artworks (p160) setting the pace with provocative shows, such as Veronika Bromová's 'HaHathor's Handbag' and the Viennafair international contemporary art show. This gallery also sponsors the annual Art Wall, a project of Prague's Centre for Contemporary Art, in which major streets are lined with traffic-stopping images.

PRAGUE BY AREA

Face to Face p156

office 7.30-11am, noon-4pm Mon-Thur; 7.30am-noon Fri. **Admission** 50-100 Kč. **Map** p155 D1 ㉑
Sparta's home ice rink was state-of-the-art when it was built; today it's showing signs of wear and tear. The team itself, though, is well-financed and always competitive. The large arena doesn't really come alive till the play-offs. Tickets can be bought in advance from the box office at entrance 30 or online through the Ticketpro agency.

Hunt Kastner Artworks
Kamenická 22 (233 376 259/www.hunt kastner.com). Metro Vltavská. **Open** noon-5pm Thur, Fri or by appointment. **Admission** free. **Map** p154 C3 ㉒
This private gallery was established to nurture the careers of a stable of over a dozen Czech contemporary artists like Tomáš Vanik and Michael Thelenová, while at the same time helping to find collectors for their works and encourage development of the fledgling art market.

Mystic Skate Park
Ostrov Štvanice 38 (222 232 027/www.mysticskates.cz). Metro Florenc or

Vltavská. **Open** *Jan-Apr, Oct-Dec* noon-9pm daily. *May-Sept* 9am-10pm daily. **Rates** *BMX, in-line skates* 80-120 Kč. *Skateboard* 50-80 Kč. **Map** p155 F4 ㉓
Popular skate park on Štvanice Island in the Vltava, which also hosts the high-profile Mystic Skate Cup. Tickets for the event sell out fast.

Stromovka
U Výstaviště & Dukelských hrdinů. Metro Nádraží Holešovice, then tram 5, 12, 14. **Map** p155 D1 ㉔
The most central of Prague's large parks. After the initial sprint to avoid the Výstaviště crowds, you can have the meadows to yourself. See if you can hear the language of birds that alchemist John Dee claimed to understand here.

T-Mobile Arena
Výstaviště, Za elektrárnou 319, Holešovice (266 727 411). Metro Nádraží Holešovice. **Map** p155 D1/E1 ㉕
A skating rink when not a concert hall, this barn has all the acoustics you'd expect from such a place. But it's the only indoor spot in Prague that can accommodate thousands.

Tenisový klub Slavia Praha
Letenské sady 32 (233 374 033). Metro Hradčanská. **Open** *Jan-Mar, Nov, Dec* (indoor only) 7am-10pm daily. *Apr-Oct* 7am-9pm daily. **Rates** *Indoor* 600 Kč/hr. *Outdoor* 200-250 Kč/hr. **Map** p154 A4 ㉖
Eight floodlit outdoor clay courts, plus a tennis bubble for the winter months in Letná park, with a handy beer garden and grill next door.

Zimní stadion Štvanice
Ostrov Štvanice 1125 (602 623 449/www.stvanice.cz). Metro Florenc or Vltavská. **Open** 10.30am-noon Mon; 10.30am-noon, 4.30-6pm Tue, Thur; 10.30am-noon, 8-9.30pm Wed, Fri; 9-10.30am, 4-5.30pm, 8-9.30pm Sat; 9-10.30am, 2.30-4pm, 8-9.30pm Sun. **Admission** 60 Kč; 80 Kč skate rental. **Map** p155 E4 ㉗
This rickety-looking structure houses two rinks, with generous opening hours, on an island in the Vltava. Bring a Czech friend, little English spoken.

PRAGUE BY AREA

Essentials

Stay at the Corinthia Towers Hotel, and a unique and breathtaking view of the Golden City is part of every experience. Enjoy the height of hospitality in your room, conference, restaurant or even the rooftop swimming pool.

Upgrade your view of Prague.

Aria Hotel p167

Hotels

Some 100 new hotels have opened in Prague in each of the past five years, meaning two things: demand is high, and an awful lot of people could be learning the trade on your dime. Add to that the fact that many of the new ones are aimed at the elite, from the clearly capable new Hotel Mandarin Oriental, to the many billing themselves as 'design hotels', and it's clear that spending what you would in Paris doesn't always mean four-star treatment. The upside, of course, is that with so much competition for your custom, occupancy rates are often too low for the owner's taste and deals abound if you know where to look. Web-only deals are frequently posted on hotel sites and a phone call may well turn up a great weekend special not mentioned in their official rates. Adventure travellers, of course, can always scare up a spare room with a family or in basic pensions, which agencies like Stop City (www.stopcity.cz) specialise in, while a newer generation of apartment bookers such as www.pragueapartment.cz carries more homely places with cooking facilities and services like laptop and mobile phone rental.

Also remember that you can often score an arched room in a restored palace, characterful villa or 17th-century inn for about the same rate as the Best Western if you book ahead. Service may not be what Prague's famous for, but that stunning architecture is. Family facilities are better than ever too, with babysitting services or free rates for kids who share your room becoming more and more common.

Visit Prague all year around and enjoy our boutique hotels at Lesser Quarter

Only few minutes walk from Charles Bridge and Prague Castle the Aria and Golden Well hotels are unique gems.

What would be Prague without music? Modern music themed Aria orchestrates your visit with tailor made programmes, creative cuisine and composition of 52 unique rooms for unique guests.

With 20 rooms only the Golden Well is smaller in size but not in service. More traditional in style this Renaissance house and former residence of Bohemian King Rudolf 2nd is a perfect hideaway.

Visit our websites our contact us directly for reservation or more information.

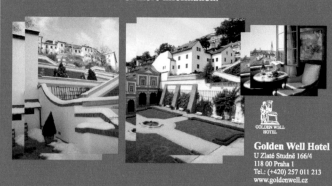

Money matters

Many hotels quote their rates in euros and, though the Czech Republic is not yet in the euro zone, will happily take them. Note that if you pay in Czech crowns, the price often won't be calculated at the official exchange rate and you'll take a hit. Many places, however, offer discounts for cash, so it may be worth proffering euro notes if you don't mind carrying them.

Many hotels quote room prices exclusive of VAT. Always check.

Hradčany & western Mala Strana

Dům U velké boty

Vlašská 30 (257 532 088/www.dum uvelkeboty.cz). Metro Malostranská. **$$**.
The Rippl family won back their 1470 Malá Strana house from the state after 1989 and, fortunately for their writer and artist regulars, opened the House at the Big Boot to guests to fund restoration. Now it's a prime bargain and the most rewarding place to stay in the area. There's no sign, just a buzzer marked Rippl, and rooms decked out in gorgeous period furniture. Family suites may include a kitchen. Breakfast is an extra 200 Kč and there's Wi-Fi connection.

Golden Horse House

Úvoz 8 (257 532 700/www.gold horse.cz). Tram 22, 23. **$**.
Prime location meets low price in these ten rooms, all en suite. Service is amiable, breakfast is available for an extra 100 Kč, and it's next door to a hip pub (U zavěšenyho kafe), where veteran Prague musos, scribes and actors hang out. You can also cook on site.

Hotel Neruda

Nerudova 44 (257 535 556/www. hotelneruda-praha.cz). Metro Malostranská. **$$$$**.
In a cosy 1348 building, designers have meshed old-world charm with an open, airy feel. Czech star designer Bořek

SHORTLIST

Best new
- Hotel Mandarin Oriental (p169)
- Riverside Hotel (p173)
- Alchymist Hotel Residence (p167)
- Courtyard by Marriott (p178)

Best for hipsters
- Hotel Josef (p174)
- Hotel Savoy (p167)

Best palace stays
- Le Palais (p179)
- Pachtův Palace (p175)

Most stellar restaurants
- Four Seasons: Allegro (p173)
- Prague Hilton: Czech House (p179)
- Hotel Schwaiger: Bistrot de Marlene (p179)

Best for families
- Mövenpick Hotel (p170)
- Dorint Don Giovanni (p178)

Cheap as chips
- U Šuterů (p178)
- Pension Accord (p175)

Most charming atmosphere
- Hotel Černy Slon (p173)
- Residence Řetězová (p176)

Superior pensions
- Dům U velké boty (p165)
- Romantik Hotel U raka (p167)

Happening hostels
- Miss Sophie's Prague (p179)
- Sir Toby's Hostel (p179)

Budget style
- Hotel Abri (p178)
- Hotel Elite (p177)

All-round winners
- Aria (p178)
- Four Seasons (p173)
- Julian (p170)
- U krále Karla (p167)

ESSENTIALS

U krále Karla

Šipek is in charge of an expansion that was at press time adding 43 rooms to the present 20. Service is attentive and friendly and you're smack bang on the main lane leading up to Prague Castle.

Hotel Questenberk

Úvoz 15 (220 407 600/www. questenberk.cz). Tram 22, 23. **$$$**.
Recently converted from a neglected monastery (there's still an imposing stone crucifix at the entrance), the 30 rooms of this quaint Baroque building, just 500 metres from the Castle, are a good bit too comfortable for monks. They're not a posh as you'd expect for the price, though, and staff, while enthusiastic, are still learning the ropes. An only-in-Prague feel.

Hotel Savoy

Keplerova 6 (224 302 430/www. hotel-savoy.cz). Tram 22, 23. **$$$$**.
First impressions are of a quiet, traditional competence, as evidenced by the library, fireplace and gliding service. Then you notice Robert Palmer in the elevator and spot a Hollywood star in the breakfast room (or, if you're lucky, in the hot tub). The plush, if not huge, 61 rooms keep the biz and showbiz crowd coming back.

Romantik Hotel U raka

Černínská 10 (220 511 100/www. romantikhotel-uraka.cz). Tram 22, 23. **$$$**.
Booking well ahead is the only way to land one of these six rooms, which date back to 1739. It's a small, rustic pension suited to couples with time to spare and located on a quiet Hradčany backstreet within earshot of the bells of the Loreto. Unique but also backed by polished service. Enchanting breakfast room/reading room with brick hearth. No children under 12.

U Červeného Lva

Nerudova 41 (257 533 832/www. starshotelsprague.com). Metro Malostranská. **$$$**.
There are few small hotels on the royal route leading up to the Castle that can boast such authentic 17th-century

decor, including colourful handpainted vaulted ceilings. This reconstructed burgher's house of just eight rooms provides guests with a sense of Renaissance Prague but service more adequate than standout.

U krále Karla

Úvoz 4 (257 532 869/www.romantic hotels.cz). Metro Malostranská. **$$$**.
Solid oak furnishings, painted vaulted ceilings, stained-glass windows and Baroque treasures lend this 19-room inn the feel of an aristocratic country house, even though it was once owned by the Benedictine order. There are discounts for cash payment and a Bohemian restaurant on site.

Eastern Malá Strana & Smíchov

Alchymist Hotel Residence

NEW *Tržiště 19, Malá Strana (257 286 011/www.alchymisthotelresidence. com). Metro Malostranská.* **$$$$**.
Humbly ensconced in the Baroque U Ježíšek Palace, the Alchymist works its magic on more than your wallet. Mottled walls, vaulted ceilings, frescoes, four-poster beds and spoiling service are complemented by one of Prague's hottest new wellness centres, with Balinese massage, a pool and a sushi bar. The US embassy is right next door.

Aria Hotel

Tržiště 9, Malá Strana (225 334 111/www.ariahotel.net). Metro Malostranská. **$$$$**.
The Aria has broken new ground and set the standard for lux boutique hostelry in Prague, with its amenities, service and location. The oddly shaped rooms (the building was previously a post office) are classically designed and jammed with audiophile toys; computers, DVD players and serious speakers are standard, and each room is dedicated to a musician, whose biog and songs are on your hard drive, and there's a music library (great books

and DVDs too) in the lobby. The roof terrace may offer the best view afforded anywhere in the city. Request a room facing the Baroque gardens. Free airport shuttle, gym and a much-lauded lobby piano café/bar.

Best Western Kampa Hotel

Všehrdova 16, Malá Strana (257 404 200/www.euroagentur.cz). Metro Malostranská. **$$$**.
Located on a quiet backstreet in Malá Strana, the Kampa Hotel has retained its 17th-century architecture and style through recent renovations, and rooms are elegantly arranged. The vaulted 'Knights Hall' dining room and adjacent pub will be a huge hit with frustrated knights. Fret not for lack of the grail, the 60 Kč beers aren't worth it anyway.

Hostel Sokol

Nosticova 2, Malá Strana (257 007 397). Metro Malostranská. **$**.
Find Hostel Sokol (the entrance is via the yard behind the Sokol sports centre) and you've found the starving student travel nerve centre of Prague. It has a great terrace for beer-sipping with a view. Many bunks are in a large gymnasium. Not far from the Castle and Charles Bridge. Breakfast not included. Book ahead via phone, or email hostelsocool@seznam.cz.

Hotel Mandarin Oriental

NEW *Nebovidská 1, Malá Strana (233 088 888/www.mandarinoriental. com/prague). Tram 6, 9, 12, 20.* **$$$$**.
The hotel event of 2006 was the opening of this 99-room gem three blocks from Charles Bridge. The former 14th-century monastery has custom rooms, a spa with holistic treatments and a grand restaurant with fine Asian and continental fare. Modern and high-tech yet cosy rooms with royal blue accents. Excellent service.

Hotel U Kříže

Újezd 20, Malá Strana (257 312 451/ www.ukrize.com). 6, 9, 12, 20, 22, 23 tram. **$$**.

Hotel Mandarin Oriental p169

Quaint enough, with 22 pleasant rooms, and great value for money. Strategically located, being across the street from Petřín hill, a quick walk from Kampa Island, one tram stop to the National Theatre, two stops to Malostranská náměstí, and just a few feet from Bohemia Bagel. Ask for a room facing the atrium; those facing the hill tend to get rattled by the street trams. Free coffee and cake can be taken in the lobby bar from noon to 6pm. The place is also pet friendly.

Hotel U páva

U Lužického semináře 32, Malá Strana (257 533 360/www.romantichotels.cz). Metro Malostranská. **$$$**.
The dark oak ceilings and crystal chandeliers don't synthesise as well here as at U krále Karla (p167; also owned by Karel Klubal), where the elegance is seamless, but the location is ideal, in a serene corner of Malá Strana. Suites 201, 301, 401 and 402 look on to the Castle. Some rooms are not accessible

ESSENTIALS

by lift, so if you need it, say so. An old-world restaurant, massage service, sauna and no-smoking rooms have kept the Peacock on the veteran travellers' lists for years.

Hotel U Zlaté Studně

U Zlaté studně 4, Malá Strana (257 011 213/www.zlatastudna.cz). Metro Malostranská. **$$$.**

The 20-room inn is nestled on a secluded street on a Malá Strana hill below the Castle. Rooms feature wood floors and ceilings and stylish furniture. If you could use a soak, ask for one of the rooms with a huge tub. Breakfast on a terrace goes with a stellar view of the city. The view from the indoor dining area is tremendous.

Hotel William

Hellichova 5, Smíchov (257 320 242/ www.euroagentur.cz). 6, 10, 12, 20 tram. **$$.**

Opened in 2001, this inconspicuous hotel of 42 rooms has a great location, a quick walk from the funicular up Petřín hill, and just one tram stop from Malostranské náměstí, the main square of the district. Decorators went a wee bit overboard trying for a 'castle feel' but rooms are comfortable and good value. Ask for one on the back side of the hotel, away from the noise of the trams.

Janáček Palace Hotel

Janáčkovo Nabřeži 19, Malá Strana (226 201 910). Tram 6, 9, 22, 23. **$$$.**

This 17-apartment 'palace' has an impressive riverside location and gabled exterior but rooms don't really live up to the name, comfortable and airy as they are. More spent on design and decor would make this exceptional building more exceptional but it still offers a taste of living well in Bohemia and the three-bedroom apartments have jacuzzis.

Julian

Elišky Peškové 11, Smíchov (257 311 150/www.julian.cz). Tram 6, 9, 12, 20. **$$.**

A bit of luxury in Smíchov, the Julian features a drawing room with fireplace and library and a non-smoking lobby bar, a rarity in Prague. Room decor is light and understated and there are apartments with kitchenettes as well as a family room, complete with toys. Not quite in the centre, but an easy tram or metro ride away from Old Town. Airport/railway station shuttle, gym, sauna and massage are all to hand.

Mövenpick Hotel

Mozartova 1, Smíchov (257 151 111/ www.movenpick-prague.com). Metro Anděl/tram 4, 7, 9. **$$.**

The not so easily accessible location is more than set off by the surrounding beauty and excellent Mövenpick-standard service. Actually two buildings (the executive wing accessible only by cable car), it's family-friendly too and has fine dining restaurants frequented by many Praguesters. Rooms are fairly standard-issue, but deep discounts are available off-season and a verdant park is next door. Good concierge and business services plus babysitting.

Pension Dientzenhofer

Nosticova 2, Malá Strana (257 311 319/www.dientzenhofer.cz). Metro Malostranská. **$$.**

This always-booked inn facing Kampa Island has a quiet courtyard and back garden that offer a lovely respite in the midst of Malá Strana. The nine rooms are not tremendously posh, but are bright, and the staff are friendly – something still not standard in Prague. Baroque architect star Kilian Ignaz Dientzenhofer was born in the 16th-century building and his work fills this quarter of the city.

Residence Nosticova

Nosticova 1, Malá Strana (257 312 513/www.nosticova.com). Metro Malostranská. **$$$.**

A classy little nook for those who plan to stay a while, this recently modernised Baroque 'residence' is on a quiet lane just off Kampa Island. The ten suites range from ample to capacious and come with antique furniture, huge bathrooms and fully equipped kitchenettes. Two have working fireplaces and one a rooftop terrace. If you

Cutting-edge cribs

Josef

Hotel Josef

One benefit of Prague jumping straight into the present day after decades of neglect is that an awful lot of radical hotel makeovers incorporate the latest technology, ideas and innovations. Guests of the city's hotels are the winners in this mass-scale makeover, as those staying at places like Nové Město's **987 Prague Hotel** (p177) will attest. For rates not out of line with ordinary places, visitors here find themselves surrounded by Philippe Starck interiors that impart a feeling of surfing the city's most exciting aesthetic developments.

Which is not to say that all the artistic conceptions work smoothly, of course; places like the **Arcotel Hotel Teatrino** (p178), in the otherwise crumbling Žižkov

district, stand out like a sore thumb, and could be accused of imposing an aesthetic on guests who'd probably just prefer a good night's sleep. The Czech nationalist art that fills this space might resonate well with locals, but this admittedly careful restoration was probably misdirected if the owners were hoping to draw in foreign visitors.

Most newly redone hotels go for a latest-thing modernist look, which can be risky territory; it's a rare designer who gets the balance right between looking great and being comfortable. The ideal is, however, achieved with panache at **Hotel Josef** (p174) in the Old Jewish Quarter; the interior, by London-based Czech architect Eva Jiřičná, is still a sensation five years after winning a place on the Condé Nast Hot List. Josef's older sister hotel, the **Maximilian** (Hastalská 14, 225 303 111, www.maximilianhotel. com), reopened in 2005 after a designer makeover of its own.

Hotel Aria (p167) and **Hotel Mandarin Oriental** (p169), both established by experienced and sophisticated global enterprises, also succeed marvelously, the former with jazzy accents and a colour palette courtesy of design specialists Spatium.

The **Hotel Neruda** (p165), meanwhile, in the shadow of Prague Castle, incorporates touches by Bořek Šípek, the local celeb glass designer who did Václav Havel's presidential office. Yet this place blends right in with the old rowhouses on Nerudova and works in harmony with the nearby Baroque-era buildings.

ESSENTIALS

don't feel like cooking your own, continental breakfast is served for an extra 9 euros. Sushi bar, massages and sauna add to the decadence.

Rezidence Lundborg

U Lužického semináře 3, Malá Strana (257 011 911/www.lundborg.se). Metro Malostranská. **$$$**.
With a prime view of Charles Bridge, and on the site of the old Juditin Bridge, this Scandinavian-owned hotel of 13 suites exudes luxury and charm. A prime example of the executive residence/hotel hybrid that's spread throughout Prague, Lundborg pampers stressed guests with apartments that successfully blend reconstructed Renaissance with business amenities. A major splashout, but every need is anticipated, from wine cellar to arranging golf programmes in Karlštejn or Konopiště resorts during summer.

Riverside Hotel

NEW *Janáčkovo nábřeží 15, Malá Strana (234 705 155/www.riverside prague.com). Metro Malostranská.* **$$$**.
A luxe little retreat that's already a fave with actors seeking an escape from the bright lights while shooting in Prague, this gem of the MaMaison group is ensconced in a lovely Baroque townhouse whose east-facing rooms overlook the Vltava. Wood floors, spacious bathrooms, Wi-Fi in the lobby, DVD library and other extras helped make Riverside an award-winner in its first year.

U Karlova mostu

Na Kampě 15, Malá Strana (257 531 430/www.archibald.cz). Metro Malostranská. **$$**.
Formerly named Na Kampě 15, the inn named At the Charles Bridge in Czech affords fine views of the bridge and Old Town, yet it's situated at a sufficient distance to offer peace and quiet. The former 15th-century tavern that brewed one of the city's pioneering beers still has homely rooms with wood floors, exposed beams and garret windows but with modern furnishings. The two cellar pubs and the beer garden out the back offer Czech trad grub and well-tapped beer.

Staré Město & northern Nové Město

Cloister Inn

Konviktská 14 (224 211 020/www. cloister-inn.com). Metro Národní třída. **$$**.
Resting behind the cheaper Pension Unitas, the Cloister Inn has attentive staff, a great location, good prices and a nearby house full of nuns should you need redemption. Bright, cheery rooms and a lobby computer with free internet, plus free coffee and tea and a lending library. Prices have risen of late, but the website offers deals.

Floor Hotel

Na Příkopě 13 (234 076 300/www. floorhotel.cz) Metro Můstek. **$$**.
An affordable addition to Prague's marquee shopping promenade but the venture capitalists kept it simple with 43 rooms over four storeys, half of which offer traditional luxury, the other half sleek and modern decor (jacuzzis optional). The upscale Italian eaterie has an impressive menu, and there's a large, crystal chandeliered conference room for the business crowd.

Four Seasons Hotel Prague

Veleslavínova 2A (221 427 000/ www.fourseasons.com/prague). Metro Staroměstská. **$$$$**.
The only fault to be found with the Four Seasons is that it's perhaps too perfect. While it's a seamless melding of restored Gothic, Baroque, Renaissance and neoclassical buildings, guests will be hardpressed to catch even a whiff of musty history. Of course, there's no shortage of that just outside the walls, so you might as well enjoy the luxurious surroundings and service. Vista seekers will want to reserve the top-flight rooms with sweeping views of Prague Castle and Charles Bridge. In-room massage and pedicures go a long way to restoring Castle-worn lower extremities.

Hotel Černý Slon

Týnská 1 (222 321 521/www.hotel cernyslon.cz). Metro Staroměstská. **$$**.

Hotel bars

In the glory days, before World War II changed the course of the Czech lands forever – and still further back, under the Habsburg Empire – Prague had as many grand bars as any cosmopolitan European capital, many of them in hotels. Such bars have experienced a resurgence since the Velvet Revolution.

The SAS Radisson, off Wenceslas Square, was once known as the Alcron, hosting jazz stars like Louis Armstrong. Neglected until 1989, it's now an art deco shrine with trios playing in the Be-Bop Lounge, where great gin is stocked. The Courtyard by Marriott may only have standard Marriott decor, but its collection of bourbon is amazing.

The Aria Hotel's lounge, with drinks and cuisine run by one of the city's best restaurateurs, Nils Jebens, has done more to revive the tradition of decadence. Called Coda, it's bathed in suffused light, has glamourous servers and does a great breakfast if you happen to be rolling in from an all-nighter.

The smoke-free Yasmin Hotel bar goes for a more modern twist, with designer plastic seats and a Noodle Bar concept. Time will tell whether this one draws the right crowds but the buzz was hot at press time. The Mandarin Oriental's Barego is another a sleek affair, with leather bar perches, Thai fish cakes and fresh drinks like the cumquatina and the raspberry breakfast martini, surely something uniquely appropriate to Prague. *Na zdraví*!

With an incredible location in the shadow of the Tyn church just off Old Town Square, this cosy 16-room inn is ensconced in a 14th-century building that's on the UNESCO heritage list. Gothic stone arches and wooden floors go with the smallish, but comfortable rooms laid out with basic amenities. Windows look out on the cobbled mews in the quieter part of Old Town, although still offering with a constant parade of characters.

Hotel Josef
Rybná 20 (221 700 111/www.hoteljosef. com). Metro Náměstí republiky. **$$$**.
Definitely the hippest (and maybe the only) designer hotel in Old Town, the Josef opened in 2002. Flash modernist interiors and unique fabrics and glass bathrooms (superior-class rooms only) are the work of London-based designer Eva Jiřičná. All this in the thick of the historic centre, with the top-floor rooms in the 'Pink House' having the best views. The fitness centre's very basic and there's no real designer bar, alas, just the overlit lobby one, but you do feel sleek here. Kids under 6 are free.

Hotel Mejstřík Praha
Jakubská 5 (224 800 055/www. hotelmejstrik.cz). Metro Náměstí Republiky. **$$$**.
This hotel, handily located in the heart of Old Town, is now back in the hands of the family that founded it in 1924. Individually decorated rooms are a hybrid of ubiquitous modern hotel decor and 1920s style. Art deco elements and wood trim are a nice touch and corner rooms offer great vantages for spying on streetlife and gables. No-smoking, disabled-adapted rooms and a reasonable trad Czech restaurant.

Hotel Paříž Praha
U Obecního domu 1 (222 195 195/ www.hotel-pariz.cz). Metro Náměstí Republiky. **$$$**.
If any hotel captures the spirit of Prague's *belle époque*, it's this one. Immortalised in Bohumil Hrabal's novel *I Served the King of England* (the film version of which was released in 2006)

Hotel U páva p169

the Paříž is ageing with remarkable grace. Guests who are weary of cookie-cutter hotels will appreciate the patina of the historic rooms and carefully preserved jazz-age dining room and café. Money no object? Try the Royal Tower Suite, with its 360-degree view of the city. Nice Wellness-spa centre too.

Hotel U Prince

Staroměstské náměstí 29 (224 213 807/www.hoteluprince.cz). Metro Staroměstská. **$$$**.
An authentic slice of history smack in the centre of Old Town Square. Opened in 2001, the hotel is a reconstruction of a 12th-century estate and boasts huge rooms with antiques and individually designed canopy beds and armoires. Marble bathrooms are nicely decadent too. There are several eateries, including a seafood cavern, a rooftop cafe with a dazzling view of Prague landmarks. Neighbouring restaurants offer better value and privacy, but U Prince is still good for breakfast or a cocktail.

Hotel U Tří Bubnů

U radnice 10 (224 214 855/www. utribubnu.cz). Metro Staroměstská. **$$**.
Just 50 metres from Old Town Square, this is another place out to prove you can just about sleep within the landmark sights of Prague. Rooms have few frills but have a nice vibe thanks to the wood furniture and ceilings. The attic suites are huge – perfect for a family. Quiet, despite the location, due to thick ancient walls. Service is worthy of the days of old as well.

Inter-Continental Praha

Náměstí Curieovych 5 (296 631 111/ www.prague.intercontinental.com). Metro Staroměstská. **$$$$**.
With 32 years as Prague's flagship for decadence, the Inter-Continental Praha may at last be getting it right. While visual traces of communist design were expunged during a $50-million refurbishment in the 1990s, only recently does the transformation seem to have taken hold in earnest, with courteous service and no reminders of

ESSENTIALS

the C-word in sight. All rooms have a dataport for your laptop and the entire hotel has Wi-Fi. The negatives? One side of the hotel faces a garish neon-lighted casino, and they hit you up for an extra 50 euros or so for a room facing the river. Kids eat for free and the fitness centre's one of Prague's best.

Pachtův Palace

Karolíny Světlé 34 (234 705 111/ www.pachtuvpalace.com). Metro Národní třída. $$$$.
With 50 deluxe, just-modernised apartments, and country managers already moving in, you'll be in powerful company here. The former residence of Count Jan Pachta is a swank stay, where biz amenities, a classy bar and babysitting go along with the timbered rooms and, well, palatial public areas.

Pension Accord

NEW *Rybná 9 (222 328 816/www. accordprague.com). Metro Náměstí republiky.* $$.
With a convenient location just three blocks from Old Town Square, and spring and summer double rates of 98 euros including breakfast (30 less in winter), this clean, basic place follows the Central Europe efficiency model. But for budget travellers who won't be in their rooms much, you could do far worse.

Residence Řetězová

Řetězová 9 (222 221 800/www. residenceretezova.com). Metro Staroměstská. $$$.
A lovely labyrinth of restored Renaissance rooms, some with timbered ceilings and lofts, make up this easy-to-miss Old Town gem. Genial service, an incredible location and a homely feel make it easy to imagine retiring to this abode to live a quiet life. The significant spread in rates reflects, aside from deep seasonal discounts, a variety of room sizes – all tastefully appointed charmers.

Travellers' Hostel

Dlouhá 33 (224 826 662/www. travellers.cz). Metro Náměstí Republiky. $.
No lock-out nonsense, all branches open 24hrs, dorm rooms starting at 280 Kč per person, and, at this location, the hottest club in Old Town (the Roxy, p115) right next door. There's a romantic suite with beamed ceilings, plus internet access. Both apartments and the suite feature kitchens but book ahead. This is also the booking office for a network of hostels (www.czechhostels.com), many scattered around Prague. The seventh night is free of charge.

U Medvídků

Na Perštyně 7 (224 211 916/www. umedvidku.cz). Metro Národní třída. $$.
The iron doors on some rooms recall Gothic dungeons, while the rudimentary bathrooms evoke the benighted years of communism. The traditional inn's a pub – one of the first to serve Budvar – that keeps a constant stream of tourists and locals fed on roasted pig, beer-basted beef and dumplings. Damn handy for carousing.

U zlaté studny

Karlova 3 (222 220 262/www.uzlate studny.cz). Metro Staroměstská. $$.

Hotel U Zlaté Studně p170

Arcanery abounds in this 16th-century building named for the well in its cellar. Exquisitely furnished with Louis XIV antiques and replicas, the four suites and two doubles are cavernous by Old Town standards. Halfway between Charles Bridge and Old Town Square on the Royal Route. Children 15 and under free.

Central Nové Město & Vyšehrad

987 Prague Hotel

Senovážné náměstí 15 (255 737 100/ www.designhotelscollection.com). Metro Hlavní nádraží. **$$**.

987 Prague Hotel was transformed by Philippe Starck from a 19th-century apartment building – the façade of which is the only aspect unchanged. Interiors are infused with contemporary brightness and have a sleek, comfortable 1960s/70s feel. A good option for late rail arrivals.

Andante

Ve Smečkách 4 (222 210 021/ www.andante.cz). Metro Muzeum/IP Pavlova. **$$$**.

A fairly spartan modern exterior hides a warm, welcoming interior. A recent renovation improved the decor and infrastructure; it's still clean and simple. The excellent location and super staff are the main draw here. The 32 rooms are small, but you're a block from the most lively street in town. A bookish retreat it ain't, though rooms are quiet. Concierge and airport transit.

Carlo IV

Senovážné náměstí 13 (224 593 111/ www.boscolohotels.com). Metro Hlavní nádraží. **$$$**.

The locale, a well-placed but not picture-pretty street, makes this palace look out of place. Boscolo Hotels made over the former bank with unrestrained Italian opulence, complete with cigar bar, pool, gym, wooden floors and a colour-palette of sage, gold and mahogany, but the service is classic Mediterranean, alas. There's also a spa and wellness centre.

Hotel Adria Prague

Václavské náměstí 26 (221 081 111/ www.hoteladria.cz). Metro Můstek **$$**.

In olden times a nunnery for the Carmelites, the Adria now sits in sin city central on Wenceslas Square, the only sign of the virtuous days being the placid Franciscan Gardens. Newly modernised, like so much of Prague, has young and (mostly) eager staff, plus a memorable restaurant (in a faux grotto) and bar with fairly standard-issue offerings. Concierge, sauna, massage and summer garden are further draws.

Hotel Elite

Ostrovní 32 (224 932 250/www.hotel elite.cz). Metro Národní třída. **$$**.

Elite is part of the Small Charming Hotels group, and fits perfectly into this brand's specs. The 14th-century building, carefully renovated to retain its character, is protected by the Town Hall as a historical monument and the former barracks is right downtown with loads of hip restaurants and bars nearby.

Hotel Palace Praha

Panská 12 (224 093 111/www.palace hotel.cz). Metro Můstek. **$$$$**.

Just off Wenceslas Square, yet still close to everything, especially the city's tonier high street, Na příkopě. The Palace seems a world apart with understated, old-style formal service and solid creds among business travellers. There's a meeting centre with interpreting services, no-smoking floors and a sauna.

Ibis Praha City

Kateřinská 36 (222 865 777/www. accorhotels.com). Metro IP Pavlova. **$$**.

For familiarity and reliability (read predictability?) in travel, the Ibis does offer deals on clean, new rooms in good locations – and at press time was planning another 430-room branch on handy Na Poříčí just east of Old Town. Unlike many wannabe exclusive places in Prague, it also knows its customer service. There's disabled access, a gym and an all-night restaurant.

ESSENTIALS

Radisson SAS Alcron

Štěpánská 40 (222 820 000/www.
radisson.com/praguecs). Metro
Muzeum. **$$$$**.

Originally known as a jazz hotel when
built in 1930, the Alcron celebrates the
heritage of Duke and Satchmo, who both
passed through, with art deco motifs. It's
also kept up its rep as one of the city's
first luxe hotels and has the finest
seafood restaurant in the country off the
lobby. The higher up you go, the better
the views, but the high ceilings and period appointments make every room a
classic. Lobby jazz bar, concierge, gym
and no-smoking floors are further draws.

U Šuterů

Palackého 4 (224 948 235/www.
usuteru.cz). Metro Můstek. **$**.

A winner for seekers of small and cosy
in the Wenceslas Square area. The
building dates back to 1383, and rooms
were last renovated in 2004. Yet the
whole interior is a time trip back to pre-
World War II days, and the formal but
solid service highlights this. The pub
restaurant downstairs is popular
throughout the city for its cheap and
classic Czech fare and venison goulash.

Vinohrady & Žižkov

Arcotel Hotel Teatrino

Bořivojova 53, Žižkov (221 422 211/
www.arcotel.at). Metro Jiřího z
Poděbrad. **$$$**.

Rough and ready Žižkov is rapidly
being turned into Prague's Greenwich
Village, largely down to places like
this big shrine to nationalist art.
Austrian designer, architect and
painter Harald Schreiber is to blame
for the interiors – the lobby sports his
epic, a giant rendering of about 100
Czech heroes, which contributes much
to the odd mixture meant to 'animate
the hotel's guests for a journey
through the art and history of the city'.

Clown & Bard

Bořivojova 102, Žižkov (222 716 453/
www.clownandbard.com). Metro Jiřího
z Poděbrad. **$**.

More or less a free-for-all, this hostel's bar
is well known in Prague with the party-
hearty set. Located in the always colour-
ful Žižkov district, it's a good choice if
you're after some after-dark action. No
lock-out, no reservations, no hassles.
Breakfast is available, as is a laundry.

Courtyard by Marriott

NEW *Lucemburská 46, Žižkov*
(236 088 088/www.marriott.com).
Metro Flora. **$$**.

Adjacent to a green line metro stop and
the city's trendiest shopping mall, this
surprisingly solid-value spot is a good
option for families or those on biz trips,
with the usual Marriott service standards. With 161 rooms, it's a good back-
up if there's no room at the inn. Disabled
access and non-smoking rooms.

Dorint Don Giovanni

Vinohradská 157A, Žižkov (267
031 111/www.dorint.de). Metro
Želivského. **$$$**.

Not in the livelier west end of Žižkov but
this 397-room mammoth makes up for it
with a borderline sci-fi lobby and rooms
that could almost be described as whim-
sical. Dependable top-notch Dorint ser-
vice, and a good option for families – up
to two kids free and an indoor and out-
door playground factor in. Deep dis-
counts can shave loads from the price as
well – check the website. There's a
concierge, disabled-adapted rooms, a
gym, a sauna and massages availabe.

Hotel Abri

Jana Masaryka 36, Vinohrady (222
515 124/www.abri.cz). Metro Náměstí
Míru. **$$**.

This small but lovely hotel is well-situ-
ated in a quiet Vinohrady neighbourhood, about five minutes from the
metro station, and two minutes from a
tram stop. The staff is unflappable,
rooms are large, the lobby is spacious
and the terrace entices in warm weather. A modern Czech restaurant is onsite.

Hotel Anna

Budečská 17, Vinohrady (222 513 111/
www.hotelanna.cz). Metro Náměstí
Míru/tram 4, 10, 16, 22, 23. **$$**.

The Anna, with modernised amenities but an art nouveau interior and wall-to-wall warmth, is a Prague veteran-visitor trump card. Simply but classily furnished, these 24 rooms, some admittedly a squeeze, feature Wi-Fi internet access.

Hotel Tříska
Vinohradská 105, Žižkov (222 727 313/www.hotel-triska.cz). Metro Jiřího z Poděbrad. **$**.
Whitewashed baroque meets Czech murals, art deco and imperial but it's a dead bargain and the owners have lovingly designed each room individually. It's also in the heart of the district, with great bar and club offerings nearby. If possible, request a courtyard facing room; the street gets noisy.

Le Palais
U Zvonařky 1, Vinohrady (234 634 111/ www.palaishotel.cz) Metro IP Pavlova/ Náměstí míru/tram 4, 16, 22, 23. **$$$$**.
This gorgeous belle époque palace was once a meat-processing plant, but that's now hard to imagine in this idyllic corner of Vinohrady. It was originally decorated by 19th-century Czech artist Luděk Mařold in exchange for rent, and many of his touches remain, including the frescoed ceilings and staircase. Service is excellent and the rooms are classically posh (mind the movie crews). A well-equipped fitness centre, a buzzing restaurant and a lovely summer terrace, plus massage services, add appeal.

Miss Sophie's Prague
Melounova 3, Vinohrady (296 303 530/www.miss-sophies.com). Metro IP Pavlova. **$**.
Dorms, private rooms and apartments, all in uptempo style in an uptempo district. Miss Sophie's, just a year old, has fitted its apartments with full kitchens, the dorm rooms with wooden floors and the private rooms with elegant marble bathrooms. A helpful vibe prevails. The more elegant end of the budget hotel scale, with a terrace and a cellar lounge.

Prague Hilton
Pobřežní 1, Karlín (224 841 111/ www.hilton.com). Metro Florenc. **$$$$**.

This glass box behemoth is very un-Prague like from the outside but hides an airy atrium and the trademark five-star luxury inside. You won't want for much, except for Prague charm, but it's just east of the old centre so an escape is easy to make. The lauded Czech House restaurant is another plus, and there are disabled-adapted rooms.

Holešovice & north

Diplomat Hotel Praha
Evropská 15, Dejvice (296 559 111/ www.diplomatpraha.cz). Metro Dejvická. **$$$$**.
On the city end of the airport road (20 minutes from Ruzyně), the Diplomat's still close enough to downtown (ten minutes by metro) to be considered central. Business-like, with serious meeting rooms, it's also big with families and has regular specials. Accommodating and helpful staff plus disabled-adapted rooms, a gym, no-smoking floors and interpreting services are further draws.

Hotel Schwaiger
Schwaigerova 3, Bubeneč (233 320 271/www.villaschwaiger.cz). Metro Hradčanská. **$$$**.
The former villa of a 19th-century Bohemian painter, the Schwaiger is located in a leafy, hushed part of town close to Stromovka park, but a ten-minute cab ride from downtown. Recently redone in what could be described as Tuscan-meets-zen style, it now accommodates the new branch of Prague's French regional shrine, Bistrot de Marlene. Staff are pleasant and there's a lovely back garden and sauna.

Sir Toby's Hostel
Dělnická 24, Holešovice (283 870 635/ www.sirtobys.com). Metro Vltavská or Nádraží Holešovice. **$**.
Friendly, accommodating staff make Sir Toby's a winner, with 70 beds in an art nouveau building that's been stylishly done over so that you nearly forget you're in a hostel. Also in the heart of a happening neighbourhood, with handy galleries and youth-orientated nightlife.

ESSENTIALS

Getting Around

Arriving & leaving

By air

Ruzyně Airport

239 007 576/www.czechairlines.com/ en. About 20 km (12.5 miles) north- west of central Prague, off Evropská.
There's no metro access to Ruzyně; the quickest way into town is **ČEDAZ** (220 114 296, www.cedaz.cz) to the Dejvická metro station and Náměstí Republiky, which takes 20 minutes and runs from 6am to 9pm daily. Singles cost 90 Kč to Dejvická, and 120 Kč to Náměstí Republiky.

The English-speaking **Prague Airport Shuttle** (602 395 421, www.prague-airport-shuttle.com) runs daily, providing door-to-door transport, as well as shuttles in Prague. Transport to your hotel is 600 Kč for up to three people, 900 Kč for 4-6 passengers, 1,200 Kč for 7-8 passengers. Book online.

Public bus (www.dp-praha.cz) service runs between Ruzyně and the Dejvická metro, with the 119 running every 20 minutes from 4.16am to midnight daily. It takes about 15 minutes, at 20 Kč for a single, with tickets available from the machine at the bus stop but not onboard.

AAA Taxi (14014, www.aaata xi.cz) charges about 350 Kč for a ride to the centre and, to the relief of many passengers, now has a rank outside the arrivals hall. Just be careful to avoid the other taxis waiting at the airport, which are likely to rip you off.

By rail

Czech Rail

Trains run everywhere, are highly affordable, and are generally threadbare but reliable. For info in English on train times, call 221 111 122, www.cd.cz. For ticket prices, call 840 112 113. The website gives online timetable information for all busses as well. You cannot buy tickets online but staff at the train stations speak English. All the major stations are served by the metro.

Main line stations

Hlavní nádraží

Main Station, Wilsonova, Nové Město (972 241 100/www.idos.cz). Metro Hlavní nádraží.
Most international trains arrive at Hlavní nádraží, two blocks north of Wenceslas Square, situated on the red metro line C.

Nádraží Holešovice

Holešovice Station, Vrbenského, Holešovice (220 806 790/www. idos.cz). Metro Nádraží Holešovice.
A few international trains stop only at Nádraží Holešovice, in the Holešovice district and on the red metro line C, a ten-minute metro ride north of the cen- tre of Prague, but many more stop at Nádraží Holešovice then continue on to the main station, Hlavní nádraží, so be sure not to hop off early.

Smíchovské nádraží

Smíchov Station, Nádraží (221 111 122, www.idos.cz). Metro Smíchovské nádraží/tram 12.
Some trains arriving from the west stop at Smíchovské nádraží, which is situated on the yellow metro line B, but usually also at Hlavní nádraží.

By coach

Florenc station

Křižíkova 4, Prague 8 (infoline 900 144 444/www.csad.cz). Metro Florenc.
International buses arrive at Florenc, a grimy and unprepossessing station, but lying a ten-minute walk east of hotels on the much more civilised Na Poříčí street on the edge of Old Town.

Public transport

Prague public transport – its metro, trams, buses, night trams, night buses and funicular – is run by Prague Public Transit, or **Dopravní podnik**, whose website provides maps and information that can be downloaded and printed. Service generally runs from 5am to midnight daily, with night trams and buses running at other times. At the information offices below employees usually have at least a smattering of English and German and provide free information, night transport booklets and individual tram and bus schedules and sell tickets (cash only).You can also find maps for sale from agents and the routes posted in metro stations. Tram stops, meanwhile, have posted schedules but not handy route maps for the taking. At tram stops, the times posted apply to the stop where you are – which is highlighted on the schedule. If your destination is listed below the highlighted stop, you are in the right place. Call 296 191 817 for more information, 7am-9pm daily, or check dpp.cz.

Information Offices

Anděl metro station Smíchov (222 646 055). Open 7am-6pm Mon-Fri.
Ruzyně Airport (220 115 404). Open 7am-10pm daily.
Ruzyně Airport Terminal North (296 667 072). Open 7am-10pm daily.
Muzeum metro station Nové Město (222 623 777). Open 7am-9pm daily.
Můstek metro station Nové Město (222 646 350). Open 7am-6pm Mon-Fri.
Nádraží Holešovice metro station Holešovice (220 806 790). Open 7am-6pm Mon-Fri.

Prague Card

The **Prague Card** is a four-day sightseeing admissions card that comes with an optional transport pass good for all modes of public transit for the same period. The Prague Card, sold at the offices of Čedok, the state tourism company, covers entrance to some 50 museums and attractions, including Prague Castle and the Astronomical Clock in Old Town, for a fee of 740 Kč for adults or 490 Kč for students. Add on the transport card for a further 220 Kč. If you're planning to take in several museums and galleries it's worth the price, but note that the Jewish Museum and some excellent galleries like the Rudolfinum and the House of the Stone Bell in Old Town are not covered. The travel pass is worthwhile no matter how many journeys you make and valid for the entire centre. The Prague Card is available at travel information centres and at the office of the Prague Information Service on Old Town Square (www.pis.cz), though not at metro stations.

To use the transport pass with your Prague Card, fill out your name and sign it (they're non-transferable), and just keep it with you while you ride – no need to pass it hrough card readers.

Travelcards

Day or multi-day travel cards are also available from the metro stations with **Dopravní podnik** offices listed above. Rates are 80 Kč for a 24-hour pass and 220 Kč for a 72-hour pass, which cover all travel on public transport in the centre of the city, including metro, trams, buses and the funicular on Petřín hill in Malá Strana. They're good for any time of day or night and also cover night trams and night buses.

Travelcards start to save you money with the three-day version, if you plan to be on the road a lot. One-day and three-day travelcards come as standard printed tickets that you insert into the slot in metro station entry gates, or in the yellow ticket boxes on trams

ESSENTIALS

or buses, which time-stamp your pass. To validate a short-term pass, fill in your full name and date of birth on the reverse and then stamp it as you would an ordinary ticket. The dates go into effect from the time you first stamp it. Once that's done, you can ride any bus or tram and only need show your pass to a driver or inspector if asked.

For longer visits, a weekly pass, for 280 Kč, or 15-day pass, for 320 Kč, will save hassle and money.

Metro

The Prague metro, constructed during the evil days of Soviet 'normalisation', is one of the old regime's best achievements. It's fast, clean, reliable, and roomier than most in Europe, probably because it was built so late in the city's history. Stations are deep underground and the city's three colour-coded lines are a cinch to sort out. The system, heavily subsidised by the state as it is, is also cheap, with a 20 Kč ticket getting you anywhere you'd need to go, including transfers (just remember to stamp it as you enter the metro or board surface transport) lest you face the wrath of the city's generally unpleasant and sometimes dodgy inspectors, who may fine you 400 Kč, cash only, on the spot.

Using the system

A one-day travel card or **Prague Card** is the best way to pay for your metro transport if you're going to make more than four round trips or travel on an unpredictable schedule. Otherwise, single tickets can be purchased from a ticket office or machine in the metro station (annoyingly, they're almost never installed at tram or bus stops).

Metro timetable

The metro runs daily from around 5am. Generally, you won't have to wait more than ten minutes for a train, and during peak times services should run every six to eight minutes. But they can slow to every 20 minutes on weekends and holidays. Last trains are usually around midnight daily.

Fares

A 20 Kč ticket is good for 75 minutes at peak times (5am-8pm Mon-Fri) and 90 minutes at off-peak (8pm-5am Mon-Fri and all of Sat, Sun, public holidays), allowing unlimited travel throughout Prague, including transfers between metros, buses and trams.

Buses and trams

Prague buses and trams require you to buy a ticket before boarding. Do so: there are inspectors about, who can fine you 400 Kč. You can buy one (or a one-day pass) from ticket machines, though, frustratingly, they're usually only located in metro stations. English-speaking operators are available round the clock (900 144 444) with bus information. Calls cost 14 Kč per minute.

Night buses and trams

The latest-running regular trams and buses operate only until about 20 minutes after midnight, so night trams and buses, which are popular with a party-loving crowd, can be a lifesaver. They generally run from around 11.30pm to 5am, seven days a week but come less frequently on weekends and holidays. Night trams have numbers in the 50s and night buses are numbered in the 500s. Most services run every 30 to 45 minutes so it may serve you well to check the schedule before going out for the night, especially in winter.

Taxis

Prague taxis have a well-deserved reputation for rip-offs and, despite frequent campaigns announced to clean them up, you're still just about guaranteed to be overcharged if you get in any taxi you see at a rank in a prominent downtown location. Your odds are slightly improved if you hail a moving taxi (those with a yellow roof-top sign switched on are available) but you really should call a reputable company and order a cab, which will generally be able to fetch you in five minutes or so. Starting rates are 34 Kč plus 25 Kč per kilometre and 5 Kč per minute waiting.

To book an honest taxi, call **AAA** 14014, **ProfiTaxi** 844 700 800, or **Halo Taxi** 244 114 411. They generally don't take credit cards, but you'll pay nothing extra for the call-out service.

Water transport

There are no commuter boat services in Prague, but for leisure cruises, see Jazz Boat (p117).

Driving

Parking

Driving can be a nightmare in Prague, it has one of Europe's highest accident rates, combined with narrow, cobbled streets, trams (which always have right of way and use special traffic signals of their own), and frequent rain, ice and snow. Street parking in the centre without a residents' permit is not permitted either, and is likely to end up getting you clamped with one of Prague's infamous yellow boots (call the number on the boot or 158 to pay up and get yourself freed).

Blue zones are reserved for local residents and companies. Orange zones are for stops of up to two hours and cost a minimum of 10 Kč for 15 minutes and 40 Kč for one hour; and green zones are for stays of up to six hours and cost cost 15

Kč for 30 minutes, 30 Kč for an hour and 120 Kč for six hours.

You'll need to pay at coin-operated parking meters, which dispense tickets that must be displayed face up on the dashboard, visible through the windscreen.

There are increasing numbers of underground private car parks of paid parking in central Prague but they are expensive, often short-term and usually full.

Vehicle removal

If your (illegally parked) car has mysteriously disappeared, chances are it's been taken to a car pound. Penalty and release fees are stiff. To find out where your car has been taken and how to retrieve it, call 158, 24hrs daily.

Vehicle hire

Alimex (800 150 170, www.alim ex.cz) offers competitive rates, just so long as you don't mind driving a branded car around town. Otherwise, try **Europcar** 224 811 290, www.europcar.cz. **Czechocar** 800 179 534, www.czechocar.cz. **Alimex** 800 150 170, www.alim excr.cz. **Budget** 235 325 713, www.budget.cz.

Cycling

Pedalling in Prague is hellish: no cycle lanes, drivers oblivious to your presence and pedestrians who yell at you if you ride on the pavement. If you must:

City Bike

Královdvorská 5, Staré Město (mobile 776 180 284, www.citybike-prague.com). Metro Náměstí Republiky. **Open** *Apr-Oct* 9am-7pm daily. *Hire* 290-490 Kč for two hours. Cycle tours of the city, leaving three times a day (11am, 2pm and 5pm), with reasonable rental fees.

ESSENTIALS

Resources A-Z

Accident & emergency

Prague's general emergency phone number is 112.

The following hospitals have 24-hour emergency facilities.

Canadian Medical Care *Veleslavínská 30, Dejvice (235 360 133/ emergency 724 300 301). Metro Dejvická.*
Medicover Clinic *Pankrác House, Lomnického 1705, Pankrác (234 630 111/emergency 603 555 006). Metro Pražského povstání.*
Motol Hospital *(Fakultní nemocnice v Motole) V Úvalu 84, Smíchov, Prague 5 (224 431 111/emergency 224 438 590-8). Anděl Metro, then tram 7, 9, 10, 58, 59.*
Na Homolce Hospital *(Nemocnice Na Homolce) Roentgenova 2, Smíchov, Prague 5 (257 271 111, emergencies 257 272 191). Anděl Metro, then tram 7, 9, 10, 58, 59.*

Credit card loss

American Express *222 412 241*
Diners Club *267 197 450*
JCB *0120 500 544*
MasterCard/Eurocard/ Visa *800 111 055.*

Customs

For allowances, see www.cs.mfcr.cz.

Dental emergencies

Dental Emergencies *Palackého 5, Nové Město (224 946 981). Metro Můstek.* **Open** 7pm-6.30am Mon-Fri; 7am-6pm Sat, Sun.

European Dental Center *Václavské náměstí 33, Nové Město (224 228 984). Metro Můstek.* **Open** 8am-11pm Mon-Fri; 9am-6pm Sat, Sun.

Disabled

Prague is a difficult city for disabled visitors, though legislation is gradually improving access. Some buses are getting more wheelchair-accessible and new trams with wheelchair access are being phased in, but the metro is mostly escalator-dependent. A guide showing stations with lift is available free of charge from ticket offices.

Electricity

The Czech Republic uses the standard European 220-240V, 50-cycle AC voltage via Continental three-pin plugs.

Embassies & consulates

Also refer to the *Zlaté stránky* (or Yellow Pages), which has an index in English at the back.

American Embassy *Tržiště 15, Malá Strana (257 022 000/emergency 257 532 716/www.usembassy.cz). Metro Malostranská*
Australian Trade Commission & Consulate *Klimentská 10, Nové Město (251 018 350). Metro Náměstí Republiky.*
British Embassy *Thunovská 14, Malá Strana (257 402 111/www.brit ain.cz). Metro Malostranská.*
Canadian Embassy *Muchova 6, Dejvice (272 101 800/www.canada.cz). Metro Hradčanská.*
Irish Embassy *Tržiště 13, Malá Strana (257 530 061). Metro Malostranská.*
New Zealand Consulate *Dykova 19, Vinohrady (222 514 672). Metro Náměstí Míru.*

Internet

There are lots of cybercafés around town, and many bars, such as Jáma

ESSENTIALS

(p129), feature free Wi-Fi. For more, check www.cybercafes.com. For locations, check with your provider or visit www.wi-fihotspotlist.com.
Internet Café Pl@neta *Vinohradska 102, Vinohrady (www.planeta.cz). Metro Jiřího z Poděbrad.* **Open** 8am-11pm daily. **Terminals** 24.

Opening hours

Banks 8am or 9am-5pm or 6pm Mon-Fri.
Businesses 9am-5pm Mon-Fri.
Shops 10am-6pm Mon-Sat; some to 8pm. Many are also open on Sunday, usually 11am-5pm or noon-6pm.

Pharmacies (Lekárna)

Belgická 37 *Vinohrady (222 519 731). Metro Náměstí Míru.* **Open** 24-hrs daily.
Palackého 5 *Nové Město (224 946 982). Metro Můstek.* **Open** 24 hrs daily.

Police

The main police station (Na Perštýně and Bartolomějská streets, Staré Město, Metro Náměstí Republiky) should have an English-speaking person available to help but many visitors have found this lacking and police to be generally unhelpful. The emergency number is 158.

Post

Post offices are usually open 9am to 5.30pm Monday-Friday and 9am to noon Saturday, although the main Post Office on Jindřišská street is open from 2am-midnight daily, shutting only for two hours. For general post office enquiries, call the central information line on 800 104 410 or consult www.ceskaposta.cz.

Main post offices

Hybernska 15 *Nové Město (222 240 271). Metro Náměstí Republiky.*

Jindřišská 14 *Nové Město (221 131 111). Metro Můstek.*
Kaprova 12 *Staré Město (222 329 003). Metro Staroměstská.*

Public phones

Public payphones take coins or pre-paid cards, available at newsstands in denominations of 50-100 units, or credit cards (sometimes both). Local calls cost 2 Kč for two minutes during peak hours. Note that most public phones in the city centre are in a poor state of repair, however, because Czechs have embraced mobile phones with a passion.

Operator services

Call 800 123 456 for the operator if you have difficulty in dialling or for help with international person-to-person calls. Dial 155 for the international operator if you need to reverse the charges (call collect) or if you can't dial direct.

Directory enquiries

For help in finding a number, dial 1180 or the international operator at 1181. Online, many of the most useful contacts for visitors are at www.expats.cz and www.prague.tv.

Safety

Prague is not a particularly dangerous city for visitors, but its crowded spots – buses, busy streets, metro trains and stations – attract the usual complement of petty crooks. Keep valuables in your hotel or room safe and make sure the cash and cards you carry with you are well tucked away in your bag.

Smoking

In 2006, a law banned smoking in restaurants during peak times, but permitting it at others. It also bars

ESSENTIALS

smoking at tram stops, the area of which the law fails to define. At press time the scuffle to amend the vague law was continuing. Many hotels offer smoking rooms.

Telephones

The Czech Republic's dialling code is 420. If you're calling from outside the country, dial your international access code, then this number, then the full Prague number. To dial abroad from the Czech Republic, dial 00, then the country code.

Tickets

With the exception of the major cultural institutions, which have in-house box offices and offer phone and web ticketing services at no significant premium, most venues subcontract their ticket sales out to agencies. To find out which, consult the venue's website. Between them, Ticketpro and Bohemia Ticket International represent most venues, but note that Bohemia Ticket accepts no credit cards.

Bohemia Ticket International

Malé náměstí 13, Staré Město (224 227 832/www.ticketsbti.cz). Metro Můstek. **Open** *9am-5pm Mon-Fri; 9am-1pm Sat.*

Ticket Pro

Old Town Hall, Staré Město (224 223 613/www.ticketpro.cz). Metro Staroměstská. **Open** *10am-7pm Mon-Fri; 10am-5pm Sat; 10am-3pm Sun.*

Time

The Czech Republic operates on Central European time, which is one hour later than Greenwich Mean Time (GMT), and six hours ahead of the US's Eastern Standard time. In spring (30 March 2008) clocks go forward by one hour. In autumn (28 October 2007) they go back to CET.

Tipping

Tip in taxis, restaurants, hotels, hairdressers, bars and pubs. Ten per cent is normal, but some restaurants add as much as 15 per cent.

Tourist information

Čedok is the city's official tourist information company. There is also a Prague Information Service office on Old Town Square.

Čedok

Na Příkopě 18, Nové Město (221 447 242/www.cedok.cz). Metro Náměstí Republiky. **Open** *9am-6pm Mon-Fri; 9am-5pm Sat, Sun.*

Prague Information Service

Staroměstské Náměstí, Staré Město (221 714 444/www.pis.cz). Metro Staroměstská. **Open** *9am-6pm Mon-Fri; 9am-5pm Sat, Sun.*
Other locations: *Main Station (Hlavní nádraží)*

Visas

EU citizens do not require a visa to visit the Czech Republic nor do those of the USA. At press time citizens of Canada, Australia, South Africa and New Zealand require a visa, which cannot be obtained at an entry point but must be arranged with a Czech consulate or embassy abroad. Use www.ukvisas.gov.uk to check your visa status well before you travel.

What's on

Numerous free listings magazines are distributed around town and with newspapers, but *The Prague Post* (www.praguepost.com), available from central newsagents on Wednesdays and containing a week's worth of listings, is the best reference. For gay listings, look out for www.gayguide.net.

Vocabulary

Pronunciation

a – as in gap; á – as in father;
e – as in let; é – as in air;
i, y – as in lit; í, ý – as in seed;
o – as in lot; ó – as in lore;
u – as in book; ú, ů – as in loom;
c – as in its; č – as in chin;
ch – as in loch; ď – as in duty;
ň – as in onion; ř – as a standard
r, but with a forceful buzz like ž;
š – as in shin; ť – as in stew;
ž – as in pleasure; dž – as in George

The basics

Czech words are always stressed
on the first syllable.
hello/good day *dobrý den*
good evening *dobrý večer*
good night *dobrou noc*
goodbye *nashledanou*
yes *ano*
no *ne*
please *prosím*
thank you *děkuji*
excuse me *promiňte*
sorry *pardon*
help! *pomoc!*
attention! *pozor!*
I don't speak Czech
nemluvím česky
I don't understand *nerozumím*
do you speak English?
mluvíte anglicky?
sir *pán*
madam *paní*
open *otevřeno*
closed *zavřeno*
I would like... *chtěl bych...*
how much is it? *kolik to stojí?*
may I have a receipt, please?
účet, prosím
can we pay, please?
zaplatíme, prosím
where is... *kde je...*
go left *doleva*
go right *doprava*

straight *rovně*
far *daleko*
near *blízko*
good *dobrý*
bad *špatný*
big *velký*
small *malý*
no problem *to je v pořádku*
rip-off *zlodějina*

Street names etc

avenue *třída*
bridge *most*
church *kostel*
embankment *nábřeží* or *nábř*
gardens *sady* or *zahrada*
monastery, convent *klášter*
square *náměstí* or *nám*
station *nádraží* or *nádr*
street *ulice* or *ul*

Numbers

0 *nula*; 1 *jeden*; 2 *dva*; 3 *tři*; 4 *čtyři*;
5 *pět*; 6 *šest*; 7 *sedm*; 8 *osm*; 9 *devět*;
10 *deset*; 20 *dvacet*; 30 *třicet*;
40 *čtyřicet*; 50 *padesát*; 60 *šedesát*;
70 *sedmdesát*; 80 *osmdesát*; 90
devadesát; 100 *sto*; 1,000 *tisíc*

Days & months

Monday *pondělí*; **Tuesday** *úterý*;
Wednesday *středa*; **Thursday**
čtvrtek; **Friday** *pátek*; **Saturday**
sobota; **Sunday** *neděle*

Pick-up lines

What a babe! *To je kost!*
What a stud! *Dobrej frajer!*
Another drink? *Ještě jedno?*

Put-down lines

Give me a break! *Dej mi pokoj!*
Kiss my arse! *Polib mi prdel!*

ESSENTIALS

Menu Glossary

You'll find that Czech menus generally list two categories of main dishes: *minutky*, cooked to order (which may take ages), and *hotová jídla*, ready-to-serve fare. The usual accompaniments to these dishes are rice, potatoes or the fried béchamel dough known as *krokety*, all of which should be ordered separately. When dining in pubs, the closest thing served to fresh vegetables is often *obloha*, which is a garnish of pickles, or a tomato on a single leaf of cabbage. Tasty appetisers to try are Prague ham with horseradish or rich soups (*polévka*), while a dessert staple is *palačinky*, filled pancakes.

Meals (jídla)

snídaně *breakfast*; **oběd** *lunch*; **večeře** *dinner*.

Preparation (příprava)

bez masa/bezmasá jídla *without meat*; **čerstvé** *fresh*; **domácí** *home-made*; **dušené** *steamed*; **grilované** *grilled*; **míchaný** *mixed*; **na roštu** *roasted*; **pečené** *baked*; **plněné** *stuffed*; **smažené** *fried*; **špíz** *grilled on a skewer*; **uzené** *smoked*; **vařené** *boiled*.

Basics (základní)

chléb *bread*; **cukr** *sugar*; **drůbež** *poultry*; **karbanátek** *patty of unspecified content*; **máslo** *butter*; **maso** *meat*; **ocet** *vinegar*; **olej** *oil*; **omáčka** *sauce*; **ovoce** *fruit*; **pepř** *pepper*; **rohlík** *roll*; **ryby** *fish*; **smetana** *cream*; **sůl** *salt*; **sýr** *cheese*; **vejce** *eggs*; **zelenina** *vegetables*.

Drinks (nápoje)

čaj *tea*; **káva** *coffee*; **mléko** *milk*; **pivo** *beer*; **pomerančový džus** *orange juice*; **sodovka** *soda*; **víno** *wine*; **voda** *water*; **slivovice** *plum brandy*; **Becherovka** *herbal liqueur*; **Fernet** *bitters*; **červené víno** *red wine*; **bílé víno** *white wine*; **perlová** *carbonated*; **neperlová** *still*.

Appetisers (předkrmy)

boršč *Russian beetroot soup (borscht)*; **chlebíček** *meat open-sandwich*; **hovězí vývar** *beef broth*; **kaviár** *caviar*; **paštika** *pâté*; **polévka** *soup*; **uzený losos** *smoked salmon*.

Meat (maso)

biftek *beefsteak*; **hovězí** *beef*; **játra** *liver*; **jehně** *lamb*; **jelení** *venison*; **kančí** *boar*; **klobása, párek, salám, vuřt** *sausage*; **králík** *rabbit*; **ledvinky** *kidneys*; **slanina** *bacon*; **srnčí** *roebuck*; **šunka** *ham*; **telecí** *veal*; **tlačenka** *brawn*; **vepřové** *pork*; **zvěřina** *game*.

Poultry & fish (drůbež a ryby)

bažant *pheasant*; **husa** *goose*; **kachna** *duck*; **kapr** *carp*; **křepelka** *quail*; **krocan** *turkey*; **kuře** *chicken*; **losos** *salmon*; **pstruh** *trout*.

Main meals (hlavní jídla)

guláš *goulash*; **řízek** *schnitzel*; **sekaná** *meat loaf*; **smažený sýr**

fried cheese; **svíčková** *beef in cream sauce*; **vepřová játra na cibulce** *pig's liver stewed with onion*; **vepřové koleno** *pork knee*; **vepřový řízek** *fried breaded pork*.

Side dishes (přílohy)

brambor *potato*; **bramborák** *potato pancake*; **bramborová kaše** *mashed potatoes*; **hranolky** *chips*; **kaše** *mashed potatoes*; **knedlíky** *dumplings*; **krokety** *potato or béchamel dough croquettes*; **obloha** *small lettuce and tomato salad*; **rýže** *rice*; **salát** *salad*; **šopský salát** *cucumber, tomato and curd salad*; **tatarská omáčka** *tartar sauce*; **zelí** *cabbage*.

Cheese (sýr)

balkán a saltier *feta*; **eidam** *hard white cheese*; **hermelín** *soft, similar to bland brie*; **Madeland** *Swiss cheese*; **niva** *blue cheese*; **pivní sýr** *beer-flavoured semi-soft cheese*; **primátor** *Swiss cheese*; **tavený sýr** *packaged cheese spread*; **tvaroh** *soft curd cheese*.

Vegetables (zelenina)

česnek *garlic*; **chřest** *asparagus*; **cibule** *onion(s)*; **čočka** *lentils*; **fazole** *beans*; **feferonky** *chilli peppers*; **hrášek** *peas*; **kukuřice** *corn*; **květák** *cauliflower*; **mrkev** *carrot*; **okurka** *cucumber*; **petržel** *parsley*; **rajčata** *tomatoes*; **salát** *lettuce*; **špenát** *spinach*; **žampiony** *mushrooms*; **zelí** *cabbage*.

Fruit (ovoce)

ananas *pineapple*; **banány** *banana*; **borůvky** *blueberries*; **broskev** *peach*; **hrozny** *grapes*; **hruška** *pear*; **jablko** *apple*; **jahody** *strawberries*; **jeřabina** *rowanberries*; **mandle** *almonds*; **meruňka** *apricot*; **ořechy** *nuts*; **pomeranč** *orange*; **rozinky raisins**; **švestky** *plums*; **třešně** *cherries*.

Desserts (moučník)

buchty *traditional curd-filled cakes*; **čokoláda** *chocolate*; **dort** *layered cake*; **koláč** *cake with various fillings*; **ovocné knedlíky** *fruit dumplings*; **palačinka** *crêpe*; **pohár** *ice-cream sundae*; **šlehačka** *whipped cream*; **zákusek** *cake*; **závin** *strudel*; **žemlovka** *bread pudding with apples and cinnamon*; **zmrzlina** *ice-cream*.

Useful phrases

May I see the menu? *Mohu vidět jídelní lístek?* **Do you have...?** *Máte...?* **I am a vegetarian** *Jsem vegetarián/vegetariánka (m/f).* **How is it prepared?** *Jak je to připravené?* **Did you say 'beer cheese'?** *Říkal jste 'pivní sýr'?* **Wow, that smells!** *Páni, to smrdí!* **Can I have it without...?** *Mohu mít bez...?* **No ketchup on my pizza, please** *Nechci kečup na pizzu, prosím.* **I didn't order this** *Neobjednal jsem si to.* **How much longer will it be?** *Jak dlouho to ještě bude?* **The bill, please** *Účet, prosím.* **I can't eat this and I won't pay for it!** (use with extreme caution) *Nedá se to jíst a nezaplatím to.* **Takeaway/to go** *S sebou.* **A beer, please** *Pivo, prosím.* **Two beers, please** *Dvě piva, prosím.* **Same again, please** *Ještě jednou, prosím.* **What'll you have?** *Co si dáte?* **Not for me, thanks** *Pro mě ne, děkuji.* **No ice, thanks** *Bez ledu, děkuji.* **He's really smashed** *Je totálně namazaný.*

ESSENTIALS

Index

Sights & Museums

ESSENTIALS